# THE BIRTH OF
# ROCK & ROLL

## MUSIC IN THE 1950s THROUGH THE 1960s

# POPULAR MUSIC
## THROUGH THE DECADES

# THE BIRTH OF
# ROCK & ROLL
## MUSIC IN THE 1950s THROUGH THE 1960s

EDITED BY JEFF WALLENFELDT, MANAGER, GEOGRAPHY AND HISTORY

Britannica®
Educational Publishing

IN ASSOCIATION WITH

ROSEN
EDUCATIONAL SERVICES

Published in 2013 by Britannica Educational Publishing
(a trademark of Encyclopædia Britannica, Inc.) in association with Rosen Educational Services, LLC

29 East 21st Street, New York, NY 10010.

Distributed exclusively by Rosen Educational Services.
For a listing of additional Britannica Educational Publishing titles, call toll free (800) 237-9932.

First Edition

Britannica Educational Publishing
J.E. Luebering: Senior Manager
Marilyn L. Barton: Senior Coordinator, Production Control
Steven Bosco: Director, Editorial Technologies
Lisa S. Braucher: Senior Producer and Data Editor
Yvette Charboneau: Senior Copy Editor
Kathy Nakamura: Manager, Media Acquisition
Jeff Wallenfeldt: Manager, Geography and History

Rosen Educational Services
Hope Lourie Killcoyne: Executive Editor
Nelson Sá: Art Director
Cindy Reiman: Photography Manager
Karen Huang: Photo Researcher
Brian Garvey: Designer, Cover Design
Introduction by Jeff Wallenfeldt

**Library of Congress Cataloging-in-Publication Data**

The birth of rock & roll: music in the 1950s through the 1960s/edited by Jeff Wallenfeldt.—1st ed.
    p. cm.—(Popular music through the decades)
"In association with Britannica Educational Publishing, Rosen Educational Services."
Includes bibliographical references and index.
ISBN 978-1-61530-906-1 (library binding)
1. Rock music—United States—To 1961—History and criticism—Juvenile literature. 2. Rock music—United States—1961–1970—History and criticism—Juvenile literature. 3. Rock musicians—United States—Biography—Juvenile literature. I. Wallenfeldt, Jeffrey H. II. Title: Birth of rock and roll.
ML3534.3.B52 2013
781.6609'045—dc23

2012019294

*Manufactured in the United States of America*

**On the cover, p. iii :** Elvis Presley performing on Elvis, his eponymous NBC TV "comeback special" in June of 1968. *Michael Ochs Archives/Getty Images*

Pages 1, 12, 27, 44, 54, 62, 88, 99, 115, 143, 156, 165, 174, 182, 199 Ethan Miller/Getty Images (Fender Stratocaster guitar), © iStockphoto.com/catrinka81 (treble clef graphic); interior background image © iStockphoto.com/hepatus; back cover © iStockphoto.com/Vladimir Jajin

# CONTENTS

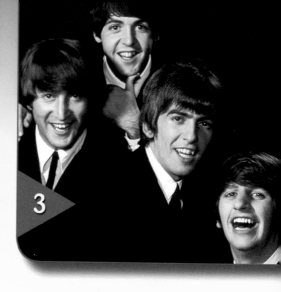

52

58

74

83

89

104

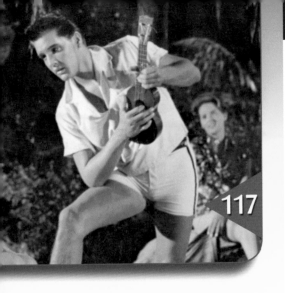

117

122

151

185

190

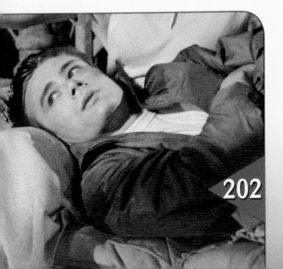
202

# Introduction

From the perspective of the early 21st century, it is difficult to appreciate both how threatening rock and roll was to mainstream culture and how exciting it was for young people at its inception in the 1950s. It is not really surprising that J. Edgar Hoover, the longtime director of the Federal Bureau of Investigation (FBI), a man given to anything but calm assessment of social change, believed rock and roll was "repulsive to right-thinking people." But even Frank Sinatra, who had whipped his own young bobby-soxer fans into a frenzy in the 1940s, called rock and roll "phony and false, and sung, written, and played for the most part by cretinous goons." For many in the 1950s, rock and roll was nothing less than an unholy, salacious communist plot to undermine the American way of life.

Cold War paranoia aside, in a way, they were right. Rock and roll did undermine the status quo. It was a huge agent for social change, certainly in the role it played in the creation of a youth culture grounded in questioning authority, but even more so in its contribution to transforming the way that black and white Americans related to each other. It is too simplistic to say that rock and roll is nothing more than rhythm and blues played by people whose ancestors came from Europe rather than Africa. It does not go too far, though, to say that rhythm and blues and rock and roll bridged the gap between black and white culture in ways that jazz only hinted at, or that in doing so R&B and rock 'n' roll—consciously and unconsciously—fostered a common cause among many black and white Americans of a magnitude unseen since Reconstruction. In the process, rock and roll and its more developed form, rock (including soul and hip-hop) became the world's dominant popular music and, arguably, even more than motion pictures, America's most influential cultural export. But we are getting ahead of the story this book is here to tell.

It is a story that one could easily begin in the early 1950s with a radio, played long after sundown, the nighttime ionosphere conducive to relaying a faraway signal carrying supercharged rhythms, impassioned vocals, and the exotic patter of a deejay to the bedroom of a teenager in Missouri or Minnesota, Ohio or Texas. The music was blues or rhythm and blues. The station was most likely in the South. The jive-talking disc jockey an Africa American or a white hipster who to some ears sounded black. Before the teenage Bob Dylan was captivated by Buddy Holly's performance at the Armory in Duluth, Minnesota, on January 31, 1959 (just three days prior to Holly's death in a plane crash), both Dylan and Holly had listened late at night to the same disc jockey, Frank "Brother Gatemouth" Page, broadcasting from Shreveport, Louisiana. Dylan, in Hibbing, Minnesota, on the Mesabi Iron Range, had the benefit of an antenna mounted by his father, whose family ran an appliance store. Because his devout parents would not have approved, Holly sneaked out of the house and off with the car to listen in it, continually repositioning the vehicle for the best reception. As a boy in St. Louis, Chuck Berry heard the music of the black church on the radio, but he also listened to big bands, jump combos, pop ballads, and country music.

But the story of rock and roll does not really begin with the radio, or with Ike Turner banging out boogie-woogie piano to back Jackie Brenston on "Rocket 88" in 1951, the electrification of blues in Chicago in the early 1950s, or at the famous session at the Memphis Recording Service in 1954 at which Elvis Presley, Scotty Moore, and Bill Black cut loose on "That's All Right," though these are all important chapters. Instead it begins in the holds of the ships that transported captured Africans to slavery in North America and with the first rhythmic call-and-response chant of unpaid labour and the secret language and rituals that proclaimed the undying humanity of people inhumanly treated. Likewise its origins can be found in the contracts that bound members of the British underclass to seven years of indentured servitude in exchange for their passage to the new world, in the Scots driven to North America by the Highland Clearances that forced them off the land to make way for large-scale sheep farming, and in the Irish immigrants displaced by the potato famine. It is the story of the music that these people brought with them and how the intermingling of that music in an American melting pot seldom on full boil still managed to produce rock and roll and an ever-expanding bounty of inventive hybrid genres. The banjos that became the engine of bluegrass came to the hills of Kentucky by way of Africa; the girl group harmonies of Motown's Supremes owed a debt to the music of the black church but also to European choral singing. Jimmy Rodgers's blues yodel echoed the work songs the "Singing Brakeman" heard sung by African American railroad workers, the melody for Chuck Berry's chugging "Maybelline" first emerged in the country ditty "Ida Red," and after he played gospel through the doors of the church, secularized as soul, Ray Charles turned his genius, at least temporarily, to country music. The prerequisite for Rock and Roll 101 is an introduction to the blues, country, traditional pop, and rhythm and blues. This book provides just that.

Arguably the most important early instructor of the course was Alan Freed. He was only one of a number of disc jockeys who first championed rhythm and blues; however, his place in the history popular music was cemented by his coining of the term *rock and roll*, though his contribution to the spread of the music went far beyond that. Leo Mintz, a record store owner who noticed a spike in the sales of "race" music (rechristened *rhythm and blues* in *Billboard* magazine by journalist and later producer Jerry Wexler), convinced Freed to begin playing the music on a radio show on WJW in Cleveland in 1951. As the "King of the Moon Doggers," Freed, who was white, sang, howled, and beat out the praises of "blues and rhythm" music on a telephone book, cultivating a mostly black listenership. Moving to New York City, he excitedly broadened his audience to include ever more young white listeners, who increasingly joined African Americans in the audiences of the live shows Freed staged. Many were outraged by this "race-mixing," bemoaned the "artless" music, and month after month and year after year predicted its imminent demise as a fad. In the meantime, Freed presided as the adult who "got it," spreading the word by playing himself in a series of R&B performance-filled movies and taking package shows on the road before becoming the biggest victim of the payola scandal, in which deejays were taken to task for accepting payments from independent labels to play their records on the air (long the standard practice in the industry).

Much of rock and roll's most raucous and iconoclastic attitude was learned at the movies in the what-have-you-got–to-rebel-against defiance of *The Wild One*, *Rebel Without a Cause*, and *Blackboard Jungle*. The last of these films featured Bill Haley's "Rock Around the Clock" on its soundtrack, solidifying the link between the music and rebellion. Yet as the 1950s came to a close, rebellion drained away from rock and roll as the music, or at least the music that was charting, seemed to lose its edge, not least because Presley's manager, Col. Tom Parker, encouraged his charge to tone it down so that he might appeal to an ever-broader audience, but also because the music had died in the roadside crash in England that took the life of Cochran and the plane crash in Iowa in which Holly perished and because Little Richard had found God and Chuck Berry found himself incarcerated. In the process the little pantheon of independent record labels that had risen with R&B and early rock and roll—most notably Chess, Sun, and Specialty Records—found it harder to make a go of it. Payola brought down Alan Freed, but Dick Clark, host of television's most famous rock-and-roll dance party, *American Bandstand*—who had used the show to promote performers who recorded for labels in which he had interests—not only emerged from the scandal largely unscathed but took a seat on top of the pop world as the clean-cut, close-to-the-surface performers who were *Bandstand* regulars assaulted the charts.

It was an era when polish was everything. In the 1950s producers such as Phillips and Norman Petty (who worked with Holly) had made their mark, but in the early 1960s Phil Spector elevated

Buddy Holly, innovative and inspirational rock-and-roll pioneer, here without his trademark glasses. Michael Ochs Archives/Getty Images

the role of the producer to another wildly creative level with his in-studio construction of the "Wall of Sound" on recordings by girl groups such as the Ronettes and the Crystals.

Brian Wilson, Spector's most adept disciple, began crafting his own studio masterpieces after first dominating surf music with his southern California band of brothers (cousins and friends), the Beach Boys, whose songs about sun, sand, cars, and girls were drenched in harmonies Wilson adapted from the vocal group the Four Freshman and driven by the careening guitar licks his brother Carl had borrowed from Berry. But perhaps the period's musical polish gleamed brightest in Detroit at Motown Records. There songwriter-entrepreneur Berry Gordy, Jr., and a staff on incomparable writers and producers, including Smokey Robinson, Norman Whitfield, and the team of Holland-Dozier-Holland, along with choreographer Cholly Atkins, and a remarkable house band known as the Funk Brothers, set the table for one of the most extraordinarily talented stables of performers ever assembled, who themselves had benefited from the Detroit school system's dedication to quality music education. The mere mention of but a few of Motown's brightest stars—Marvin Gaye, the Temptations, the Supremes, the Four Tops, Stevie Wonder, and Martha and the Vandellas—can put the musical memory of several generations of pop music fans on a shuffle filled with delight. Motown's sweet soul ranks among the most accomplished and most beloved popular music ever created.

The 1950s had produced remarkable changes in American music and stoked the kindling of social change that would blaze in the 1960s. It is important to note, though, that it was not just Americans who were listening. Across the Atlantic, young Britons in particular were smitten with the blues, R&B, and rock and roll, and in the decade that was beginning to unfold they would become protagonists in the story of rock music in their own extraordinary right.

# CHAPTER 1

# What Is Rock?

**I**t is certainly arguable that by the end of the 20th century rock was the world's dominant form of popular music. Originating in the United States in the 1950s, it spread to other English-speaking countries and across Europe in the '60s, and by the '90s its impact was obvious globally (if in many different local guises). Rock's commercial importance was by then reflected in the organization of the multinational recording industry, in the sales racks of international record retailers, and in the playlist policies of music radio and television. If other kinds of music—classical, jazz, easy listening, country, folk, etc.—are marketed as minority interests, rock defines the musical mainstream. And so over the last half of the 20th century it became the most inclusive of musical labels—everything can be "rocked"—and in consequence the hardest to define. To answer the question, What is rock?, one first has to understand where it came from and what made it possible. And to understand rock's cultural significance, one has to understand how it works socially as well as musically.

## THE DIFFICULTY OF DEFINITION

Dictionary definitions of rock are problematic, not least because the term has different resonance in its British and American usages (the latter is broader in scope). There is basic agreement that rock "is a form of music with a strong beat," but it is difficult to be much more explicit. The *Collins*

*Cobuild English Dictionary*, based on a vast database of British usage, suggests that "rock is a kind of music with simple tunes and a very strong beat that is played and sung, usually loudly, by a small group of people with electric guitars and drums," but there are so many exceptions to this description that it is practically useless.

Legislators seeking to define rock for regulatory purposes have not done much better. The Canadian government defined "rock and rock-oriented music" as "characterized by a strong beat, the use of blues forms and the presence of rock instruments such as electric guitar, electric bass, electric organ or electric piano." This assumes that rock can be marked off from other sorts of music formally, according to its sounds. In practice, though, the distinctions that matter for rock fans and musicians have been ideological. *Rock* was developed as a term to distinguish certain music-making and listening practices from those associated with pop; what was at issue was less a sound than an attitude. In 1990 British legislators defined pop music as "all kinds of music characterized by a strong rhythmic element and a reliance on electronic amplification for their performance." This led to strong objections from the music industry that such a definition failed to appreciate the clear sociological difference between pop ("instant singles-based music aimed at teenagers") and rock ("album-based music for adults"). In pursuit of definitional clarity, the lawmakers misunderstood what made rock music matter.

## CRUCIAL ROCK MUSICIANS

For lexicographers and legislators alike, the purpose of definition is to grasp a meaning in order to hold it in place so that people can use a word correctly—for example, to assign a track to its proper radio outlet (rock, pop, country, jazz). The trouble is that the term *rock* describes an evolving musical practice informed by a variety of nonmusical arguments (about creativity, sincerity, commerce, and popularity). It makes more sense, then, to approach the definition of rock historically, with examples. The following musicians were crucial to rock's history. What do they have in common?

Elvis Presley, from Memphis, Tennessee, personified a new form of American popular music in the mid-1950s. Rock and roll was a guitar-based sound with a strong (if loose) beat that drew equally on African American and white traditions from the southern United States, on blues, church music, and country music. Presley's rapid rise to national stardom revealed the new cultural and

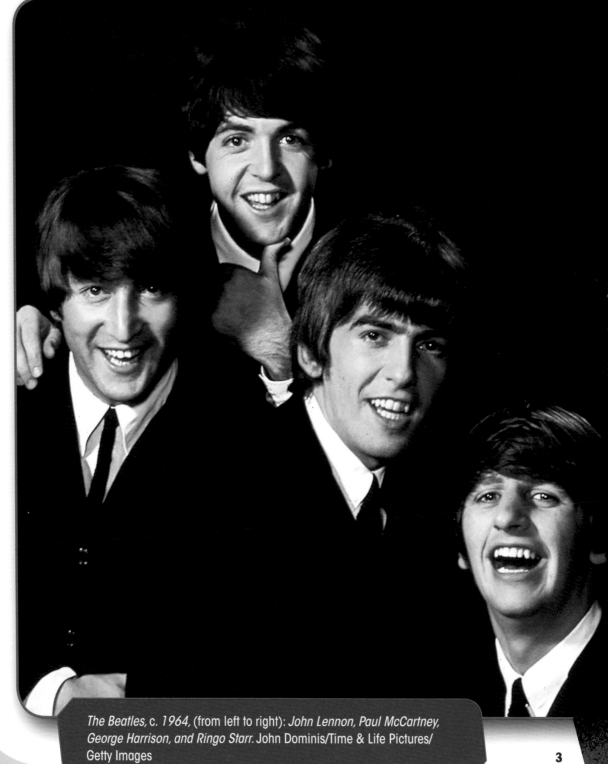

*The Beatles, c. 1964,* (from left to right): *John Lennon, Paul McCartney, George Harrison, and Ringo Starr.* John Dominis/Time & Life Pictures/ Getty Images

economic power of both teenagers and teen-aimed media—records, radio, television, and motion pictures.

The Beatles, from Liverpool, England (via Hamburg, Germany), personified a new form of British popular music in the 1960s. Merseybeat was a British take on the black and white musical mix of rock and roll: a basic lineup of lead guitar, rhythm guitar, bass guitar, and drums (with shared vocals) provided local live versions of American hit records of all sorts. The Beatles added to this an artistic self-consciousness, soon writing their own songs and using the recording studio to develop their own—rather than a commercial producer's—musical ideas. The group's unprecedented success in the United States ensured that rock would be an Anglo-American phenomenon.

Bob Dylan, from Hibbing, Minnesota (via New York City), personified a new form of American music in the mid-1960s. Dylan brought together the amplified beat of rock and roll, the star imagery of pop, the historical and political sensibility of folk, and—through the wit, ambition, and obscurity of his lyrics—the arrogance of urban bohemia. He gave the emerging rock scene artistic weight (his was album, not Top 40, music) and a new account of youth as an ideological rather than a demographic category.

Jimi Hendrix, from Seattle, Washington (via London), personified the emergence of rock as a specific musical genre in the late 1960s. Learning his trade as a guitarist in rhythm-and-blues bands and possessing a jazzman's commitment to collective improvisation, he came to fame leading a trio in London and exploring the possibilities of the amplifier as a musical instrument in the recording studio and on the concert stage. Hendrix established versatility and technical skill as a norm for rock musicianship and gave shape to a new kind of event: the outdoor festival and stadium concert, in which the noise of the audience became part of the logic of the music.

Bob Marley, from Kingston, Jamaica (via London), personified a new kind of global popular music in the 1970s. Marley and his group, the Wailers, combined sweet soul vocals inspired by Chicago groups such as the Impressions with rock guitar, a reggae beat, and Rastafarian mysticism. Marley's commercial success established Jamaica as a major source of international talent, leaving a reggae imprint not just on Western rock but also on local music makers in Africa, Asia, and Australia.

Madonna, from suburban Detroit, Michigan (via New York City), personified a new sort of global teen idol in the 1980s. She combined the sounds and technical devices of the New York City disco club scene with the new sales and image-making opportunities

*Jimi Hendrix performing at Woodstock.* Barry Z. Levine/Premium Archive/
Getty Images

offered by video promotion—primarily by Music Television (MTV), the music-based cable television service. As a star, Madonna had it both ways: she was at once a knowing American feminist artist and a global sales icon for the likes of Pepsi-Cola.

Public Enemy, from New York City, personified a new sort of African American music in the late 1980s. Rap, the competitive use of rhyming lines spoken over an ever-more-challenging rhythmic base, had a long history in African American culture; however, it came to musical prominence as part of the hip-hop movement. Public Enemy used new digital technology to sample (use excerpts from other recordings) and recast the urban soundscape from the perspective of African American youth. This was music that was at once sharply attuned to local political conditions and resonant internationally. By the mid-1990s rap had become an expressive medium for minority social groups around the world.

What does this version of rock's history—from Presley to Public Enemy—reveal? First, that rock is so broad a musical category that in practice people organize their tastes around more focused genre labels: the young Presley was a rockabilly, the Beatles a pop group, Dylan a folkie, Madonna a disco diva, Marley and the Wailers a reggae act, and Public Enemy rappers. Even Hendrix,

the most straightforward rock star on this list, also has a place in the histories of rhythm and blues and jazz. In short, while all these musicians played a significant part in the development of rock, they did so by using different musical instruments and textures, different melodic and rhythmic principles, and different approaches to lyrics and performing.

## MUSICAL ECLECTICISM AND THE USE OF TECHNOLOGY

Even from a musicological point of view, any account of rock has to start with its eclecticism. Beginning with the mix of country and blues that comprised rock and roll (rock's first incarnation), rock has been essentially a hybrid form. African American music was at the centre of this mix, but rock resulted from what white musicians, with their own folk histories and pop conventions, did with African American music—and with issues of race and race relations.

Rock's musical eclecticism reflects (and is reflected in) the geographic mobility of rock musicians, back and forth across the United States, over the Atlantic Ocean, and throughout Europe. Presley was unique as a rock star who did not move away from his roots; Hendrix was more typical in his restlessness. And if rock and roll had rural origins, the rock audience was from the start urban, an anonymous crowd seeking an idealized sense of community and sociability in dance halls and clubs, on radio stations, and in headphones. Rock's central appeal as a popular music has been its ability to provide globally an intense experience of belonging, whether to a local scene or a subculture.

Rock is better defined, then, by its eclecticism than by reference to some musical essence, and it is better understood in terms of its general use of technology rather than by its use of particular instruments (such as the guitar). Early rock-and-roll stars such as Presley and Buddy Holly depended for their sound on engineers' trickery in the recording studio as much as they did on their own vocal skills, and the guitar became the central rock instrument because of its amplified rather than acoustic qualities. Rock's history is tied up with technological shifts in the storage, retrieval, and transmission of sounds: multitrack tape recording made possible an experimental composition process that turned the recording studio into an artist's studio; digital recording made possible a manipulation of sound that shifted the boundaries between music and noise.

Rock musicians pushed against the technical limits of sound amplification and inspired the development of new electronic instruments, such as the drum machine. Even relatively primitive technologies, such as the double-deck turntable, were tools for new sorts of music making in the hands of the "scratch" deejay, and one way rock marked itself off from other popular musical forms was in its constant pursuit of new sounds and new sound devices. With the advent of sophisticated digital recording software, more and more musicians have become their own producers and sound engineers.

## RURAL MUSIC IN URBAN SETTINGS

Selling the various forms of rural American music (blues, folk, country, and gospel) had always been the business of small rather than corporate entrepreneurs, but World War II changed the markets for them—partly because of the hundreds of thousands of Southerners who migrated north for work, bringing their music with them, and partly because of the broadening cultural horizons that resulted from military service. Rural music in urban settings became, necessarily, louder and more aggressive (the same thing had happened to jazz in the early 1920s). Instruments, notably the guitar, had to be amplified to cut through the noise, and, as black dance bands got smaller (for straightforward economic reasons), guitar, bass, and miked-up voice replaced brass and wind sections, while

# ROCK AND RECORDING TECHNOLOGY

In the early 1940s, recording sessions took place to document musical performances. Except for the presence of a microphone (and, perhaps, the absence of an audience), the procedure was exactly the same as a live performance: all members of the ensemble played and sang together "live," and the music was etched onto an acetate disc. This was the master from which copies were made for commercial release. No editing was possible; corrections and revisions could be made only on subsequent performances. After World War II, however, the much-improved medium of magnetic tape offered both superior sound quality and the crucial advantage of editability. From the simple tape splice to the more recent cutting and pasting of digital audio, the ability to edit gave rise to a "record consciousness," an approach that sought to move beyond the simple documentary function of the recording studio to exploit its potential for composition and experimentation.

Multitrack technology brings an additive dimension to recording: individual instruments, or groups of instruments, can be recorded separately and not necessarily simultaneously. All tracks are then fed through a mixing console where individual volumes are set relative to the sound as a whole. For the mixing stage, signal modifying devices are used to enhance or, in some cases, transform the original timbre of the recorded material. Sam Phillips's "slapback" delay treatment of Elvis Presley's voice, Phil Spector's distinctive use of the echo chamber, and the extraordinary innovations produced by digital sampling illustrate how seemingly "natural" sounds are technologically effected in the composition of popular music. Technology has therefore increased the control recording artists have over the process of creating popular music to the extent that the studio itself has become the primary site of the compositional process. Pop musicians often begin a recording project with little, if any, material beyond a broad conceptual framework and some digitally recorded or taped sketches. As the work progresses, the artist will shape the music through considerable experimentation with different structural and timbral (sound quality) possibilities. Thus, the recording apparatus is used as a notating device, and the principal mode of communication is oral. (Jimi Hendrix, for example, was known to leave the tape machine running for the entire recording session.) Moreover, most of the traditional distinctions between performer and composer, technician and artist have blurred as creative input comes from all participants regardless of their official role: a guitarist might suggest a bass line; an engineer might offer a useful critique of one take over another that results in a change in the music.

keyboards and saxophone became rhythm instruments used to swell the beat punched out by the drums. Country dance bands, emerging from 1940s jazz-influenced western swing, made similar changes, amplifying guitars and bass, giving the piano a rhythmic role, and playing up the personality of the singer.

Such music—rhythm and blues and honky-tonk—was developed in live performance by traveling musicians who made their living by attracting dancers to bars, clubs, and halls. By the late 1940s it was being recorded by independent record companies, always on the lookout for cheap repertoire and aware of these musicians' local pulling power. As the records were played on local radio stations, the appeal of this music—its energy, humour, and suggestiveness—reached white suburban teenagers who otherwise knew nothing about it. Rhythm-and-blues record retailers, radio stations, and deejays (most famously Alan Freed) became aware of a new market—partying teenagers—while the relevant recording studios began to be visited by young white musicians who wanted to make such music for themselves. The result was rock and roll, the adoption of these rural-urban, black and white sounds by an emergent teenage culture that came to international attention with the success of the film *Blackboard Jungle* in 1956.

## MARKETING ROCK AND ROLL

Rock and roll's impact in the 1950s reflected the spending power of

# AMERICAN BANDSTAND

From 1957 through 1963 Philadelphia was the "Home of the Hits," a reflection of the power of Dick Clark's *American Bandstand* television show, carried nationally on the American Broadcasting Company network. The program's format was simple: singers mimed (lip-synched) to their records, and the show's teenage audience danced. Before the advent of *Bandstand,* no Philadelphia-based label had ever been consistently successful; in the wake of the show, several labels based in the city—including Cameo, Chancellor, Jamie, and Swan—were regularly on the charts.

In 1960, during the congressional hearings on payola (money or gifts given by record labels to disc jockeys to air their records), it was revealed that Clark (who was inducted into the Rock and Roll Hall of Fame in 1993) had part ownership of the labels as well as shares in local pressing plants and distribution companies that out-of-town independent labels were allegedly encouraged to use. Under Clark's patronage several local singers of modest talent emerged as national stars—Frankie Avalon, Bobby Rydell, and Fabian—while a succession of banal dance records, including "The Twist" by Chubby Checker, became hits. There were talented Philadelphia-based musicians untainted by all this—notably John Coltrane, Earl Bostic, and Bill Doggett—but they all recorded elsewhere. It was not until the emergence of producer-songwriters Thom Bell, Kenny Gamble, and Leon Huff later in the 1960s and the tremendous success of Philadelphia International Records in the '70s that the city could proudly claim its own sound.

young people who, as a result of the '50s economic boom (and in contrast to the prewar Great Depression), had unprecedented disposable income. That income was of interest not just to record companies but to an ever-increasing range of advertisers keen to pay for time on teen-oriented, Top 40 radio stations and for the development of teen-aimed television shows such as *American Bandstand*. For the major record companies, Presley's success marked less the appeal of do-it-yourself musical hybrids than the potential of teenage idols: singers with musical material and visual images that could be marketed on radio and television and in motion pictures and magazines. The appeal of live rock and roll (and its predominantly black performers) was subordinated to the manufacture of teenage pop stars (who were almost exclusively white). Creative attention thus swung from the performers to the record makers— that is, to the songwriters (such as those gathered in the Brill Building in New York City) and producers (such as Phil Spector) who could guarantee the teen appeal of a record and ensure that it would stand out on a car radio.

## A BLACK AND WHITE HYBRID

Whatever the commercial forces at play (and despite the continuing industry belief that this was pop music as transitory novelty), it became clear that the most successful writers and producers of teenage music were themselves young and intrigued by musical mixability and the technological possibilities of the recording studio. In the early 1960s teenage pop ceased to sound like young adult pop. Youthful crooners such as Frankie Avalon and Fabian were replaced in the charts by vocal groups such as the Shirelles. A new rock-and-roll hybrid of black and white music appeared: Spector derived the mini-dramas of girl groups such as the Crystals and the Ronettes from the vocal rhythm-and-blues style of doo-wop, the Beach Boys rearranged Chuck Berry for barbershop-style close harmonies, and in Detroit Berry Gordy's Motown label drew on gospel music (first secularized for the teenage market by Sam Cooke) for the more rhythmically complex but equally commercial sounds of the Supremes and Martha and the Vandellas. For the new generation of record producer, whether Spector, the Beach Boys' Brian Wilson, or Motown's Smokey Robinson and the team of Holland-Dozier-Holland, the commercial challenge—to make a record that would be heard through all the other noises in teenage lives—was also an artistic challenge. Even in this most commercial of scenes (thanks in part to its emphasis on fashion), success depended on a creative approach to technological DIY(do-it-yourself).

# CHAPTER 2

# Roots: Part 1, the Blues

In an earlier era, blues, country, and European-derived traditional folk music all were considered "folk" music. All three musical styles, however, not only served as the inspiration and building blocks for rock and roll but became popular commercial music in their own right. It is hard to imagine the rock music of today without any one of these antecedents or without the tradition of deliberate popular music stretching from Stephen Foster to the crooners of mid-20th century. Of the number of musical sources in which rock is rooted, none is more fertile or seminal than the blues.

## BLUES BASICS

From its origin in the South, the blues' simple but expressive forms had become by the 1960s one of the most important influences on the development of popular music throughout the United States. Although instrumental accompaniment is almost universal in the blues, the blues is essentially a vocal form. Blues songs are lyrical rather than narrative; blues singers are expressing feelings rather than telling stories. The emotion expressed is generally one of sadness or melancholy, often due to problems in love. To express this musically, blues performers use vocal techniques such as melisma (sustaining a single syllable across several pitches), rhythmic techniques such as syncopation, and instrumental techniques such as "choking" or bending guitar strings on the neck or applying a metal slide or bottleneck to the guitar strings to create a whining, voicelike sound.

As a musical style, the blues is characterized by expressive "microtonal" pitch inflections (blue notes), a three-line textual stanza of the form AAB, and a 12-measure form. Typically the first two and a half measures of each line are devoted to singing, the last measure and a half consisting of an instrumental "break" that repeats, answers, or complements the vocal line. In terms of functional (i.e., traditional European) harmony, the simplest blues harmonic progression is described as follows (I, IV, and V refer, respectively, to the first or tonic, fourth or subdominant, and fifth or dominant notes of the scale):

Phrase 1 (measures 1–4) I–I–I–I

Phrase 2 (measures 5–8) IV–IV–I–I

Phrase 3 (measures 9–12) V–V–I–I

African influences are apparent in the blues tonality, the call-and-response pattern of the repeated refrain structure of the blues stanza, the falsetto break in the vocal style, and the imitation of vocal idioms by instruments, especially the guitar and harmonica.

## CLASSIC BLUES

Although the origins of the blues are poorly documented, it is known that the blues developed in the southern United States after the American Civil War (1861–65). It was influenced by work songs and field hollers, minstrel show music, ragtime, church music, and the folk and popular music of the white population. Blues derived from and was largely played by Southern black men, most of whom were agricultural workers. The earliest references to blues date back to the 1890s and early 1900s. In 1912 black bandleader W.C. Handy's composition "Memphis Blues" was published. It became very popular, and thereafter many other Tin Pan Alley songs entitled blues—Tin Pan Alley being a genre of U.S. popular music that arose in New York in the late 19th century—began to appear.

## W.C. HANDY

W.C. Handy (born William Christopher Handy, November 16, 1873, Florence, Alabama, U.S.—died March 28, 1958, New York, New York) was a son and grandson of Methodist ministers, and he was educated at Teachers Agricultural and Mechanical College in Huntsville, Alabama. Going against family tradition, he began to cultivate his interest in music at a young age and learned to play several instruments, including the organ, piano, and guitar. He was a particularly skilled cornetist and trumpet player. Longing to experience

*Birthplace of W.C. Handy, Florence, Ala.* Carol M. Highsmith/Library of Congress, Washington, D.C. (LC-DIG-highsm-08585)

the world beyond Florence, Alabama, Handy left his hometown in 1892. He traveled throughout the Midwest, taking a variety of jobs with several musical groups. He also worked as a teacher in 1900–02. He conducted his own orchestra, the Knights of Pythias from Clarksdale, Mississippi, from 1903 to 1921. During the early years of this period of his life, Handy was steeped in the music of the Mississippi Delta and of Memphis, and he began to arrange some of those tunes for his band's performances. Unable to find a publisher for the songs he was beginning to write, Handy formed a partnership with Harry Pace and founded Pace & Handy Music Company (later Handy Brothers Music Company).

Handy worked during the period of transition from ragtime to jazz.

Drawing on the vocal blues melodies of African American folklore, he added harmonizations to his orchestral arrangements. His work helped develop the conception of the blues as a harmonic framework within which to improvise. With his "Memphis Blues" (published 1912) and especially his "St. Louis Blues" (1914), he introduced a melancholic element, achieved chiefly by use of the "blue" or slightly flattened seventh tone of the scale, which was characteristic of African American folk music.

## MA RAINEY

The first blues recordings were made in the 1920s by black women such as Mamie Smith, Ma Rainey, Ida Cox, and Bessie Smith. These performers were primarily stage singers backed by jazz bands; their style is known as classic blues.

Ma Rainey (born Gertrude Malissa Nix Pridgett, April 26, 1886, Columbus, Georgia, U.S.—died December 22, 1939, Rome, Georgia) and her husband, William "Pa" Rainey, toured with African American minstrel groups as a song-and-dance team. In 1902, in a small Missouri town, she first heard the sort of music that was to become known as the blues. She soon began singing blues songs and contributed greatly to the evolution of the form

and to the growth of its popularity. In her travels she appeared with jazz and jug bands throughout the South. While with the Tolliver's Circus and Musical Extravaganza troupe, she exerted a direct influence on young Bessie Smith. Her deep contralto voice, sometimes verging on harshness, was a powerful instrument by which to convey the pathos of her simple songs of everyday life and emotion.

In 1923 Ma Rainey (who was inducted into the Rock and Roll Hall of Fame as an early influence in 1990) made her first phonograph recordings for the Paramount company. Over a five-year span she recorded some 92 songs for the label—such titles as "See See Rider," "Prove It on Me," "Blues Oh Blues," "Sleep Talking," "Oh Papa Blues," "Trust No Man," "Slave to the Blues," "New Boweavil Blues," and "Slow Driving Moan"—that later became the only permanent record of one of the most influential popular musical artists of her time. She continued to sing in public into the 1930s.

## BESSIE SMITH

Bessie Smith (born Elizabeth Smith, April 15, 1898?, Chattanooga, Tennessee, U.S.—died September 26, 1937, Clarksdale, Mississippi) grew up in poverty and obscurity. She may

*Bessie Smith.* Gilles Petard/Redferns/Getty Images

in 1989) traveled through the South singing in tent shows and bars and theatres in small towns and in such cities as Birmingham, Alabama; Memphis, Tennessee; and Atlanta and Savannah, Georgia. After 1920 she made her home in Philadelphia, and it was there that she was first heard by Clarence Williams, a representative of Columbia Records. In February 1923 she made her first recordings, including the classic "Down Hearted Blues," which became an enormous success, selling more than two million copies. She made 160 recordings in all, in many of which she was accompanied by some of the great jazz musicians of the time, including Fletcher Henderson, Benny Goodman, and Louis Armstrong.

Bessie Smith's subject matter was the classic material of the blues: poverty and oppression, love—betrayed or unrequited—and stoic acceptance of defeat at the hands of a cruel and indifferent world. The great tragedy of her career was that she outlived the topicality of her idiom. In the late 1920s her record sales and her fame diminished as social forces changed the face of popular music and bowdlerized the earthy realism of the sentiments she expressed in her music. Her gradually increasing alcoholism caused managements to become wary of engaging her, but there is no evidence that her actual

have made a first public appearance at the age of eight or nine at the Ivory Theatre in her hometown. About 1919 Smith was discovered by Ma Rainey, from whom she received some training. For several years Smith (who was inducted into the Rock and Roll Hall of Fame as an early influence

singing ability ever declined. Known in her lifetime as the "Empress of the Blues," Smith was a bold, supremely confident artist who often disdained the use of a microphone and whose art expressed the frustrations and hopes of a whole generation of black Americans. Her tall figure and upright stance, and above all her handsome features, are preserved in a short motion picture, *St. Louis Blues* (1929), banned for its realism and now preserved in the Museum of Modern Art, New York City. She died from injuries sustained in a road accident. It was said that, had she been white, she would have received earlier medical treatment, thus saving her life, and Edward Albee made this the subject of his play *The Death of Bessie Smith* (1960).

## RURAL BLUES

The rural blues developed in three principal regions, Georgia and the Carolinas, Texas, and Mississippi. The blues of Georgia and the Carolinas is noted for its clarity of enunciation and regularity of rhythm. Influenced by ragtime and white folk music, it is more melodic than the Texas and Mississippi styles. Blind Willie McTell and Blind Boy Fuller were representative of this style. The Texas blues is characterized by high, clear singing accompanied by supple guitar

lines that consist typically of single-string picked arpeggios rather than strummed chords. Blind Lemon Jefferson was by far the most influential Texas bluesman.

## BLIND LEMON JEFFERSON

Blind from birth and the youngest of seven children, Lemon Jefferson (born September 1893, Couchman, Texas, U.S.—died *c.* December 1929, Chicago, Illinois) became an itinerant entertainer in his teens, learning a repertoire of prison songs, blues, moans, spirituals, and dance numbers. He worked in the streets and in brothels, saloons, and at parties in Texas, Louisiana, Mississippi, Alabama, and Virginia. In the 1920s he went to Chicago.

Jefferson's high voice, shouting style, and advanced guitar technique, which used melodic lead lines, bent notes, and imitative effects, as well as his lyrics and themes, became staples of the blues through such disciples as Leadbelly (Huddie Ledbetter), who worked with Jefferson for a time, and through his recordings for the Paramount label (1926–29). Jefferson also recorded spiritual songs, using the pseudonym Deacon L.J. Bates. Among his best-known songs are "Black Snake Moan," "Matchbox Blues," and "See That My Grave Is Kept Clean." The circumstances of Jefferson's death are uncertain, though there were reports that he suffered a heart attack on the street and died of exposure. He was buried in the Wortham (Texas) Negro Cemetery, and his grave went unmarked until October 15, 1967, when blues devotees placed a metal marker on the plot; in 1997 it was replaced by a granite headstone.

## DELTA BLUES

The Mississippi Delta style of blues—or, simply, Delta blues—emphasized solo performances by singers accompanying themselves on guitar and relying on a host of distinctive techniques, such as the sliding of a bottleneck or metal object (such as a knife) along the fingerboard to bend notes, the use of melodic phrases on the guitar to respond to the voice in an improvised call-and-response pattern, and a reliance on vamps (repeated chord progressions that precede the entrance of the voice) and melodic and rhythmic figures that often deviated from the typical chord progressions and formal 12-bar (measure) structure found in most blues performances. Above all, Delta blues music was marked by a particular intensity of vision that was both projected through the lyrics of the songs and underscored by the players' often aggressive attack on the guitar strings. Song topics encompassed familiar laments of failed romance, stories of sexual escapades (often described in double-entendre references), and tales of rambling and life on the road, as well as apocalyptic musings on salvation and damnation.

Performance venues were often informal and happenstance. W.C. Handy recalled an early encounter with blues music about 1903 at a train station in Tutwiler, Mississippi, where he heard a man dressed in rags singing while playing the guitar with a knife. Performances also took place at juke joints (informal roadside taverns for drinking and dancing) on plantations and street corners. Folk music scholars John and Alan Lomax, meanwhile, documented Delta blues music in field recordings made at the Mississippi State Penitentiary, colloquially known as "Parchman Farm," in Sunflower County, Mississippi.

Scattered accounts by travelers and researchers indicate the prevalence of blues music in the Delta region since at least the turn of the 20th century, although no commercial recordings were made until the late 1920s. Associated primarily with male singer-guitarists, the Delta sound stood in marked contrast to earlier recordings of the "classic" blues singers, which had emphasized female vocalists working with small combo accompaniment. The Paramount record label enjoyed great success with the Delta blues recordings of Charley Patton.

## CHARLEY PATTON

Charley Patton (born *c.* 1887–91, Hinds County, Mississippi, U.S.—died April 28, 1934, Indianola, Mississippi) spent most of his life in the Delta region of northwestern Mississippi, and from about 1900 he was often based at Dockery's plantation in Sunflower County. There he and other early blues performers, such as Tommy Johnson and Willie Brown, shared songs and ideas. Patton spent most of his career playing blues and ragtime-based popular songs for dancers at rural parties and barrelhouses, where his singing and clowning made him a popular entertainer.

In the nearly 70 recordings he made between 1929 and 1934, Patton sang in a coarse, strained, sometimes unintelligible voice while providing himself with a changing, heavily percussive guitar accompaniment. His lyrics range from personal to topical. He also recorded some gospel songs. His best-known recording is "Pony Blues," among the first of his to be issued, and others such as "Down the Dirt Road," "Shake It and Break It," "High Water Everywhere," and "Moon Going Down" helped secure his popularity.

The aggressive intensity of Patton's performances is particularly notable, a quality that influenced his successors such as Howlin' Wolf (Chester Arthur Burnett), Son House, and Bukka White.

In 1930, Paramount made a series of recordings by Eddie ("Son") House, whose music failed to find a large audience at the time but exerted a powerful influence on later blues performers, notably Robert Johnson and Muddy Waters. Tommy Johnson, who recorded for both the Victor and Paramount labels, also contributed to the Delta legacy with his widely emulated guitar style.

## TOMMY JOHNSON

Tommy Johnson (born *c.* 1896, Terry, Mississippi, U.S.—died November 1, 1956, Crystal Springs, Mississippi) grew up in Crystal Springs, Mississippi, and learned to play guitar from one of his brothers. He ran away from home to play in the Mississippi Delta region, where he encountered other early blues singers, most notably Charley Patton. Subsequently, he spent much of his life there, playing at parties, dances, picnics, and juke joints, performing for donations on town streets, and sometimes taking nonmusical jobs; he also played in neighbouring states.

Johnson's only two recording sessions, in 1928 and 1930, reveal his sweet voice, with near-yodeling falsetto phrases, over a simple but active guitar accompaniment. Lyrics from his songs, including "Maggie Campbell Blues," "Big Road Blues," and "Cool Drink of Water Blues," became standard features of the blues repertoire, while one of his most compelling works, "Canned Heat Blues," was autobiographical: Johnson was severely alcoholic, a factor that narrowed his career.

## SKIP JAMES AND BUKKA WHITE

The recording of blues music was sharply curtailed during the Great Depression, yet a few traditional blues musicians from Mississippi continued to find opportunities to record. Skip James developed a deeply personal blues style on guitar—often using an unconventional tuning—as well as on piano. Although his 1931 recordings for Paramount sold poorly at the time, songs such as "Hard Time Killing Floor Blues," "Devil Got My Woman," and "I'm So Glad" later gained recognition as blues classics; the latter song was featured on a 1966 hit album by the rock-music trio Cream. Booker ("Bukka") White, another prominent Mississippi guitarist, enjoyed commercial success with his 1937 recording "Shake 'Em on Down," and in 1940 he recorded an especially influential group of songs, including "Parchman Farm Blues" and "District Attorney Blues," both of which addressed issues of social justice that were typically avoided in traditional blues music.

## ROBERT JOHNSON

Robert Johnson was the most important Delta blues musician of the era. His eerie falsetto singing voice and masterful, rhythmic slide guitar influenced both his contemporaries and many later blues and rock musicians.

Johnson (born c. 1911, Hazlehurst, Mississippi, U.S.—died August 16, 1938, near Greenwood, Mississippi) was the product of a confusing childhood, with three men serving as his father before he reached age seven. Little is known about his biological father (Noah Johnson, whom his mother never married), and the boy and his mother lived on various plantations in the Mississippi Delta region before settling briefly in Memphis, Tennessee, with her first husband (Robert Dodds, who had changed his surname to Spencer). The bulk of Johnson's youth, however, was spent in Robinsonville, Mississippi, with his mother and her second husband (Dusty Willis). There Johnson learned to play the Jew's harp and harmonica before taking up the guitar. In 1929 he married 16-year-old Virginia Travis, whose death in childbirth (along with that of their baby) in April 1930 devastated Johnson.

In Robinsonville he came in contact with masters of the Mississippi Delta blues Willie Brown, Charley Patton, and Son House—all of whom

*Blues musician Skip James in Washington Square Park, New York City,* c. *1965.* Bernard Gotfryd/Premium Archive/Getty Images

influenced his playing and none of whom was particularly impressed by his talent. They were dazzled by his musical ability, however, when he returned to town after spending as much as a year away. That time away is central to Johnson's mythic status. According to legend, during that period Johnson made a deal with Satan at a crossroads, acquiring his prodigious talent as a guitarist, singer, and songwriter in exchange for the stipulation that he would have only eight more years to live. (A similar story circulated in regard to Tommy Johnson.) Music historian Robert Palmer, in his highly regarded book *Deep Blues* (1981), instead ascribes Robert Johnson's remarkable musical attainments to the time he had to hone his skills as a guitarist under the instruction of Ike Zinneman as a result of the financial support he received from the older woman he married near Hazlehurst, Mississippi (Johnson's birthplace), and to the wide variety of music to which he was exposed during his hiatus from Robinsonville, including the single-string picking styles of Lonnie Johnson and Scrapper Blackwell.

After returning briefly to Robinsonville, Robert Johnson settled in Helena, Arkansas, where he played with Elmore James, Robert Nighthawk, and Howlin' Wolf, among others. He also became involved with Estella Coleman and informally adopted her son, Robert Lockwood, Jr., who later became a notable blues musician under the name Robert Jr. Lockwood. Johnson traveled widely throughout Mississippi, Arkansas, Texas, and Tennessee and as far north as Chicago and New York, playing at house parties, juke joints, lumber camps, and on the street. In 1936–37 he made a series of recordings in a hotel room in San Antonio, Texas, and a warehouse in Dallas. His repertoire included several blues songs by House and others, but Johnson's original numbers, such as "Me and the Devil Blues," "Hellhound on My Trail," "Sweet Home Chicago," "I Believe I'll Dust My Broom," "Ramblin' on My Mind," and "Love in Vain" are his most compelling pieces. Unlike the songs of many of his contemporaries—which tended to unspool loosely, employing combinations of traditional and improvised lyrics—Johnson's songs were tightly composed, and his song structure and lyrics were praised by Bob Dylan. Despite the limited number of his recordings, Johnson (who was inducted into the Rock and Roll Hall of Fame as an early influence in 1986) had a major impact on other musicians, including Muddy Waters, Elmore James, Eric Clapton, and the Rolling Stones. Johnson died of poisoning after drinking

# LONNIE JOHNSON

One of a large family of musicians, Lonnie Johnson (born Alonzo Johnson, February 8, 1889?, New Orleans, Louisiana, U.S.—died June 16, 1970, Toronto, Ontario, Canada) played violin in his father's string band, and he also played guitar in New Orleans in the early 20th century. He traveled with a musical revue to London in 1917, returning home two years later. Johnson performed in the Mississippi riverboat bands of Fate Marable and Charlie Creath (1920–22) and on vaudeville tours before beginning his recording career, which lasted some 40 years and yielded about 500 recordings. Though he also played often in theatres and nightclubs and on radio, he supported himself with nonmusical work during several lean periods.

Johnson did much of his major work during his first recording period, 1925–32. He was among the first guitarists to play single-string solos, and his energy, swing, melodic ingenuity, and good taste were important elements in recordings by Louis Armstrong's Hot Five ("Hotter Than That"), Duke Ellington, The Chocolate Dandies, McKinney's Cotton Pickers, and King Oliver. He also recorded guitar solos and exceptional duets with the other major early jazz guitarist, Eddie Lang ("A Handful of Riffs").

Despite his urban style, Johnson's blues also influenced rural performers, most notably Robert Johnson. An unusually gifted lyricist, his subject matter ranged from highly serious to amusing ("Blue Ghost Blues"). In time his blues often became repetitious, and he added sentimental ballads to his repertoire; one ballad, "Tomorrow Night" (1948), was a million-record-selling hit.

strychnine-laced whiskey in a juke joint.

## URBAN BLUES

The Great Depression and the World Wars caused the geographic dispersal of the blues as millions of African Americans left the South for the cities of the North. The blues became adapted to the more sophisticated urban environment. Lyrics took up urban themes, and the blues ensemble developed as the solo bluesman was joined by a pianist or harmonica player and then by a rhythm section consisting of bass and drums. The electric guitar and the amplified harmonica created a driving sound of great rhythmic and emotional intensity.

Among the cities in which the blues initially took root were Atlanta, Memphis, and St. Louis. John Lee Hooker settled in Detroit, and on the West Coast Aaron ("T-Bone") Walker

# SWEET HOME CHICAGO IN THE 1950S

Then the second most populous city in the United States, by the 1950s Chicago had the potential talent and market to sustain a substantial music industry—but it rarely did so. The city did support a vibrant jazz scene during Prohibition and was the leading recording centre for artists supplying the "race" market during the 1930s: Big Bill Broonzy, Georgia Tom (who, as Thomas A. Dorsey, went on to even greater success as a gospel composer), Tampa Red, and many more. During the 1940s Mercury Records was founded from a Chicago base and emerged as a viable rival to the established major companies. But the most creative period for the city was the 1950s, when rivals Chess and Vee Jay battled for supremacy in the rhythm-and-blues market. The few blues artists who chose other labels later looked back in regret—when it came to getting records played on the radio, Chess and Vee Jay had no peers in Chicago.

developed a style later adopted by Riley ("B.B.") King. It was Chicago, however, that played the greatest role in the development of urban blues. In the 1920s and '30s Memphis Minnie, Tampa Red, Big Bill Broonzy, and John Lee ("Sonny Boy") Williamson were popular Chicago performers. After World War II they were supplanted by a new generation of bluesmen that included Muddy Waters, Chester Arthur Burnett (Howlin' Wolf), Elmore James, Little Walter Jacobs, Buddy Guy, and Koko Taylor.

In the years following World War II, traditional blues fell out of favour with the public. The Delta musicians, however, continued to exert a strong influence on the music world, although often from new home bases outside the region. Muddy Waters and Howlin' Wolf both left Mississippi and played a key role in defining the emerging Chicago style of blues. These two artists also helped establish Chess Records as one of the leading independent labels in the United States. In its new setting, the solo performance approach of the Delta was replaced by a high-energy ensemble style that featured electric guitar, anticipating both the sound and the instrumentation of 1960s rock music.

B.B. King also contributed to this mainstreaming of the Delta blues legacy and stood out as one of the most influential electric guitarists of his generation. He created an expansive guitar style that mixed blues with elements of jazz, rhythm and blues, and other popular-music idioms. By contrast, John Lee Hooker retained the most overtly traditional approach of the Delta players. He achieved crossover success during the postwar period, using solo guitar with voice—the approach typical of earlier Delta players—for his hit record "Boogie Chillen" in 1948. Hooker did, however, incorporate elements of rock and soul music into his later releases

The blues have influenced many other musical styles. Blues and jazz are closely related; such influential jazzmen as Jelly Roll Morton and Louis Armstrong employed blues elements in their music. Soul music and rhythm and blues also show obvious blues tonalities and forms. The blues have had their greatest influence on rock music. Early rock singers such as Elvis Presley often used blues material. British rock musicians in the 1960s, especially the Rolling Stones, Eric Clapton, and John Mayall, were strongly influenced by the blues, as were such American rock musicians as Mike Bloomfield, Paul Butterfield, and the Allman Brothers Band.

Meanwhile, resurgent interest in the earlier Delta tradition during the 1960s led to unexpected career revivals for Son House, Skip James, Bukka White, and others. In many instances, these artists found larger audiences and greater commercial success in their final years than they ever did as young men. The most striking sign of the enduring importance of the Delta tradition, however, came via the work of prominent rock artists of the period. The Rolling Stones, the Beatles, and Bob Dylan were among those who, in creating their own music, tapped the legacy of early blues musicians and ultimately inspired many of their fans to seek out the work of the leading exponents of the Delta tradition.

# CHAPTER 3

# Roots: Part 2, Country and Western

**A**mong the branches of rock's family tree is country music, and ultimately, country music's roots lie in the ballads, folk songs, and popular songs of the English, Scots, and Irish settlers of the Appalachians and other parts of the South. In the early 1920s the traditional string-band music of the Southern mountain regions began to be commercially recorded, with Fiddlin' John Carson garnering the genre's first hit record in 1923. The vigour and realism of the rural songs, many lyrics of which were rather impersonal narratives of tragedies pointing to a stern, Calvinist moral, stood in marked contrast to the often mawkish sentimentality of much of the popular music of the day.

More important than recordings for the growth of country music was broadcast radio. Small radio stations appeared in the larger Southern and Midwestern cities in the 1920s, and many devoted part of their airtime to live or recorded music suited to white rural audiences. Two regular programs of great influence were the "National Barn Dance" from Chicago, begun in 1924, and the "Grand Ole Opry" from Nashville, Tennesse.

The immediate popularity of such programs encouraged more recordings and the appearance of talented musicians from the hills at radio and record studios. These early

# "GRAND OLE OPRY"

Founded in 1925 by George Dewey Hay, who had helped organize the WLS "National Barn Dance" in Chicago, the "Grand Ole Opry" was originally known as the "WSM Barn Dance," acquiring its lasting name in 1926. It was largely Hay, called "the Solemn Ol' Judge," who determined the course of the Opry's development.

The Nashville-based show flourished through the heyday of radio and on into the television era. Such widening exposure led to tours of Opry stars and in the 1940s to Opry films. The music of the Opry developed from Uncle Dave Macon's ballads of rural labourers in the 1920s, through the string bands, cowboy music, and western swing of the 1930s, and back to the traditional music characterized by the career of Roy Acuff, who was promoted into stardom by the Opry in the

*Roy Acuff and June Carter performing onstage at the Grand Ole Opry, c. 1956.* Yale Joel/Time & Life Pictures/ Getty Images

late 1930s. After World War II, the honky-tonk style of Ernest Tubb, the bluegrass music of Bill Monroe with Earl Scruggs, the honky-tonk music of Hank Williams, the crooning of Eddy Arnold and Tennessee Ernie Ford, and the singing of such female vocalists as Kitty Wells were all Opry staples, as were comedy routines, notably by Minnie Pearl. In 1941 the Opry became a live stage show at the Ryman Auditorium in Nashville; in 1974 the show moved to its current venue, the Grand Ole Opry House in Nashville's Music Valley area. The Opry initiated and promoted the creation of Nashville as the centre of country music.

recordings were of ballads and country dance tunes and featured the fiddle and guitar as lead instruments over a rhythmic foundation of guitar or banjo. Other instruments occasionally used included Appalachian dulcimer, harmonica, and mandolin; vocals were done either by a single voice or in high close harmony. Among the musicians who first made a mark were the Carter Family and Jimmie Rodgers, whose performances strongly influenced later musicians.

## CARTER FAMILY

The Carter Family was a leading force in the spread and popularization of the songs of the Appalachian Mountain region of the eastern United States. The group consisted of A.P. Carter (born Alvin Pleasant Carter, April 15, 1891, Maces Spring, Virginia, U.S.—d. November 7, 1960, Kentucky), his wife, Sara (born Sara Dougherty, July 21, 1898, Flatwoods, Virginia—d. January 8, 1979, Lodi, California), and his sister-in-law Maybelle Carter (born Maybelle Addington, May 10, 1909, Nickelsville, Virginia—d. October 23, 1978, Nashville, Tennessee).

The family's recording career began in 1927 in response to an advertisement placed in a local newspaper by a talent scout for Victor Records. Over the next 16 years, with two of Sara's children and three of Maybelle's (Helen, June, and Anita) also appearing, they recorded more than 300 songs for various labels, covering a significant cross section of the mountain music repertory, including old ballads and humorous songs, sentimental pieces from the 19th and early 20th centuries, and many religious pieces. They later performed extensively on radio and popularized many songs that became

# THE LOUVIN BROTHERS

Remembered for their simple but pure gospel-tinged style and extraordinary harmonies, the Louvin Brothers were among country music's most distinctive stylists. Growing up in rural northeastern Alabama, Ira Loudermilk (born April 21, 1924, Henagar, Alabama, U.S.—d. June 20, 1965, Williamsburg, Missouri) and his brother, Charlie (born July 7, 1927, Henagar—died January 26, 2011, Wartrace, Tennessee), were exposed to a variety of early country music influences, including the Carter Family, Charlie and Bill Monroe, and the Blue Sky Boys, as well as to shape-note hymnal singing. From the early 1940s the Loudermilks sang devoutly Christian songs in an artless, heartfelt manner, their high-pitched harmonies accompanied only by Ira's mandolin and Charlie's guitar. During one of their regular stints as live performers on radio stations in the Southeast, they changed their name to the Louvin Brothers. Commercial success came when they adopted secular themes; among their hits were "When I Stop Dreaming," released in 1955—the year they joined the Grand Ole Opry—and "I Don't Believe You've Met My Baby" (1956). On later recordings their record companies imposed lush, elaborate accompaniments far removed from their original style. Each brother pursued a solo career after the partnership broke up in 1963.

Often called the greatest duet act in country music, the Louvin Brothers influenced such artists as the Everly Brothers, Gram Parsons, and Emmylou Harris. The Louvin Brothers also were much-revered songwriters, and their compositions have been covered by many performers.

standards of folk and country music; some of these were "Jimmy Brown, the Newsboy," "Wabash Cannonball," "It Takes a Worried Man to Sing a Worried Song," and "Wildwood Flower."

The Carter Family was remarkable not only for its prolific recording but also for the musical accomplishment—and balance—of its members. A.P. was the group's songsmith. He was an avid collector of oral tradition, as well as an adept arranger of rural regional repertoire for consumption by a broader audience. A.P. also composed many new songs for the group, replicating the style of the traditional material. Sara, with her strong soprano voice, was typically the lead singer, supported by Maybelle's alto harmonies and A.P.'s bass and baritone interjections. The instrumental anchor of the Carter Family was Maybelle, who was a skilled performer on guitar, banjo, and autoharp. She also developed a unique finger-picking technique on guitar that continues to be emulated by many guitarists today.

## JIMMIE RODGERS

Remembered as the "Singing Brakeman" and "America's Blue Yodeler," singer, songwriter, and guitarist Jimmie Rodgers (born James Charles Rodgers, September 8, 1897, Pine Springs Community, near Meridian, Mississippi, U.S.—died May 26, 1933, New York, New York) was another of the principal figures in the emergence of the country and western music.

Rodgers, whose mother died when he was a young boy, was the son of an itinerant railroad gang foreman, and his youth was spent in a variety of southern towns and cities. Having already run away with a medicine show by age 13, he left school for good at age 14. He began working on railroad crews, initially as a water carrier, and during this time was likely exposed to the work songs and early blues of African American labourers. As a young man he held a number of jobs with the railroad, including those of baggage master, flagman, and brakeman, crisscrossing the Southwest but especially working the line between New Orleans and Meridian, Mississippi. Early on, Rodgers aspired to be an entertainer, and the life of the railroad worker provided him ample opportunity to develop and exercise his musical skills, to absorb a mixture of musical styles, and to catalogue the experiences of working people and southern small-town life that would later be at the heart of so many of his songs. He learned to play the guitar and banjo, honing what became his characteristic sound—a blend of traditional country, work, blues, hobo, and cowboy songs.

After contracting tuberculosis, Rodgers was forced to give up railroad work in 1924 or 1925 and began pursuing a performing career, playing everything from tent shows to street corners but with little success. He relocated to Asheville, North Carolina, and began appearing on local radio in 1927, backed by a string band formerly known as the Tenneva Ramblers. The group (renamed the Jimmie Rodgers Entertainers) also performed at resorts and traveled to nearby Bristol, Tennessee, in the hope of making a field recording for the visiting Victor Talking Machine Company. A disagreement resulted in the Ramblers' going it on their own, but Rodgers was still recorded by Victor's Ralph Peer as a guitar-playing solo artist. The popularity of his first recording, "Sleep, Baby, Sleep," earned Rodgers the opportunity to record again for Victor, this time in New Jersey. It also sparked a long series of hits from among more than 110 recordings he would make in what proved to be a relatively short career (1928–33) that coincided with the beginning of the Great Depression. Rodgers toured widely in the South (also playing the vaudeville circuit) and, seeking a dry climate for his health, eventually settled in Texas, with which he became intimately associated, borrowing the aura of the cowboy to put the "country" in

country and western and to prefigure "Singing Cowboy" Gene Autry.

Rodgers helped establish the template for country music and the model for country singers, infusing his performances and compositions with personality, humour, and heightened emotion, delivered in a unique vocal style at a time when, as biographer Nolan Porterfield put it, "The emerging 'hillbilly music' consisted largely of old-time instrumentalists and lugubrious vocalists who sounded much alike." Rodgers is perhaps best remembered for his distinctive blue yodel (whose origins have been ascribed to everything from Tyrolese minstrels to work-gang calls to attempts to imitate a train whistle); it was popularized in "Blue Yodel No. 1" and was at the heart of some dozen other recorded versions. Most of Rodgers's original compositions were written with a variety of collaborators, the most prominent of whom was his sister-in-law, Elsie McWilliams. His hits, which span the emotional gauntlet and incorporate elements of a wide variety of genres, include "Miss the Mississippi and You," "Daddy and Home," "My Carolina Sunshine Girl," "Waiting for a Train," "Brakeman's Blues," "Frankie and Johnny," "Mississippi River Blues," and "My Time Ain't Long." Among the many country performers on whom his influence is most obvious are Autry, Ernest Tubb, Merle Haggard, Hank Snow, and Lefty Frizzell. Rodgers recorded right up to his premature death, resting on a cot in the studio between takes during recording sessions. He was the first person inducted into the Country Music Hall of Fame and was inducted into the Rock and Roll Hall of Fame as an early influence in 1986.

With the migration of many Southern rural whites to industrial cities during the Great Depression and World War II, country music was carried into new areas and exposed to new influences, such as blues and gospel music. The nostalgic bias of country music, with its lyrics about grinding poverty, orphaned children, bereft lovers, and lonely workers far from home, held special appeal during a time of wide-scale population shifts.

## SINGING COWBOYS AND WESTERN SWING

During the 1930s a number of "singing cowboy" film stars, of whom Gene Autry was the best known, took country music and with suitably altered lyrics made it into a synthetic and adventitious "western" music. A second and more substantive variant of country music arose in the 1930s in the Texas-Oklahoma region, where the music of rural whites was exposed to the swing jazz of black orchestras.

In response, a Western swing style evolved in the hands of Bob Wills and others and came to feature steel and amplified guitars and a strong dance rhythm.

## GENE AUTRY

While working as a telegraph agent for the railroad, Gene Autry (born September 29, 1907, Tioga, Texas, U.S.—died October 2, 1998, North Hollywood, California) journeyed briefly to New York City, where he tried unsuccessfully to become a professional singer. His real performing debut came on a local radio show in Oklahoma in 1928, and, beginning in 1931, he hosted his own radio program on WLS in Chicago. During this period he also began recording, often covering hits by Jimmie Rodgers. His first film, *In Old Santa Fe* (1934), launched his career as a cowboy actor, and he starred in 18 movies, ending with *Alias Jesse James* (1959). Aided by the popularity of his films, Autry had a string of hit recordings, including "Tumbling Tumbleweeds" (1935) and "Back in the Saddle Again" (1939). He also had hits with holiday classics such as "Here Comes Santa Claus" (1947), "Rudolph the Red-Nosed Reindeer" (1949), and "Frosty the Snow Man" (1950). The *Gene Autry Show* aired on television from 1950 to 1956.

## BOB WILLS

Taught to play the mandolin and fiddle by his father and other relatives, Bob Wills (born March 6, 1905, near Kosse, Texas, U.S.—died May 13, 1975, Fort Worth, Texas) began performing in country string bands in Texas in the late 1920s. In 1933 he formed the Playboys (later His Texas Playboys) as a traditional string band, to which he added drums, amplified steel and standard guitar, and horns—instruments theretofore foreign to country music. Gathering a stellar combination of players (whose number varied from 6 to 22), Wills became the King of Western Swing, an up-tempo country jazz that drew on Dixieland, big band, minstrelsy, pop, blues, and various ethnic (Czech, German, Cajun, and Mexican) styles. Among the key Playboys were vocalist Tommy Duncan, steel-guitarist Leon McAuliffe (famous for "Steel Guitar Rag"), and arranger Eldon Shamblin, one of the pioneers of the electric guitar. During performances Wills gleefully called out the names of the musicians as they were featured and, when the spirit moved him, hollered his trademark "ah-ha!"

After being based in Texas and Oklahoma, Wills moved the band to California in 1943, where they remained popular into the 1950s, when the advent of television diminished dance-hall attendance. In 1964,

after a second heart attack, Wills folded the Texas Playboys but continued as a solo performer until 1973, when he fell into a coma after a recording session. Best remembered for the songs "New San Antonio Rose" (1940) and "Faded Love" (1950), Wills infused his innovative, adaptable musical vision with charismatic energy, leaving an indelible mark not only on country music but also on rock and influencing such performers as Merle Haggard as well as the outlaw music of Willie Nelson and Waylon Jennings. Bob Wills and His Texas Playboys were inducted into the Rock and Roll Hall of Fame as early influences in 1999.

## HONKY-TONK

An even more important variant within country music was honky-tonk, a style that emerged in the 1940s with such figures as Ernest Tubb and Hank Williams. Honky-tonk's fiddle-steel-guitar combination and its bitter, maudlin lyrics about rural whites adrift in the big city were widely adopted by other country musicians.

### ERNEST TUBB

Singer-songwriter Ernest Tubb (born February 9, 1914, Crisp, Texas, U.S.— died September 6, 1984, Nashville, Tennessee) became one of the earliest exponents of honky-tonk with hits such as "I'm Walking the Floor Over You" (1941). He joined the Grand Ole Opry in 1942, and he became one of the first musicians to record in Nashville. He was a pioneer of the electric guitar in the early 1950s. His Nashville radio program, *Midnight Jamboree* (from 1947), helped launch many stars, including the Everly Brothers and Elvis Presley. In 1947 he starred in the first country music show at Carnegie Hall.

## HANK WILLIAMS

An immensely talented songwriter and an impassioned vocalist, Hank Williams arguably became country music's first superstar in the 1950s. He also experienced great crossover success in the popular music market. His iconic status was amplified by his death at age 29 and by his reputation for hard living and heart-on-the-sleeve vulnerability.

As a boy, Williams (born Hiram King Williams, September 17, 1923, Georgiana, Alabama, U.S—died Janurary 1, 1953, Oak Hill, West Virginia) was the musical protégé of Rufus Payne, an African American street performer who went by the name Tee-Tot and busked on the streets of Georgiana and Greenville, Alabama. Probably taught his first chords by Payne, Williams began playing the guitar at age 8. He made his radio debut at age 13; formed his first band, Hank Williams and his Drifting Cowboys, at age 14; and early on began wearing the cowboy hats and western clothing that later were so associated with him. During World War II Williams commuted between Mobile, where he worked in a shipyard, and Montgomery, where he pursued a musical career. At this stage Williams began abusing alcohol, a problem that haunted him the rest of his life but that came about partly as a result of his attempts to self-medicate agonizing back pain caused by a congenital spinal disorder. Later he would dull his physical pain with morphine, but alcohol remained his painkiller of choice when he sought to relieve the heartache of his tumultuous relationship with Audrey Sheppard, whom he married in 1942 (they divorced in 1952).

In 1946 Williams landed a songwriting contract with Acuff-Rose Publications and began composing material for singer Molly O'Day. Later that year he received his first recording contract, with Sterling Records; however, it was on the start-up label MGM that he had his first hit, "Move It on Over," in 1947. Shortly thereafter he became a regular on the newly created *Louisiana Hayride* radio program based in Shreveport, Louisiana. His breakthrough moment came in 1949 with the release of "Lovesick Blues," an old show tune that Williams parlayed into a chart-topping hit, an invitation to join the Grand Ole Opry, and international fame. More than half of the 66 recordings he would make under his own name (he also released a string of religious-themed recordings under the name Luke the Drifter) were Top Ten country and western hits, many of them reaching number one, including "Cold, Cold Heart," "Your Cheatin' Heart," "Hey, Good Lookin'," "Jambalaya (On the Bayou)," and "I'll Never Get Out of This World Alive." His extraordinary Lost Highway" peaked at number 12.

Williams, who wrote most of his songs himself, crafted direct, emotionally honest lyrics with a poetic simplicity that spoke not only to fans of country and western music but to a much broader audience, as evidenced by the pop hit crooner Tony Bennett had with his cover of "Cold, Cold Heart" in 1951. Williams's music itself was not especially groundbreaking, though he was a deft synthesizer of blues, honky-tonk country, western swing, and other genres. However, his plaintive, bluesy phrasing was unique and became a touchstone of country music. Country music historian Bill Malone wrote that Williams "sang with the quality that has characterized every great hillbilly singer: utter sincerity." Despite Williams's many well-known heartbreak songs, it should also be remembered that he was capable of writing and singing

with great joy and humour, as on, for example, "Howlin' at the Moon."

The last years of his life were suffused in increasing sadness and substance abuse. He died of a heart attack in a drug- and alcohol-induced stupor in the backseat of a car, probably in West Virginia, while being driven from Knoxville, Tennessee, to a concert in Canton, Ohio. Red Foley, Roy Acuff, and Ernest Tubb, among others, sang Williams's gospel-influenced "I Saw the Light" at his funeral, which was attended by thousands. Williams was inducted into the Rock and Roll Hall of Fame as an early influence in 1987.

## BLUEGRASS

The 1940s saw a concerted effort to recover some of country music's root values. A direct descendant of the old-time string-band music that had been widely played and recorded by such groups as the Carter Family from the late 1920s, bluegrass is distinguished from the older string-band music by its more syncopated (off-beat) rhythm, its relatively high-pitched tenor (lead) vocals, tight harmonies, and a strong influence of jazz and blues. It differs from other varieties of country and western music in its driving rhythms and its repertory, as well as in the very prominent place given to the banjo, always played in the three-finger Scruggs style (named for legendary banjo-ist Earl Scruggs), which is unique to bluegrass. Mandolin and fiddle are generally featured considerably more in bluegrass than in other country and western music, and traditional square-dance tunes, traditional religious songs, and ballads furnish a much larger part of the repertory.

The bluegrass style was originated by Bill Monroe, who by the mid-1940s had experimented considerably with new methods of presenting string-band music. He began to evolve a highly distinctive mandolin style while playing with his brothers Birch and Charlie, and after their group broke up, he formed his own group, the Blue Grass Boys. The band already showed many of the distinctive features of modern bluegrass when in 1945 Earl Scruggs, originator of the revolutionary aforementioned banjo technique, joined it. The bluegrass style emerged fully in the years 1945–48, and by the late 1940s a number of bands were playing the music; the most successful were usually led by musicians who had at one time or another played with the Blue Grass Boys and learned the style directly from Monroe.

## BILL MONROE

The youngest of eight children of a Kentucky farmer and entrepreneur, Bill Monroe (born William Smith Monroe, September 13, 1911, Rosine, Kentucky, U.S.—died September 9, 1996, Springfield, near Nashville, Tennessee) was exposed early to traditional folk music by his mother. Another important early musical influence on the young Monroe was Arnold Schultz, a local African American miner who also was an accomplished fiddler and guitarist and who played both blues and country music. Monroe began playing the mandolin professionally in 1927 in a band led by his older brothers Birch and Charlie. In 1930 they moved to Indiana, and in 1932 they joined a barn-dance touring show; their reputation grew, but, because Birch did not like to travel, Bill and Charlie maintained the Monroe Brothers as a duo, touring widely from Nebraska to South Carolina. In 1936 they made their first recordings on the RCA Victor label, and they recorded 60 songs for Victor over the next two years. In 1938 Bill and Charlie decided to form separate bands. Bill's second band, the Blue Grass Boys (his first, called the Kentuckians, played together for only three months), auditioned for the Grand Ole Opry on radio station WSM in Nashville, Tennessee, and became regular performers on that program in 1939.

Monroe's signature sound emerged fully in 1945, when banjoist Earl Scruggs and guitarist Lester Flatt joined his band. Scruggs was among the first banjoists in country music whose principal role was musical rather than comical; Monroe's original banjoist David ("Stringbean") Akeman had provided a humorous touch to the proceedings. The Blue Grass Boys established the classic makeup of a bluegrass group—with mandolin, fiddle, guitar, banjo, and upright bass—and ultimately bequeathed the band's name to the genre itself. Bluegrass is characterized by acoustic instruments; a driving syncopated rhythm; tight, complex harmonies; and the use of higher keys—B-flat, B, and E rather than the customary G, C, and D. The band played traditional folk songs and Monroe's own compositions, the most famous of which were "Blue Moon of Kentucky" (later famously covered and transformed by a young Elvis Presley), "Uncle Pen" (a tribute to another early influence on Monroe, his fiddle-playing uncle Pendleton Vandiver), and "Raw Hide." Although Monroe had sung only harmony as a member of the Monroe Brothers, his high, mournful tenor (both as lead and backing voice) established the convention of bluegrass music's "high lonesome" vocals, and his breakneck-tempo mandolin playing set the standard for other bluegrass performers.

The Blue Grass Boys enjoyed wide popularity, but Scruggs and Flatt quit in 1948 in order to form their own influential bluegrass band, the Foggy Mountain Boys. Soon other bands playing this style of music began to appear, many of them led by former members of Monroe's band, such as Sonny Osborne (the Osborne Brothers), Carter Stanley (who with his brother Ralph formed the Stanley Brothers), Don Reno, Jimmy Martin, and Mac Wiseman. Bluegrass was promoted at numerous annual festivals, such as the one founded by Monroe in 1967 at Bean Blossom, Indiana. He continued to perform until shortly before his death. He was inducted into the Rock and Roll Hall of Fame as an early influence in 1997.

Bluegrass moved from performances on the radio in small Southern communities in the 1940s to television and "hillbilly" bars in the 1950s, to college concerts, coffeehouses, and folk festivals in the 1960s; and in the 1970s the influx of younger musicians interested in bluegrass brought some influence from rock music.

## THE BIRTH OF MUSIC CITY

Commercialization proved a much stronger influence as country music became popular in all sections of the United States after World War II. Rarely has a section of the pop market been as completely dominated by the major companies as country music was during the 1950s. Only five

# RALPH STANLEY

Ralph Stanley (born February 25, 1927, Stratton, Virginia, U.S.) grew up in the mountains of far southwestern Virginia, where his mother taught him to play the banjo in the traditional clawhammer style. While other banjo-picking techniques involve the upward plucking of individual strings with the fingernails or with a plectrum, clawhammer players use a consistent downward stroke to strum the strings with the backs of the fingers. Stanley and his guitar-playing older brother, Carter, became a singing team as teenagers, and after service in World War II the duo began their career in earnest. They performed as the Stanley Brothers and formed a five-piece string band, the Clinch Mountain Boys, one of the first bands to play in the new bluegrass style, a form of country music invented by Bill Monroe. The brothers' sound was distinctive—Carter played guitar and sang lead, while Ralph played banjo and sang a mournful tenor harmony. Both wrote songs that captured the atmosphere of the stark, ancient Appalachian landscape. They toured extensively and made numerous recordings, and the 1960s folk music revival brought the Stanleys widespread popularity. In 1966, however, Carter died, and Ralph later reorganized the Clinch Mountain Boys.

Stanley played at the inaugurations of U.S. presidents Jimmy Carter (1977) and Bill Clinton (1993). In 2002 he released the solo album *Ralph Stanley*, a collection of spirituals and murder ballads that featured the production talents of American songwriter and performer T-Bone Burnett. That same year "O Death," an unaccompanied vocal from the sound track for the film *O Brother, Where Art Thou?* (2000) won Stanley his first Grammy Award. In 2003 the Clinch Mountain Boys, featuring Stanley and his son Ralph Stanley II, collected the Grammy Award for best bluegrass album. The following year the Ralph Stanley Museum and Traditional Mountain Music Center opened in Clintwood, Virginia. Stanley was awarded the National Medal of Arts in 2006.

companies—RCA, Decca, Columbia, Capitol, and MGM—reached the top spot on the best-seller charts until independent Cadence claimed it for seven weeks at the end of 1957 with the Everly Brothers' "Bye Bye Love." Hank Williams's meteoric rise to fame in the late 1940s helped establish Nashville as the undisputed centre of country music, with large recording studios and the Grand Ole Opry as its chief performing venue.

Nashville was the commercial centre of the mid-South, dominated by bank and insurance companies. It also became the home for a handful of specialist country-music publishing companies that sprung up after Acuff-Rose, the first publishing house exclusively for country music, was founded in 1942 by Fred Rose (one of country music's foremost songwriters, who had composed songs for Gene Autry's films) and vocalist, songwriter, and fiddle player Roy Acuff (who had hits with "The Great Speckled Bird" and "The Wabash Cannonball"). Peer-Southern, Tree, and the Nashville office of Hill and Range, like Acuff-Rose, employed full-time writers to provide new songs for the major labels to record and promote. Although many singers employed their own touring musicians to help define their sound, Nashville-based producers invariably preferred the city's pool of studio musicians when it came time

to record. Sessions were quicker and more efficient, but the result was a formulaic sound that normally had little impact beyond the country market.

This approach was challenged when Elvis Presley recorded "Heartbreak Hotel" with his own trio, augmented by pianist Floyd Cramer and a four-man vocal group, under the supervision of Chet Atkins at RCA's Nashville studio in January 1956. It did not sound much like any previous country record, and its worldwide success led to a redefinition of what could be done in Nashville. Presley only occasionally returned to record there, preferring New York City or Los Angeles, but during the next few years the Everly Brothers, Brenda Lee, Marty Robbins, and Johnny Cash were among the many Southern singers who made records in Nashville that broke through the fences into the world of pop.

By the 1950s and '60s country music had become a huge commercial enterprise, and Nashville became "Music City," with such leading performers as Tex Ritter, Tammy Wynette, Buck Owens, Merle Haggard, Patsy Cline, Loretta Lynn, and Charley Pride. Popular singers often recorded songs in a Nashville style.

## JOHNNY CASH

Nashville also became the home of the man who was arguably country

*Johnny Cash performing for inmates at Folsom Prison in California on January 13, 1968. The concert was recorded for his live album* Johnny Cash at Folsom Prison. *© AP Images*

music's biggest star in the 1960s, Johnny Cash (born J.R. Cash, February 26, 1932, Kingsland, Arkansas, U.S—died September 12, 2003, Nashville, Tennessee). Cash was exposed from childhood to the music of the rural South—hymns, folk ballads, and songs of work and lament—but he learned to play guitar and began writing songs during military service in Germany in the early 1950s. After military service he settled in Memphis, Tennessee, to pursue a musical career. Cash began performing with the Tennessee Two (later Tennessee Three), and appearances at county fairs and other local events led to an audition with Sam Phillips of Sun Records, who signed Cash in 1955. Such songs as "Cry, Cry, Cry," "Hey, Porter," "Folsom Prison Blues," and "I Walk the Line" brought him considerable attention, and by 1957 Cash was the top recording artist in the country and western field. His music was noted for its stripped-down sound and focus on the working poor and social and political issues. Cash, who typically wore black clothes and had a rebellious persona, became known as the "Man in Black."

In the 1960s Cash's popularity began to wane as he battled drug addiction, which would recur throughout his life. At the urging of June Carter of the Carter Family, with whom he had worked since 1961, he eventually sought treatment; the couple married in 1968. By the late 1960s Cash's career was back on track, and he was soon discovered by a wider audience. The signal event in Cash's turnaround was the album *Johnny Cash at Folsom Prison* (1968), which was recorded live in front of an audience of some 2,000 inmates at California's Folsom Prison. The performance was regarded as a risky move by record company executives, but it proved to be the perfect opportunity for Cash to reestablish himself as one of country music's most relevant artists. He used the success of that album and its follow-up, *Johnny Cash at San Quentin* (1969), to focus attention on the living conditions of inmates in American prisons, and he became a vocal champion for penal reform and social justice. Live appearances in New York and London and his television show, *The Johnny Cash Show* (1969–71), which deviated from the standard variety program by featuring such guests as Ray Charles, Rod McKuen, and Bob Dylan (who had enlisted Cash to appear on his 1969 album, *Nashville Skyline*), brought to the general public his powerfully simple songs of elemental experiences.

Although Cash had established himself as a legend in the music world, by the late 1980s he faced dwindling record sales and interest. In 1994, however, he experienced an unexpected resurgence after signing with Rick Rubin's American Recordings, which was best known for its metal and rap acts. Cash's first release on the label, the acoustic *American Recordings*, was a critical and popular success, and it won him a new generation of fans. Later records included *Unchained* (1996), *American III: Solitary Man* (2000), *American IV: The Man Comes Around* (2002), and the posthumous *American V: A Hundred Highways* (2006). The recipient of numerous awards, he won 13 Grammy Awards, including a Lifetime Achievement Award in 1999, and 9 Country Music Association Awards. Cash was inducted into the Country Music Hall of Fame in 1980 and to the Rock and Roll Hall of Fame in 1992.

# CHAPTER 4

# Roots: Part 3, Pre-rock Pop

**U**nlike traditional folk music, popular music is written by known individuals, usually professionals, and does no evolve through the process of oral transmission. Historically popular music was any nonfolk form that acquired mass popularity—from the songs of the medieval minstrels and troubadours to those elements of fine-art music originally intended for a small, elite audience but that became widely popular. After the Industrial Revolution, true folk music began to disappear, and the popular music of the Victorian era and the early 20th century was that of the music hall and vaudeville, with its upper reaches dominated by waltz music and operettas. In the United States, minstrel shows performed the compositions of songwriters such as Stephen Foster.

## STEPHEN FOSTER

Stephen Foster (born July 4, 1826, Lawrenceville [now part of Pittsburgh], Pennsylvania, U.S.—died January 13, 1864, New York, New York) grew up on the urban edge of the Western frontier. Although formally untutored in music, he had a natural musical bent and began to write songs as a young boy. He absorbed musical influences from the popular, sentimental songs sung by his sisters; from black church services he attended with the family's servant Olivia Pise; from popular minstrel show songs; and from songs sung by black labourers at the Pittsburgh warehouse where he worked for a time.

In 1842 he published his song "Open Thy Lattice, Love." In 1846 he went to Cincinnati as a bookkeeper, returning to Pittsburgh in 1850 to marry Jane McDowell, a physician's daughter. In 1848 he sold his song "Oh! Susanna" for $100; together with his "Old Uncle Ned" it brought the publisher about $10,000. In 1849 Foster entered into a contract with Firth, Pond & Co., the New York publishers to whom he had previously given the rights for "Nelly Was a Lady." He was commissioned to write songs for Edwin P. Christy's minstrel show. The most famous, "Old Folks at Home" (1851), also called "Swanee River," appeared originally under Christy's name; Foster's name appeared on the song after 1879. In 1852 he made his only visit to the South.

He vacillated between composing minstrel songs (for which he is largely remembered) and songs in the sentimental "respectable" style then popular. He was never a sharp entrepreneur for his talents, and in 1857, in financial difficulties, he sold all rights to his future songs to his publishers for about $1,900. The profits from his songs went largely to performers and publishers.

In 1860, already struggling with sinking morale and alcoholism, he moved to New York City. His songs after that date are largely sentimental songs such as "Poor Drooping Maiden." His wife left him in 1861, except for a brief reconciliation in 1862. He spent the rest of his life in debt.

He left about 200 songs, for most of which he wrote the words as well as the music. They include "Camptown Races," "Nelly Bly," "My Old Kentucky Home," "Massa's in de Cold, Cold Ground," "Old Dog Tray," "Old Black Joe," "Jeanie with the Light Brown Hair," and "Beautiful Dreamer."

## TIN PAN ALLEY

In the 1890s Tin Pan Alley emerged as the first popular song-publishing industry, and over the next half century its lyricism was combined with European operetta in a new kind of play known as the musical. Tin Pin Alley took its name from the nickname of the street on which the industry was based, being on 28th Street between Fifth Avenue and Broadway in the early 20th century; around Broadway and 32nd Street in the 1920s; and ultimately on Broadway between 42nd and 50th streets. The phrase *tin pan* referred to the sound of pianos furiously pounded by the so-called song pluggers, who demonstrated tunes to publishers. Tin Pan Alley comprised the commercial music of songwriters of ballads, dance music, and vaudeville, and its name eventually became synonymous with American popular music in general. When these genres first became prominent, the most profitable commercial product of Tin Pan Alley was sheet music for home consumption, and songwriters, lyricists, and popular performers laboured to produce music to meet the demand.

The growth of film, audio recording, radio, and television created an increased demand for more and different kinds of music, and Tin Pan Alley was rendered actually and metaphorically dead as other music-publishing centres arose to supply melodies for these genres.

Beginning with ragtime in the 1890s, African Americans began combining complex African rhythms with European harmonic structures, a synthesis that would eventually create jazz. Music audiences greatly expanded, partly because of technology. By 1930, phonograph records had replaced sheet music as the chief source of music in the home. The microphone enabled more-intimate vocal techniques to be commercially adapted.

## THE DEVELOPMENT OF THE NEW VOCAL POP STAR

If rock music evolved from 1950s rock and roll, then rock and roll itself—which at the time seemed to spring from nowhere—evolved from developments in American popular music that followed the marketing of the new technologies of records, radio, motion pictures, and the electric microphone. By the 1930s their combined effect was an increasing demand for vocal rather than instrumental records and for singing stars such as Bing Crosby and Frank Sinatra. Increasingly, pop songs were written to display a singer's personality rather than a composer's skill; they had to work emotionally through the singer's expressiveness rather than formally as a result of the score (it was *Sinatra's* feelings that were heard in the songs he sang rather than their writers').

Beginning in the 1940s, it was the singers whom jazz had helped spawn—those who used microphones in place of pure lung power and who adapted the Viennese operetta-inspired songs of the great Broadway composers (who had, in turn, already been changed by jazz)—who became the bearers of the next dominant American style. Simply to list their names is to evoke a social history of the United States since World War II: Crosby, Sinatra, Nat King Cole, Mel Tormé, Ella Fitzgerald, Billie Holiday, Doris Day, Sarah Vaughan, Peggy Lee, Joe Williams, Judy Garland, Tony Bennett, and many others. More than any other single form or sound, it was their voices that created a national sound track of longing, fulfillment, and forever-renewed hope that sounded like America to Americans, and then sounded like America to the world.

## BING CROSBY

Bing Crosby (born Harry Lillis Crosby, May 3, 1903, Tacoma, Washington, U.S —died October 14, 1977, near Madrid, Spain) became the archetypal crooner of a period when the advent of radio broadcasting and talking pictures and the refinement of sound-recording techniques made the climate ideal for the rise of such a figure. His casual stage manner and mellow, relaxed singing style influenced two generations of pop singers and made him the most successful entertainer of his day.

Crosby began to sing and to play the drums while studying law at Spokane, Washington. After a period spent singing with the Paul Whiteman orchestra in 1927, he appeared in the early sound film *King of Jazz* (1931). Crosby became a star after getting his own program on the CBS radio station in New York City in 1932. He began appearing in more films, and by the late 1930s his records were selling millions of copies. His songwriting activities included part-authorship of "A Ghost of a Chance"

*Bing Crosby* (left) *and Barry Fitzgerald in* Going My Way *(1944).* © 1944 Paramount Pictures Corporation; photograph from a private collection

and "Where the Blue of the Night" (his radio theme song). His recording of "White Christmas" became one of the most popular songs of the 20th century, exceeded in record sales only by his "Silent Night."

## FRANK SINATRA

Upon hearing Crosby's recordings, Frank Sinatra (born Francis Albert Sinatra, December 12, 1915, Hoboken, New Jersey, U.S.—died May 14, 1998, Los Angeles, California) was inspired as a teenager to become a singer. Sinatra had performed as a member of the Hoboken Four vocal group and had sung with local dance bands and for remote radio broadcasts. He was singing and waiting tables in 1939 when he was hired by trumpeter Harry James to join his band. Sinatra's warm baritone and sensitivity to lyrics were well showcased on the recordings he made during his six-month tenure with James, who graciously freed him from his contract when Sinatra received a more lucrative offer from bandleader Tommy Dorsey. The 83 commercial recordings that Sinatra made with the Dorsey band from 1940 to 1942 represent his first major body of work.

Sinatra was enormously influenced by Dorsey's trombone playing and strove to improve his breath control in order to emulate Dorsey's seamless, unbroken melodic passages. It was also during this period that Sinatra proved his mastery of both ballads and up-tempo numbers. Often teamed with singer Connie Haines, or with Dorsey's vocal group, The Pied Pipers, Sinatra was featured on memorable sides such as "I'll Never Smile Again" and "I'll Be Seeing You."

In 1942, with his fame having eclipsed that of Dorsey, Sinatra left the Dorsey organization, a risky venture in the days when few big-band singers found success on their own. Within weeks, however, Sinatra was a cultural phenomenon. Near-hysteria greeted his appearances at New York's Paramount Theatre in January 1943. Such throngs of screaming, young female fans—who became known as "bobby-soxers"—had not been seen since the days of silent-movie star Rudolph Valentino. The singer was soon dubbed "Frankieboy," "The Sultan of Swoon," and, most popularly, "The Voice."

During the period Sinatra recorded with Columbia Records (1943–52), his chief arranger was Axel Stordahl, whose spare string arrangements on beautiful recordings such as "You Go to My Head" (1945), "These Foolish Things" (1945), and "That Old Feeling" (1947) defined Sinatra's sound with Columbia.

Sinatra's success continued unabated until about 1948, when

Frank Sinatra (left) *receiving the Thomas Jefferson Award from James Waterman Wise, director of the Council Against Intolerance in America, New York City, 1947.* Encyclopædia Britannica, Inc.

his popularity suddenly declined (he later speculated that the decline came because of his reluctance to change styles and evolve musically). In 1952 his Columbia recording contract was not renewed, he was dropped by his talent agency, and his network television show was canceled. Sinatra was considered a has-been. In the 1940s, however, Sinatra had begun acting in a films, and his performance in *From Here to Eternity* (1953), for which he won the Academy Award for Best Supporting Actor, helped revive his flagging career. Indeed, he later starred in a number of acclaimed motion pictures, including musicals such as *Guys and Dolls* (1955) and dramas such as *The Manchurian Candidate* (1962).

In 1953 he signed with Capitol Records and, throughout the next nine years, issued a series of recordings widely regarded as his finest body of work. He began making albums that consisted of songs related to a single theme or mood. His new approach also demanded new arrangements, and Capitol's in-house arrangers—including Billy May and Gordon Jenkins—were among the best in the business; however, Sinatra's collaboration with arranger Nelson Riddle reached an even higher plateau. Riddle employed everything from quartets to 50-piece orchestras for ballad arrangements that were often characterized by a dominant solo instrument (particularly a mournful trombone), and by

Riddle's "private melodies," which served as counterpoint to Sinatra's highly personal approach. Virtually all of the albums the Sinatra-Riddle team made for Capitol—such as *In the Wee Small Hours* (1955), *Songs for Swingin' Lovers!* (1956), and *Only the Lonely* (1958)—are stellar.

Despite the importance of the Capitol arrangers in determining Sinatra's new sound, the resulting albums were still very much dominated by the singer himself. Sinatra's voice, which Riddle often described as having the warm timbre of a cello, had deepened and grown in power; gone was the whispery crooning of the Columbia days. His failed marriage

*Frank Sinatra (left) and Laurence Harvey in the American Cold War thriller* The Manchurian Candidate *(1962).* © 1962 United Artists Corporation; photograph from a private collection

to actress Ava Gardner infused his ballad singing with a heretofore unseen emotional urgency and plaintive quality, although he eschewed anything that approached heart-on-the-sleeve histrionics. He attacked swing numbers with abandon and displayed his jazz influences with an uncanny sense of syncopation and an innate knowledge of "blue notes," which he incorporated into the melody line.

During the late 1950s and early '60s, Sinatra frequently appeared on stage and in films with his close-knit band of friends known most popularly as "The Rat Pack," which included most prominently Sammy Davis, Jr., and Dean Martin. It was also about this time that Sinatra generated more controversy for his connections with organized crime.

In 1960 Sinatra founded Reprise Records and was allowed to record there simultaneously with his Capitol contract, which expired in 1962. Sinatra's prodigious recording during these years resulted in some quickly recorded albums of uneven quality, but he also released two masterpieces, *September of My Years* (1965) and the partnership with Brazilian songwriter Antônio Carlos Jobim, *Francis Albert Sinatra and Antonio Carlos Jobim* (1967), which rank among Sinatra's greatest albums. He also had chart success during the decade with the hit singles "Strangers in the Night"

(1966), "That's Life" (1967), and "My Way" (1969). In his last two decades as a recording artist, he chose his projects carefully and released only seven albums of new material.

## NAT KING COLE

Nat King Cole (born Nathaniel Adams Cole, March 17, 1917, Montgomery, Alabama, U.S.—died February 15, 1965, Santa Monica, California) grew up in Chicago, where, by age 12, he sang and played organ in the church where his father was pastor. He formed his first jazz group, the Royal Dukes, five years later. In 1937, after touring with a black musical revue, he began playing in jazz clubs in Los Angeles. There he formed the King Cole Trio (originally King Cole and His Swingsters), with guitarist Oscar Moore (later replaced by Irving Ashby) and bassist Wesley Prince (later replaced by Johnny Miller). The trio specialized in swing music with a delicate touch in that they did not employ a drummer; also unique were the voicings of piano and guitar, often juxtaposed to sound like a single instrument. An influence on jazz pianists such as Oscar Peterson, Cole was known for a compact, syncopated piano style with clean, spare, melodic phrases.

During the late 1930s and early '40s the trio made several instrumental recordings, as well as others that

*The King Cole Trio, 1947.* (Left to right) *Irving Ashby, guitarist; Johnny Miller, bass player; Nat King Cole, at the piano.* Encyclopædia Britannica, Inc.

featured their harmonizing vocals. They found their greatest success, however, when Cole began doubling as a solo singer. Their first chart success, "Straighten Up and Fly Right" (1943), was followed by hits such as "Sweet Lorraine," "It's Only a Paper Moon," "(I Love You) For Sentimental Reasons," and "Route 66." Eventually, Cole's piano playing took a backseat to his singing career. Noted for his warm tone and flawless phrasing, Cole was regarded among the top male vocalists, although jazz

critics tended to regret his near-abandonment of the piano. He first recorded with a full orchestra (the trio serving as rhythm section) in 1946 for "The Christmas Song," a holiday standard and one of Cole's biggest-selling recordings. By the 1950s, he worked almost exclusively as a singer, with such notable arrangers as Nelson Riddle and Billy May providing lush orchestral accompaniment. "Nature Boy," "Mona Lisa," "Too Young," "A Blossom Fell," and "Unforgettable" were among his major hits of the period. He occasionally revisited his jazz roots, as on the outstanding album *After Midnight* (1956), which proved that Cole's piano skills had not diminished.

Cole's popularity allowed him to become the first African American to host a network variety program, *The Nat King Cole Show*, which debuted on NBC television in 1956. The show fell victim to the bigotry of the times, however, and was canceled after one season; few sponsors were willing to be associated with a black entertainer. His hits of the early '60s—"Ramblin' Rose," "Those Lazy, Hazy, Crazy Days of Summer," and "L-O-V-E"—indicate that he was moving even further away from his jazz roots and concentrating almost exclusively on mainstream pop. Adapting his style, however, was one factor that kept Cole (who was inducted into the Rock and Roll Hall of Fame as an early influence in 2000) popular up to his early death from lung cancer in 1965.

The prejudices of the era in which Cole lived hindered his potential for even greater stardom. His talents extended beyond singing and piano playing: he excelled as a relaxed and humorous stage personality, and he was also a capable actor, evidenced by his performances in a number of motion pictures, including *The Nat "King" Cole Musical Story* (1955), in which he played himself. His daughter Natalie also became a popular singer who achieved her greatest chart success in 1991 with "Unforgettable," an electronically created duet with her father.

## POP GOES ECLECTIC

The ability of radio broadcasting to reach rural communities aided the dissemination of new styles, notably country music. American popular music achieved international dominance in the decades after World War II. By the 1950s the migration of African Americans to cities in the North had resulted in the cross-fertilization of elements of blues with the up-tempo rhythms of jazz to create rhythm and blues. Rock and roll, pioneered by figures such as Elvis Presley, soon developed as an amalgam of rhythm and blues with country music and other influences. In the 1960s British rock groups, including the Beatles, became internationally influential and popular. Rock and soul music (especially the sophisticated but hook-laden variety of the latter, which took its name from the company that created it, Motown) quickly attracted the allegiance of Western teenagers and eventually became the soundtrack for young people throughout the world.

# CHAPTER 5

# Rhythm and Blues

The term *rhythm and blues* (often shortened to R&B) was coined in 1947 by music journalist turned record producer Jerry Wexler when he was editing the charts at the trade journal *Billboard*. Wexler learned that the record companies issuing black popular music considered the chart names then in use (Harlem Hit Parade, Sepia, Race) to be demeaning. Accordingly, the magazine changed the chart's name in its June 17, 1949, issue, having used the term *rhythm and blues* in news articles for the previous two years. Although the records that appeared on *Billboard*'s rhythm-and-blues chart thereafter were in a variety of different styles, the term was used to encompass a number of contemporary forms that emerged at that time.

## JUMP BLUES

Perhaps the most commonly understood meaning of the term is as a description of the sophisticated urban music that had been developing since the 1930s, when saxophonist-singer Louis Jordan's small combo started making blues-based records with humorous lyrics and upbeat rhythms that owed as much to boogie-woogie as to classic blues forms. This music, sometimes called jump blues, set a pattern that became the dominant black popular music form during and for some time after World War II. Among its leading

# LOUIS JORDAN

Louis Jordan (born July 8, 1908, Brinkley, Arkansas, U.S.—died February 4, 1975, Los Angeles, California) was a seminal figure in the development both of rhythm and blues and of rock and roll. Jordan's father was a professional musician, and it was through him that Jordan absorbed the black musical traditions of the American South. As a teenager Jordan toured as a singer, dancer, comedian, and woodwind player with a variety of performing troupes including the Rabbit Foot Minstrels. He joined drummer-bandleader Chick Webb's orchestra in 1936, remaining (alongside the young Ella Fitzgerald) for two years before forming his own band. Though Jordan had developed into an accomplished alto saxophonist in the mold of Benny Carter, he did not set out to form a jazz group. His goal, instead, was to create a music that would have a broader appeal.

Jordan and his Tympany Five (a name chosen despite the fact that he was normally accompanied by six musicians, none of whom played tympani) became by 1942 one of the most popular recording acts in the country. They often combined Count Basie-style riffs with a buoyant, boogie-based shuffle, and hits such as "Ain't Nobody Here But Us Chickens" and "Choo Choo Ch'Boogie" inspired countless "jump blues" combos. Though largely retaining the sound and subject matter of his African American roots, he enjoyed celebrity status among both blacks and whites, starring in numerous Hollywood short films and receiving equal billing on recorded collaborations with Louis Armstrong and Bing Crosby.

Jordan's musical style exerted a profound influence on a wide range of performers, most notably Chuck Berry, Ray Charles, and Bill Haley. Among many others who covered his material were Woody Herman, Muddy Waters, and Eric Clapton. Jordan's popularity had faded considerably by the time of his death, but his music enjoyed a revival during the 1990s, when *Five Guys Named Moe*, a musical based on Jordan's songs, played in London and New York City. Jordan was inducted into the Rock and Roll Hall of Fame as an early influence in 1987.

practitioners were Jordan, Amos Milburn, Roy Milton, Jimmy Liggins, Joe Liggins, Floyd Dixon, Wynonie Harris, Big Joe Turner, and Charles Brown. While many of the numbers in these performers' repertoires were in the classic 12-bar A-A-B blues form, others were straight pop songs, instrumentals that were close to light jazz, or pseudo-Latin compositions.

Within this genre there were large-group and small-group rhythm and blues. The former was practiced by singers whose main experience was with big bands and who were usually hired employees of bandleaders such as Lucky Millinder (for whose band Harris sang) or Count Basie (whose vocalists included Turner and Jimmy Witherspoon). The small groups usually consisted of five to seven pieces and counted on individual musicians to take turns in the lime-light. Thus, for instance, in Milton's group, Milton played drums and sang, Camille Howard played piano and sang, and the alto and tenor saxophonists (Milton went through several of them) each would be featured at least once. Another hallmark of small-group rhythm and blues was the relegation of the guitar, if indeed there was one, to a time-keeping status, because guitar soloing was considered "country" and unsophis-ticated. The most extreme example of this was Brown, both in his early work with Johnny Moore's Three Blazers and in his subsequent work as a bandleader; in both cases the band consisted of piano, bass, and guitar, but solos almost totally were handled by Brown on the piano.

## R&B ON RECORD

Early rhythm and blues was recorded largely in Los Angeles by small independent record labels such as Modern, RPM, and Specialty. The founding of Atlantic Records in 1947 by Ahmet Ertegun, a jazz fan and the son of a Turkish diplomat, and Herb Abramson, a music industry professional, shifted the industry's centre to New York City. In 1953 they brought in Wexler as a partner, and he and Ertegun were instrumental in moving rhythm and blues forward. Atlantic hired jazz musicians as studio players and, owing to its engineer, Tom Dowd, paid particular attention to the sound quality of their recordings. It introduced some of the top female names in rhythm and blues—most notably Ruth Brown and LaVern Baker—and signed Ray Charles, who had been imitating Charles Brown, and helped him find a new direction, which eventually would evolve into soul. Wexler and Ertegun worked closely with Clyde McPhatter (both in and out of his group the Drifters) and Chuck

# J & M STUDIO: MAKING MUSICAL MAGIC IN NEW ORLEANS

Initially located in the back room of a music shop, J & M Studio moved twice en route to becoming the crucible of the New Orleans sound of the 1950s. Nearly all of the biggest hits by Fats Domino and Little Richard—as well as landmark records by Lloyd Price, Guitar Slim, and Clarence ("Frogman") Henry—were recorded at J & M under the watchful eye of owner-engineer Cosimo Matassa. Many of those recordings were supervised by Dave Bartholomew (who was inducted into the Rock and Roll Hall of Fame in 1991), Robert ("Bumps") Blackwell, or Paul Gayten and released on out-of-town labels (Imperial and Specialty in Los Angeles, Chess in Chicago). Bartholomew, a multitalented composer-arranger who had played trumpet for Duke Ellington, put together an outstanding house band that included saxophonists Lee Allen and Herb Hardesty and the influential drummer Earl Palmer. Working with minimal equipment and little separation between instruments, Matassa developed a distinctive, atmospheric sound that better-equipped studios could never replicate.

Willis, both of whom were important figures in early 1950s rhythm and blues. King Records in Cincinnati, Ohio, the Chess and Vee Jay labels in Chicago, and Duke/Peacock Records in Houston, Texas, also played pivotal roles in the spread of rhythm and blues, as did Sun Records in Memphis, Tennessee—before Sam Phillips turned his attention to Elvis Presley and rockabilly music—and J & M Studio in New Orleans, Louisiana, where a number of the most important records released on the Los Angeles-based labels were recorded.

## RHYTHM AND BLUES OR ROCK AND ROLL?

By mid-decade rhythm and blues had come to mean black popular music that was not overtly aimed at teenagers, since the music that was becoming known as rock and roll sometimes featured lyrics that concerned first love and parent-child conflict, as well as a less subtle approach to rhythm. Many doo-wop vocal groups, therefore, were considered rock-and-roll acts, as were performers such as Little Richard and Hank Ballard and the Midnighters.

*Tina Turner at the mike and Ike Turner on a Fender Stratocaster* (middle) *performing c. 1964.* Michael Ochs Archives/Getty Images

Because the distinction between rock and roll and rhythm and blues was not based on any hard-and-fast rules, most performers issued records that fit in both categories. Moreover, some vocalists who were later considered jazz performers—in particular, Dinah Washington—also appeared on the rhythm-and-blues charts, and a steady stream of saxophone-led instrumentals firmly in the rhythm-and-blues tradition continued to be produced by performers such as Joe Houston, Chuck Higgins, and Sam ("The Man") Taylor but were considered rock and roll and were often used as theme music by disc jockeys on rock-and-roll radio.

The division based on the age of the intended audience for black popular music also meant that, by the mid-1950s, much of the guitar-led electric blues music coming from Chicago and Memphis was now considered rhythm and blues, since it appealed to older buyers. Thus, although they had little to nothing in common with the earlier generation of band-backed blues shouters, performers such as Muddy Waters, Howlin' Wolf, and B.B. King (who, because he used a horn section when he could, was perhaps more like the older generation than the Chicago bluesmen) became regarded as rhythm-and-blues performers. One important figure in this transition was Ike Turner, a piano-player-turned-guitarist from Mississippi who worked as a talent scout for several labels and fronted a band called the Kings of Rhythm, which backed many of his discoveries on records. When Turner married the former Anna Mae Bullock and rechristened her Tina Turner, the Ike and Tina Turner Revue became a significant force in the modernization of rhythm and blues, dispensing with the horn section but including a trio of female backing singers who were modeled on Ray Charles's Raelettes.

By 1960 rhythm and blues was, if not a spent force, at least aging with its audience. Performers such as Washington, Charles, and Ruth Brown were appearing more in nightclubs than in the multiperformer revues in which they had made their names. Although younger performers such as Jackie Wilson and Sam Cooke clearly owed a debt to the previous generation of rhythm-and-blues performers, they were more transitional figures who were, like Charles, establishing the new genre of soul. Significantly, in the August 23, 1969, issue of *Billboard*, the black pop chart's name was changed again, to soul. Although *soul* then became the preferred term for black popular music, in some quarters *rhythm and blues* continued to be used to refer to nearly every genre of post-World War II black music.

# REPRESENTATIVE WORKS

- ► Cecil Gant, "I Wonder" (1944)
- ► Louis Jordan, "Caldonia" (1945)
- ► Joe Liggins, "The Honeydripper" (1945)
- ► Roy Milton and His Solid Senders, "Milton's Boogie" (1945)
- ► Johnny Moore's Three Blazers, "Drifting Blues" (1946)
- ► Roy Brown, "Good Rockin' Tonight" (1947)
- ► Camille Howard, "X-Temperaneous Boogie" (1947)
- ► Johnny Moore's Three Blazers, "Merry Christmas, Baby" (1947)
- ► T Bone Walker, "Call It Stormy Monday" (1947)
- ► Lonnie Johnson, "Tomorrow Night" (1948)
- ► Amos Milburn, "Chicken-Shack Boogie" (1948)
- ► Louis Jordan, "Saturday Night Fish Fry" (1949)
- ► Professor Longhair, "Mardi Gras in New Orleans" (1949)
- ► Roy Milton and His Solid Senders, "The Hucklebuck" (1949)
- ► Fats Domino, "The Fat Man" (1950)
- ► Lowell Fulson, "Every Day I Have the Blues" (1950)
- ► Ivory Joe Hunter, "I Almost Lost My Mind" (1950)
- ► Joe Liggins, "Pink Champagne" (1950)
- ► Percy Mayfield, "Please Send Me Someone to Love" (1950)
- ► Johnny Otis Quintette, "Double Crossing Blues" (1950)
- ► Tiny Bradshaw, "The Train Kept Rollin'" (1951)
- ► Jackie Brenston, "Rocket '88'" (1951)
- ► Floyd Dixon, "Telephone Blues" (1951)
- ► Big Maybelle, "Gabbin' Blues" (1952)
- ► Willie Mae ("Big Mama") Thornton, "Hound Dog" (1953)
- ► Big Joe Turner, "Shake, Rattle and Roll" (1954)
- ► Ray Charles, "I've Got a Woman" (1955)

The term *rhythm and blues*, however, attained a new meaning thanks to the British bands that followed in the wake of the Beatles. Most of these groups, notably the Rolling Stones, played a mixture of Chicago blues and black rock and roll and described their music as rhythm and blues. Thus, the Who, although a quintessential mod rock band, advertised their early performances as "Maximum R&B" to attract an audience. Although bands that followed this generation—John Mayall's Bluesbreakers and Fleetwood Mac, for example—called themselves blues bands, rhythm and blues remained the rubric for the Animals, Them, the Pretty Things, and others. Today a band that advertises itself as rhythm and blues is almost certainly following in this tradition rather than that of the early pioneers.

# CHAPTER 6

# Rhythm and Blues People

**I**t is hard to imagine African American popular culture, or American popular culture, for that matter, without the fundamental building block of the blues—the soundtrack of survival in the face of a history of dehumanization, exploitation, repression, discrimination, and depravation. Blues is a willful re-experience of personal or political pain undertaken as the strongest of reminders that despite the hurt felt one is down but not out, that to keep on keeping on is its own victory. As jazz grew increasingly complex and cerebral, the emotion, feeling, and sensuality of the blues took on new importance, and especially after incorporating the boogie-woogie stylings of pre-bop jazz, blues became dance music, transforming into rhythm and blues in the process. R&B was the product of a number of strains of evolving blues forms pioneered by musicians whose musical arrival often depended as much on where they came from and where they landed. Place played an important role in the genesis of rhythm and blues, not just in development of regional styles but in the consequences of the Great Migration of African Americans from the South to the North and from the country to the city. Economics, gender, and technology all had their role—so, too, did personal history.

# BIG BANDS, SHOUTERS, AND COMBOS

A legacy of the tremendous popularity of swing jazz, big bands were among the first vehicles for the blues that would ultimately morph into rhythm and blues. To compete with the roar of the band, vocalists adopted an emotional "shouting" style that required more than a little lung power. Smaller ensembles, or combos, usually featuring a lineup of guitar, bass, piano, drums, and saxophones, also became popular and provided the foundation for jump blues.

## BIG JOE TURNER

Singing in his youth in church choirs and informally for tips, Big Joe Turner (born Joseph Vernon Turner, May 18, 1911, Kansas City, Missouri, U.S.— died November 24, 1985, Inglewood, California) drew attention as a singing bartender, accompanied by pianist Pete Johnson, in Kansas City saloons. Discovered by jazz critic John Hammond, Turner, with his powerful baritone voice, was taken to New York City for the 1938 Carnegie Hall "Spirituals to Swing" concert and stayed on to become a popular attraction, with boogie-woogie piano accompaniment, at New York nightclubs. He began recording with

top jazz musicians and touring the United States and Canada, sometimes with blues players or Count Basie's orchestra. In 1951 he made a top-selling rhythm-and-blues record, "Chains of Love," and followed it with "Sweet 16," "Honey, Hush," "Shake, Rattle and Roll," and "Flip, Flop and Fly," which were rerecorded by young white musicians, notably Bill Haley, using expurgated lyrics. Turner (who was inducted into the Rock and Roll Hall of Fame as an early influence in 1991) appeared in several movies (including the documentary *Last of the Blue Devils*, 1979), at major jazz and folk festivals in the United States and Europe, on television, and in jazz clubs, recording continually into the 1980s.

## JOHNNY OTIS

Bandleader, drummer, vibraphonist, singer, producer, and promoter Johnny Otis (born John Alexander Veliotes, December 28, 1921, Vallejo, California, U.S.—d. January 17, 2012, Altadena, California) was instrumental in furthering the careers of a number of important rhythm-and-blues performers.

While growing up as part of a Greek immigrant family in Berkeley, California, Otis began a lifelong attraction and commitment to African American culture. He celebrated the vibrancy of African American music and its power to unite people across racial boundaries, coming to think of himself as "black by persuasion." Otis dropped out of school to play with bands throughout the Midwest and settled in Los Angeles in 1943. He performed with Charlie Parker, Lester Young, Count Basie, and Art Tatum, but his main impact was in rhythm and blues. He discovered and promoted Big Mama Thornton (on whose "Hound Dog" record [1953] he played drums), Little Willie John, and Little Esther Phillips; he also had a hand in developing the careers of Hank Ballard and Jackie Wilson. As leader of his own band, Otis (who was inducted into the Rock and Roll Hall of Fame in 1994) had 15 Top 40 rhythm-and-blues hits from 1950 to 1952; his biggest success was with "Willie and the Hand Jive" in 1958. An artist, a pastor, and a civil rights activist, Otis wrote *Listen to the Lambs* (1968), an insightful account of the 1965 Watts riots, and *Upside Your Head! Rhythm and Blues on Central Avenue* (1993).

## CHARLES BROWN

One of the most influential singers of his day, Charles Brown (born September 13, 1922, Texas City, Texas, U.S.—died January 21, 1999, Oakland, California) was an accomplished classical pianist whose career began in 1943 after he moved to Los Angeles. He played with the Bardu Ali band before joining Johnny Moore's Three Blazers, a piano-guitar-bass combo that rose to stardom with "Driftin' Blues," recorded at their first session for Aladdin Records in 1946. The next year they recorded Brown's "Merry Christmas, Baby," which became a holiday favourite. Irked that he was not receiving the same billing or money as guitarist Moore, who neither wrote nor sang, Brown left the group in 1948 to form his own trio and continued to record for Aladdin through 1952. His smooth, quiet vocals (he rarely recorded up-tempo material) were perfect for the sophisticated urban blues audience of the day, and he managed to produce two number one rhythm-and-blues hits, "Trouble Blues" (1949) and "Black Night" (1951), during this period.

As rhythm and blues became more raucous and laid the foundations for rock and roll, Brown, who was too gritty to follow Nat King Cole (whom he superficially resembled) into the pop arena, continued to record with less success, although "Please Come Home for Christmas" was a hit in 1961. Eventually he retired, occasionally performing in lounges and giving piano and organ lessons. Rediscovered by blues enthusiasts in the early 1980s and helped financially by one of the first grants from the Rhythm and Blues Foundation, he found a new audience, recorded several albums that showed his powers undiminished by time, and toured with Bonnie Raitt in 1990. Brown was posthumously inducted into the Rock and Roll Hall of Fame in 1999.

# ELECTRIC BLUESMEN

The generation of post-World War II electric bluesmen often shared Southern roots, an early immersion in acoustic country blues, and a sense of dislocation that was the result of their journey from the rural environments of their youth to the reality of life in bustling cities such as Memphis, Detroit, and Chicago. To be heard above the cacophony of the crowded bars in which they performed, they crafted a raw, powerful style of blues. Setting was crucial to the development of this style, but it was not everything; without the technological innovation of the electric guitar, urban blues as we know them would have been unimaginable, not just because of the necessary amplification of sounds they provided but also because of the sustained notes and noises they enabled, which would become essential ingredients for R&B and rock and roll.

## MUDDY WATERS

Muddy Waters (born McKinley Morganfield, April 4, 1915, Rolling Fork, Mississippi, U.S.—d. April 30, 1983, Westmont, Illinois), whose nickname came from his proclivity for playing in a creek as a boy, grew up in the cotton country of the Mississippi Delta, where he was raised principally by his grandmother on the Stovall plantation near Clarksdale, Mississippi. He taught himself to play harmonica as a child and took up guitar at age 17. He eagerly absorbed the classic Delta blues styles of Robert Johnson, Son House, and others while developing a style of his own. As a young man, he drove a tractor on the sharecropped plantation, and on weekends he operated the cabin in which he lived as a "juke house," where visitors could party and imbibe moonshine whiskey made by Waters. He performed both on his own and in a band, occasionally earning a little money playing at house parties. He was first recorded in 1941, for the U.S. Library of Congress by archivist Alan Lomax, who had come to Mississippi in search of Johnson (who had already died by that time).

In 1943 Waters—like millions of other African Americans in the South who moved to cities in the North and West during the Great Migration from 1916 to 1970—relocated to Chicago. There he began playing clubs and bars on the city's South and West sides while earning a living working in a paper mill and later

*Muddy Waters, c. 1950.* Tom Copi/Michael Ochs Archives/Getty Images

driving a truck. In 1944 he bought his first electric guitar, which cut more easily through the noise of crowded bars. He soon broke with country blues by playing electric guitar in a shimmering slide style. In 1946 pianist Sunnyland Slim, another Delta native, helped Waters land a contract with Aristocrat Records, for which he made several unremarkable recordings. By 1948 Aristocrat had become Chess Records (taking its name from Leonard and Phil Chess, the Polish immigrant brothers who owned and operated it), and Waters was recording a string of hits for it that began with "I Feel Like Going Home" and "I Can't Be Satisfied." His early, aggressive, electrically amplified band—including pianist Otis Spann, guitarist Jimmie Rodgers, and harmonica virtuoso Little Walter—created closely integrated support for his passionate singing, which featured dramatic shouts, swoops, and falsetto moans. His repertoire, much of which he composed, included lyrics that were mournful ("Blow Wind Blow," "Trouble No More"), boastful ("Got My Mojo Working," "I'm Your Hoochie Coochie Man"), and frankly sensual (the unusual 15-bar blues "Rock Me"). In the process Waters became the foremost exponent of modern Chicago blues.

Tours of clubs in the South and Midwest in the 1940s and '50s gave way after 1958 to concert tours of the United States and Europe, including frequent dates at jazz, folk, and blues festivals. Over the years, some of Chicago's premier blues musicians did stints in Waters's band, including harmonica players James Cotton and Junior Wells, as well as guitarist Buddy Guy. Toward the end of his career, Waters concentrated on singing and played guitar only occasionally. A major influence on a variety of rock musicians—most notably the Rolling Stones (who took their name from his song "Rollin' Stone" and made a pilgrimage to Chess to record)—Waters was inducted into the Rock and Roll Hall of Fame in 1987.

## SONNY BOY WILLIAMSON

Vocalist and harmonica virtuoso Sonny Boy Williamson (born John Lee Williamson, March 30, 1914, Jackson, Tennessee, U.S.—died June 1, 1948, Chicago, Illinois) traveled through Tennessee and Arkansas with mandolinist Yank Rachell and guitarist Sleepy John Estes, working in bars, on the streets, and at parties from the late 1920s until he settled in Chicago in 1934. Williamson began recording in 1937, using small bands composed of a guitar, string bass, and sometimes a piano. Characteristically, he alternated vocal phrases with harmonica phrases, built melodic solo choruses, and preferred fast "jump" tempos. Every aspect of his style, including his slight speech impediment, has been imitated. Working in Chicago blues clubs, Williamson prefigured the post-World War II electric blues; he performed with Muddy Waters, an adherent of electronic amplification, in 1943. At the height of his popularity, Williamson was robbed and murdered while walking home from a blues bar.

Alex ("Rice") Miller, also a blues singer and harmonica player, took Sonny Boy Williamson's name, insisting that he had invented it. He performed, toured, and recorded under it from 1941, when he began playing on the popular King Biscuit Time radio broadcasts in Helena, Ark., until his death in 1965.

## JOHN LEE HOOKER

The child of a Mississippi sharecropping family, John Lee Hooker (born August 22, 1917, Clarksdale, Mississippi, U.S.—d. June 21, 2001, Los Altos, California) learned to play the guitar from his stepfather and developed an interest in gospel music as a child. In 1943 he moved to Detroit, Michigan, where he made his mark as a blues musician. On such early records as "Boogie Chillen," "Crawling King Snake," and "Weeping Willow (Boogie)" (1948–49), Hooker, accompanied only by an electric guitar, revealed his best qualities: aggressive energy in fast boogies and

no less intensity in stark, slow blues. A primitive guitarist, he played simple harmonies, pentatonic scales, and one-chord, modal harmonic structures. Later hits included "Dimples" (1956) and "Boom Boom" (1962). He toured widely from the 1950s and appeared in the motion pictures *The Blues Brothers* (1980) and *The Color Purple* (1985). Hooker, whose music influenced such bands as the Rolling Stones and the Animals, was inducted into the Rock and Roll Hall of Fame in 1991. Among the more than 100 albums he recorded are *The Healer* (1989), which features appearances by Bonnie Raitt and Carlos Santana; the Grammy Award-winning *Don't Look Back* (1997); and *The Best of Friends* (1998).

## HOWLIN' WOLF

Howlin' Wolf (born Chester Arthur Burnett, June 20, 1910, West Point, Mississippi, U.S.—died January 10, 1976, Hines, Illinois) was brought up on a cotton plantation; the music he heard was the traditional tunes of the region. He started singing professionally when quite young and in the 1920s and '30s performed throughout Mississippi, playing in small clubs. He was influenced by the music of Blind Lemon Jefferson, Sonny Boy Williamson, and Charley Patton. In the 1940s he went to Arkansas, where there was a flourishing blues tradition, and formed his own group, which included James Cotton and Little Jr. Parker, both of whom became noted blues performers in their own right. Wolf accompanied himself on guitar and harmonica, but his main instrument was his guttural and emotionally suggestive voice, which gave his songs power and authenticity. After his first record, *Moanin' at Midnight* (1951), became a hit, Wolf moved to Chicago, where he, along with Muddy Waters, made the city a centre for the transformation of the (acoustic) Mississippi Delta blues style into an electrically amplified style for urban audiences. His work was known only to blues audiences until the Rolling Stones and other British and American rock stars of the 1960s and '70s acknowledged his influence. Wolf (who was inducted into the Rock and Roll Hall of Fame as an early influence in 1991) was noted for his brooding lyrics and his earthy, aggressive stage presence.

## LITTLE WALTER

Raised on a Louisiana farm, Little Walter (born Marion Walter Jacobs, May 1, 1930, Marksville, Louisiana, U.S.—died February 15, 1968, Chicago, Illinois) began playing harmonica in childhood, and by the time he was 12 he was playing for a living on New Orleans street corners and in clubs. In his teens he gradually worked northward, settling in Chicago about 1946; there he began recording in 1947 and played in Muddy Waters's blues band (1948–52).

After Little Walter's 1952 harmonica solo "Juke" became a popular record, he successfully led his own bands in Chicago and on tours. In the 1960s alcoholism curtailed his career, and he died following a street fight.

Little Walter was one of the major figures in postwar Chicago blues. Influenced by guitarists as well as by senior harmonica players, he brought a singular variety of phrasing to the blues harmonica. His solos were cunningly crafted, alternating riffs and flowing lines; he was a pioneer of playing a harmonica directly into a handheld microphone and developed expressive techniques to enhance his playing. Though his vocal range was small, his singing often emulated Waters's style. His most popular recording was "My Babe," and his finest work included "Sad Hours," "Off the Wall," and "Can't Hold Out Much Longer." In 2008 Little Walter was inducted into the Rock and Roll Hall of Fame.

## B.B. KING

B.B. King (born Riley B. King, September 16, 1925, Itta Bena, near Indianola, Mississippi, U.S.) was reared in the Mississippi Delta region, and gospel music in church was the earliest influence on his singing. To his own impassioned vocal calls, King played lyrical single-string guitar responses with a distinctive vibrato; his guitar style was influenced by T-Bone Walker, by delta blues players (including his cousin Bukka White), and by such jazz guitarists as Django Reinhardt and Charlie Christian. King worked for a time as a disc jockey in Memphis, Tennessee (notably at station WDIA), where he acquired the name B.B. (for Blues Boy) King. In 1951 he made a hit record of "Three O'Clock Blues," which led to virtually continuous tours of clubs and theatres throughout the country. He often played 300 or more one-night stands a year with his 13-piece band. A long succession of hits, including "Every Day I Have the Blues," "Sweet Sixteen," and "The Thrill Is Gone," enhanced his popularity. By the late 1960s rock guitarists acknowledged his influence and priority; they introduced King and his guitar, Lucille, to a broader white public, who until then had heard blues chiefly in derivative versions.

King's relentless touring strengthened his claim to the title of undisputed king of the blues, and he was a regular fixture on the Billboard charts through the mid-1980s. His strongest studio albums of this era were those that most closely tried to emulate the live experience, and he found commercial success through a series of all-star collaborations. On *Deuces Wild* (1997), King enlisted such artists as

Van Morrison, Bonnie Raitt, and Eric Clapton to create a fusion of blues, pop, and country that dominated the blues charts for almost two years. Clapton and King collaborated on the more straightforward blues album *Riding with the King* (2000), which featured a collection of standards from King's catalog. He recaptured the pop magic of *Deuces Wild* with *80* (2005), a celebration of his 80th birthday that featured Sheryl Crow, John Mayer, and a standout performance by Elton John. King returned to his roots with *One Kind Favor* (2008), a collection of songs from the 1940s and '50s including blues classics by the likes of John Lee Hooker and Lonnie Johnson. Joining King in the simple four-part arrangements on the T-Bone Burnett-produced album were stalwart New Orleans pianist Dr. John, ace session drummer Jim Keltner, and stand-up bassist Nathan East. The album earned King (who was inducted into the Rock and Roll Hall of Fame in 1987) his 15th Grammy Award.

In 2008 the B.B. King Museum and Delta Interpretive Center opened in Indianola, with exhibits dedicated to King's music, his influences, and the history of the Delta region.

## JIMMY REED

Jimmy Reed (born Mathis James Reed, born September 6, 1925, Dunleith,

Mississippi, U.S.—died August 29, 1976, Oakland, California) began recording with the Chicago-based label Vee Jay in 1953 and had a string of hits in the 1950s and '60s that included "Honest I Do," "Baby, What You Want Me to Do," "Big Boss Man," and "Bright Lights, Big City." They almost invariably featured the same basic, unadorned rural boogie-shuffle rhythm accompanied by his thickly drawled, "mush-mouth" vocals and high, simply phrased harmonica solos. Much of his repertoire was composed by his wife, Mary Lee ("Mama") Reed, who occasionally sang duets with him, and his childhood friend Eddie Taylor often provided the intricate guitar work that fueled Reed's music. Despite his limitations, Reed was an energetic performer, a favourite on college and theatre tours in the late 1950s and early 1960s, and a leading influence on later rock and southern-styled blues musicians. In 1991 he was inducted into the Rock and Roll Hall of Fame.

## BUDDY GUY

Buddy Guy (born George Guy, July 30, 1936, Lettsworth, Louisiana, U.S.) made his own guitar at age 13 and taught himself to play by trying to reproduce the sounds of blues-men such as John Lee Hooker that he heard on the radio. He started play-ing clubs in Baton Rouge, Louisiana,

while still a teenager and in 1957 went on to Chicago. There he was discov-ered by blues great Muddy Waters, who helped him find work at the 708 Club, where he met other legendary bluesmen, including B.B. King and Willie Dixon. In 1960–67 he recorded several hits for the Chess label, includ-ing "Leave My Girl Alone" and "Stone Crazy." He also worked as a sideman (supporting instrumentalist) for such artists as Howlin' Wolf, Little Walter, and Koko Taylor.

In the 1970s and '80s Guy con-tinued to record and performed often with blues harmonica player Junior Wells, but he fell victim to the growing popularity of rock music. It was not until younger white musicians, among them Eric Clapton, Stevie Ray Vaughn, Keith Richards, and Jeff Beck, acknowl-edged their debt to Guy and other bluesmen that his fortunes again began to rise. He made several Grammy-winning albums in the 1990s, including *Damn Right, I've Got the Blues* (1991), *Feels Like Rain* (1993), and *Slippin' In* (1994). In 2003 Guy released his first acoustic blues recording, *Blues Singer*, and in 2011 he won another Grammy, for his album *Living Proof* (2010).

In addition to his work as a musi-cian, Guy (who was inducted into the Rock and Roll Hall of Fame in 2005) has owned two renowned blues clubs in Chicago, the Checkerboard

Lounge (1972–85) and (since 1989) Buddy Guy's Legends.

# WOMEN

Just as women played crucial roles in the development of classic blues, so, too, were they central to the popularization of rhythm and blues. To get a sense of the importance of their contributions, one need only remember that Atlantic Records, rhythm and blues' preeminent label, was often characterized simply as the "House That Ruth [Brown] Built." And long before Elvis Presley famously belittled the "Hound Dog," Big Mama Thornton had called out the cavorting canine.

## DINAH WASHINGTON

As a child, Ruth Jones (born August 29, 1924, Tuscaloosa, Alabama, U.S.—died December 14, 1963, Detroit, Michigan) moved with her family to Chicago. She sang in and played the piano for her church choir and in 1939 began to sing and play piano in various Chicago nightclubs, in addition to touring with Sallie Martin's gospel group. About 1942–43 she adopted the stage name Dinah Washington. From 1943 to 1946 she sang with the Lionel Hampton band and in 1946 began a successful solo career. During the period from 1949 to 1955, her recordings were consistently among the Top Ten hits of the rhythm-and-blues charts. Even after she crossed over to the popular (pop) music market, in which she had her greatest commercial success, Washington (who was inducted into the Rock and Roll Hall of Fame as an early influence in 1993) retained many of her earlier fans because of her passionate, supple style.

## BIG MAMA THORNTON

Singer and songwriter Big Mama Thornton performed in the tradition of classic blues singers such as Bessie Smith and Memphis Minnie. Her work inspired imitation by Elvis Presley and Janis Joplin, who recorded popular cover versions of Thornton's "Hound Dog" and "Ball and Chain," respectively. The daughter of a minister, Thornton (born Willie Mae Thornton, December 11, 1926, Montgomery, Alabama, U.S.—died July 25, 1984, Los Angeles, California) was introduced to church music at an early age. A skilled singer and dancer and a self-taught drummer and harmonica player, she toured the American South as a member of Sammy Green's Hot Harlem Revue during the 1940s. Settling in Houston, Texas, in 1948, she came under the influence of blues greats Lightnin' Hopkins, Lowell Fulson, Junior Parker, and Clarence ("Gatemouth") Brown. In the early 1950s she began performing with bandleader Johnny Otis, with whom she recorded many songs for Peacock Records, including the Jerry Leiber and Mike Stoller composition "Hound Dog," a number one rhythm-and-blues hit for Thornton in 1953 and an even bigger pop hit in 1956 for Presley, whose rock-and-roll version owed much to Thornton's original.

As interest in blues declined, Thornton ceased recording but continued to perform in the San Francisco Bay area, where she came to the attention of Joplin, whose late 1960s version of the Thornton-written "Ball and Chain" revived interest in the blues singer called "Big Mama" because of her girth and larger-than-life voice and stage presence.

## RUTH BROWN

By dominating the rhythm-and-blues charts throughout the 1950s singer Ruth Brown earned the sobriquet "Miss Rhythm." Her success helped establish Atlantic Records ("The House That Ruth Built") as the era's premier rhythm-and-blues label. The oldest of seven children, Brown (born January 12, 1928, Portsmouth, Virginia, U.S.—died November 17, 2006, Las Vegas, Nevada) was steered away from "the devil's music" by her father, a church choir director, but by her late teens she was singing in clubs in Virginia's Tidewater region and had

begun to perform with touring bands. In 1949, after spending nine months in a hospital recovering from an automobile accident, Brown released her first recording, "So Long." Abetted by Atlantic's cofounder Herb Abramson and songwriter Rudy Toombs, she became the most popular female rhythm-and-blues singer of the 1950s with a string of number one hits that included "Teardrops from My Eyes" (1950), "5-10-15 Hours" (1952), and her signature tune, "(Mama) He Treats Your Daughter Mean" (1953). After years of having her records covered by white performers, she experienced crossover pop success with "Lucky Lips" (1957) and "This Little Girl's Gone Rockin'" (1958).

Brown's career began a long decline in the early 1960s. Having survived four failed marriages, she spent the next decade driving a bus and cleaning houses while raising two sons. She began acting in the mid-1970s, first in television situation comedies and then in films and on the stage. In 1989 she won a Tony Award for best performance by a leading actress for the musical *Black and Blue,* and in 1990 she won a Grammy Award for best jazz vocal by a female. A champion of musicians' rights, she spoke out against exploitative contracts, and in the 1980s she eventually received some back royalties from Atlantic. Brown, whose principal influences were Ella

Fitzgerald and Billie Holiday, was inducted into the Rock and Roll Hall of Fame in 1993.

## LAVERN BAKER

At age 17 LaVern Baker (born Delores Williams, November 11, 1929, Chicago, Illinois, U.S.—died March 10, 1997, New York, New York) performed as Little Miss Sharecropper. Her 1955–65 tenure with Atlantic Records yielded 15 rhythm-and-blues hits, most notably "Tweedle Dee" (1955), "Jim Dandy" (1957), and "I Cried a Tear" (1959). Popular imitations of her recordings by white singers in the mid-1950s temporarily slowed her career. Typically her hits were novelty songs, but her only jazz album, *LaVern Baker Sings Bessie Smith* (1958), revealed her mastery of drama, expression, and soul. She retired to the Philippines in the 1970s and '80s and returned to performing in concerts and clubs in the United States in the 1990s. Baker was inducted into the Rock and Roll Hall of Fame in 1991.

## ETTA JAMES

With bandleader Johnny Otis, Etta James as a teenager composed a reply song to Hank Ballard and the Midnighters' suggestive hits "Work

*Etta James*, c. 2006. PRNewsFoto/RCA Records/AP Images

with Me, Annie" and "Annie Had a Baby." Originally titled "Roll with Me, Henry," that song, retitled "The Wallflower," became a rhythm-and-blues hit for James and then a million-seller in a sanitized cover version ("Dance with Me, Henry") by Georgia Gibbs. A veteran of grueling tours on the rhythm-and-blues theatre circuit, James (born Jamesetta Hawkins, January 25, 1938, Los Angeles, California, U.S.—d. January 20, 2012, Riverside, California) battled drug addiction for much of her career. Her highly dramatic qualities became evident on her 1960s ballads such as "All I Could Do Was Cry," "I'd Rather Go Blind," and the sensuous "At Last." Over the years James's voice changed—growing rougher and deeper and losing its little-girl quality—and she became one of the first women to sing in the style that became soul. She continued to perform and record into the early 21st century. James was inducted into the Rock and Roll Hall of Fame in 1993.

## TINA TURNER

Tina Turner (born Anna Mae Bullock, November 26, 1939, Brownsville, Tennessee, U.S.) was the child of a sharecropping family in rural Tennessee. She began singing as a teenager and, after moving to St. Louis, Missouri, immersed herself in the local rhythm-and-blues scene. She met Ike Turner at a performance by his band, the Kings of Rhythm, in 1956 and soon became part of the act. She began performing as Tina Turner, and her electric stage presence quickly made her the centrepiece of the show. The ensemble, which toured as the Ike and Tina Turner Revue, was renowned for its live performances but struggled to find recording success. That changed in 1960, when "A Fool in Love" hit the pop charts, and a string of hit singles followed. Ike and Tina were married in 1962, although the date is subject to some speculation (during the couple's divorce proceedings in 1977, Ike claimed that the two were never legally married). The Phil Spector-produced album *River Deep—Mountain High* (1966) was a hit in Europe, and its title track is arguably the high point of Spector's "wall of sound" production style, but it sold poorly in the United States. Ike and Tina's final hits as a couple were the cover version of Creedence Clearwater Revival's "Proud Mary" (1971) and "Nutbush City Limits" (1973).

Tina divorced Ike in 1978, alleging years of physical abuse and infidelity. After a series of guest appearances on the albums of other artists, she released her debut solo album, *Private Dancer*, in 1984. It was a triumph, both critically and commercially, garnering three

Grammy Awards and selling more than 20 million copies worldwide. She followed her musical success with a role in the film *Mad Max Beyond Thunderdome* (1985), and she wrote her autobiography, *I, Tina* (1986; adapted as the film *What's Love Got to Do with It,* 1993). Later albums include *Break Every Rule* (1986), *Foreign Affair* (1989), and *Wildest Dreams* (1996). Her greatest-hits compilation *All the Best* was released in 2004, and Turner continued touring into the 21st century. Ike and Tina were inducted into the Rock and Roll Hall of Fame in 1991.

## R&B

The big tent provided by the term *rhythm and blues* makes room for a wide variety of styles and stylists. For many listeners it stretches to include not only the soul music of the 1960s and '70s but even the most contemporary "urban" music of the 21st century. Indeed, several of the artists who gained popularity in the 1950s with records filed in stores under rhythm and blues had already begun inventing soul, most notably Sam Cooke, Ray Charles, and Jackie Wilson. Finally, tellingly, often in the 1950s the dividing line between rhythm and blues and rock and roll was in the eye rather than the ear of the beholder, the crucial distinction being the complexion of the performer.

## IKE TURNER

Ike Turner (born Izear Luster Turner, Jr., November 5, 1931, Clarksdale, Mississippi, U.S.—died December 12, 2007, San Marcos, California) began playing piano as a child and by the late 1940s had played with a number of the leading blues musicians in the Mississippi Delta region. While in high school he formed a band, the Kings of Rhythm. Their first recording, "Rocket 88"—made at Sam Phillips's Memphis (Tennessee) Recording Service but released on the Chess label—was a number one rhythm-and-blues hit in 1951, though it was credited to saxophonist Jackie Brenston (who provided the lead vocal) and the Delta Cats. After Brenston's departure, Ike served as a talent scout in the Memphis region for Los Angeles-based Modern Records and played as a session musician on early recordings by Howlin' Wolf, B.B. King, and others.

In St. Louis, where Ike had relocated in 1956, he expanded a new lineup of the Kings of Rhythm to include Anna Mae Bullock, who had begged to sing with the band. Even before marrying Ike, she changed her name to Tina Turner, and, as the Ike and Tina Turner Revue, the ensemble, which included a trio of female backing vocalists known as the Ikettes, thrived as a live act—largely because of Tina's fiery stage presence and Ike's

# REPRESENTATIVE WORKS

▶ *It's Gonna Work Out Fine* (1962)
▶ *Dynamite* (1963)
▶ *Live! The Ike and Tina Turner Show* (1965)

rubber-faced guitar-playing antics. Recording success eluded them, however, until the New York-based Sue label released a series of singles— "A Fool in Love" (1960), "I Idolize You" (1960), and "It's Gonna Work Out Fine" (1961)—that won them a national following. In 1966 Phil Spector made *River Deep—Mountain High* with Tina (he paid Ike to stay out of the studio). Easily the most complex and nuanced of Spector's famous "wall of sound" productions, it was a hit in Britain, but it attracted little American attention and is usually cited as the end of Spector's early career.

Repositioning themselves to appeal to the growing rock market in the late 1960s, Ike and Tina Turner began to sell records again with their energetic reworkings of other people's songs, most notably Creedence Clearwater Revival's "Proud Mary"

(1971), which, along with "Nutbush City Limits" (1973), written by Tina, proved to be their last major success. Tina began to realize that she, not Ike, was the attraction, and she divorced him—alleging beatings, cocaine addiction, and infidelity on his part. Ike's career was hurt by Tina's revelations, and, after imprisonment for cocaine possession (1989–91), he undertook a comeback. In 2007 he received a Grammy Award for his album *Risin' with the Blues* (2006).

## LLOYD PRICE

Singer, songwriter, and entrepreneur Lloyd Price (born March 9, 1933, New Orleans, Louisiana, U.S.) made his mark in rock music history with his exuberant tenor and his flair for recasting rhythm and blues as irrepressible pop music, often working with seminal New Orleans producer

Dave Bartholomew. Price's recording of his composition "Lawdy Miss Clawdy" (with Fats Domino on piano) topped the rhythm-and-blues charts in 1952 and was later a hit for Elvis Presley. "Personality" (1959) remains one of the most delightful of all New Orleans rhythm-and-blues hits, and his cover of the traditional ballad "Stagolee," which tells of a turn-of-the-century murder, became the best-known version of that often-recorded song. Price renamed it "Stagger Lee" (1958), turned the song's cautionary theme on its head with an uproarious arrangement, and wrote a delicate introduction reminiscent of haiku: "The night was clear / The moon was yellow / And the leaves...came...tumbling / Down." Price turned out hits throughout the 1960s and appeared on the oldies circuit well into his 60s. He also established three record companies and ran a booking agency and limousine service. In 1998 he was inducted into the Rock and Roll Hall of Fame.

## THE DRIFTERS

The Drifters were actually two groups—one built around lead singer Clyde McPhatter, the other an entirely different group that took the name Drifters, to which manager George Treadwell held the copyright, after he dismissed the original contingent. The principal members of the first incarnation were Clyde McPhatter (born November 15, 1932, Durham, North Carolina, U.S.—d. June 13, 1972, New York, New York), Billy Pinckney (born August 15, 1925, Sumter, South Carolina—died July 4, 2007, Daytona Beach, Florida), Andrew Thrasher (born Wetumpka, Alabama), Gerhart Thrasher (born Wetumpka), "Little David" Baughan (born New York—died 1970), and Johnny Moore (born 1934, Selma, Alabama). Principal members of the second incarnation included Ben E. King (born Benjamin Earl Nelson, September 28, 1938, Henderson, North Carolina), Charlie Thomas, Elsbeary Hobbs, Rudy Lewis, and Moore.

The Drifters were formed in 1953 at the behest of Atlantic Records cofounder Ahmet Ertegun, who approached McPhatter when the popular vocalist was dropped from Billy Ward and the Dominoes. After serving in the army, McPhatter left the Drifters in 1955 to pursue a solo career—but not before the group had reached number one on the rhythm-and-blues charts with "Money Honey" (1953) and scored several other hits, including "White Christmas" (1954). Three lead singers later, in 1959, Treadwell replaced the entire group with another ensemble, the Five Crowns, led by King. Still recording for Atlantic, now under the guidance of writer-producers Jerry

# DOC POMUS

Songwriter Doc Pomus teamed with Mort Shuman to write some of the most memorable rock and pop songs in the Brill Building style of the early 1960s.

Pomus (born Jerome Felder, January 27, 1925, New York, New York, U.S.—died March 14, 1991, New York) began singing in jazz and blues clubs as a teenager and met pianist Shuman during a recording session. Together (Shuman wrote most of the music and Pomus the lyrics) they crafted bluesy teen-oriented songs that were recorded primarily by Atlantic Records artists, notably the Drifters ("Save the Last Dance for Me" and "This Magic Moment"). They also wrote more than 20 songs for Elvis Presley, including "Little Sister," "Viva Las Vegas," and "Surrender." The author of more than 1,000 songs, Pomus was inducted into the Rock and Roll Hall of Fame in 1992.

Leiber and Mike Stoller, the Drifters cracked the pop Top Ten in 1959 with "There Goes My Baby" (remembered for its innovative use of strings and Latin rhythms) and took "Save the Last Dance for Me" (1960) to number one.

King, too, left and became a successful soloist, scoring hits with "Spanish Harlem" (1960) and "Stand by Me" (1961). However, the Drifters continued their string of hits, benefiting from the Brill Building–style songwriting prowess of teams such as Carole King and Gerry Goffin and Mort Shuman and Doc Pomus. Lewis sang lead on "Up on the Roof" (1962) and "On Broadway" (1963), while Moore took the lead on "Under the Boardwalk" (1964). Although the group's popularity waned in the mid-1960s, a changing membership carried the Drifters' gospel-tinged sound into the early 21st century. The Drifters were inducted into the Rock and Roll Hall of Fame in 1988.

## CLYDE MCPHATTER

One of the most dramatic vocalists of his generation, Clyde McPhatter (born November 15, 1932, Durham, North Carolina, U.S.—d. June 13, 1972, New York, New York) grew up in a devout Christian family that moved from North Carolina to New Jersey in the mid-1940s. There, together with some high school friends (including two of author James Baldwin's brothers), he formed the Mount Lebanon Singers, who quickly found success on the gospel circuit. In 1950 a talent contest brought him to the attention of vocal coach Billy Ward, whose group he joined. With McPhatter singing lead, Billy Ward and the Dominoes became one of the era's preeminent vocal groups, but the martinetish Ward fired McPhatter in 1953 (replacing him with Jackie Wilson). Shortly thereafter, Atlantic Records' Ahmet Ertegun sought to establish a new group around McPhatter, eventually recruiting former members of the Thrasher Wonders. As Clyde McPhatter and the Drifters, this group soon had a hit with "Money Honey," which perfectly showcased McPhatter's melismatic, gospel-derived style. In 1954 their recording of Irving Berlin's classic "White Christmas" was banned from the radio because of alleged lewdness, yet it became a perennial seller. That fall McPhatter was drafted into the army but, stationed in New Jersey, was able to continue recording and appear in the film *Mister Rock and Roll* (1957).

Upon his discharge he became a soloist, with the Drifters continuing with other lead singers (most notably Ben E. King). Thereafter, he began to record increasingly pop-oriented material, including the pop Top 20 hits "Without Love (There Is Nothing)" (1956) and "A Lover's Question" (1958) as well as the rhythm-and-blues hit "Lovey Dovey." In 1960 he switched record labels, signing first with MGM, then with Mercury. His new material was so pop-oriented that his 1962 hit "Lover Please" did not even show up on the rhythm-and-blues charts, and, after a mild success in 1965 with "Crying Won't Help You Now," the hits stopped coming, although his voice would have been perfect for the emerging style of soul. Slipping into alcoholism, he played the oldies circuit and died before his 40th birthday. McPhatter was inducted into the Rock and Roll Hall of Fame in 1987.

## HANK BALLARD

Singer and songwriter Hank Ballard is best remembered for songs that were frequently as scandalous as they were inventive, most notably the salacious "Work with Me, Annie" (1954). He also wrote "The

Twist" (1959), which sparked a dance craze in the United States. Ballard (born November 18, 1936, Detroit, Michigan, U.S.—died March 2, 2003, Los Angeles, California) grew up in Alabama but returned to his birthplace when he was a teenager, and there he worked at an automobile assembly plant before joining the vocal group that would record for Federal and King first as the Royals and then, more successfully, as the Midnighters. In addition to Ballard, the principal members of the Midnighters included Henry Booth (born March 7, 1934, Montgomery, Alabama, U.S.—died 1978), Cal Green (born June 22, 1935, Liberty, Texas—died July 2, 2004, Lake View Terrace, California), Charles Sutton, and Sonny Woods (born March 6, 1935, Detroit, Michigan—died 1984). Although he was responsible for "The Twist," a crossover sensation when later covered by *American Bandstand* stalwart Chubby Checker, Ballard's popularity was confined primarily to a wildly appreciative black audience that made the Midnighters a hit on the chitlin circuit (music venues that attracted African American audiences). "Work with Me, Annie"—which prompted a raft of answer songs, most notably "Roll with Me, Henry" by Etta James— was opposed by radio programmers who disapproved of its "explicit lyrics." However, it and the similarly criticized "Sexy Ways" and "Annie Had a Baby" were Top Ten rhythm-and-blues hits for the Midnighters in 1954. Later hits included "Finger Poppin' Time" and "Let's Go, Let's Go, Let's Go" (both 1960).

Both the gospel phrasing with which Ballard infused his high tenor and the scorching guitar of the Midnighters' backing band played important roles in the development of rock and roll. Ballard pursued a solo career after 1963, performing regularly with the James Brown Revue. After years of relative obscurity, he was inducted into the Rock and Roll Hall of Fame in 1990; the Midnighters were selected for induction in 2012.

## THE COASTERS

Another of the most popular rhythm-and-blues vocal quartets of the 1950s was the Coasters. The principal members were Carl Gardner (born April 29, 1928, Tyler, Texas, U.S.— died June 12, 2011, Port St. Lucie, Florida), Bobby Nunn (b. June 25, 1925, Birmingham, Alabama—died November 5, 1986, Los Angeles, California), Billy Guy (born June 20, 1936, Itasca, Texas—died November 12, 2002, Las Vegas, Nevada), Leon Hughes (born 1938), Will ("Dub") Jones (born May 14, 1928, Shreveport, Louisiana—died January 16, 2000, Long Beach, California), Cornelius Gunter (born November

THE BIRTH OF ROCK & ROLL: MUSIC IN THE 1950S THROUGH THE 1960S

14, 1938, Los Angeles—died February 26, 1990, Las Vegas), Ronnie Bright (born October 18, 1938), and Earl ("Speedo") Carroll (born November 2, 1937, New York, New York).

Originally from Los Angeles, the Coasters began as the Robins; instead of singing the usual ballads and rhythm pieces, they sang novelty songs by Jerry Leiber and Mike Stoller ("Riot in Cell Block No. 9" and "Smokey Joe's Cafe"). In 1955, with a change in personnel (most notably the loss of Richard Berry, who would later write the rock classic "Louie, Louie"), they became the Coasters. The group had a series of rock-and-roll hits—largely for Atlantic Records' subsidiary label Atco—with witty Leiber-Stoller songs directed at teenage listeners: "Searchin'" and "Young Blood" (both 1957), "Yakety Yak" (1958), and "Charlie Brown" and "Poison Ivy" (both 1959). The Coasters alternated lead singers and featured clever arrangements, including amusing bass replies and tenor saxophone solos by King Curtis, who played a crucial role in creating Atlantic's rhythm-and-blues sound. With further personnel changes they continued performing in "oldies" shows into the 1990s. The Coasters were inducted into the Rock and Roll Hall of Fame in 1987.

## LITTLE WILLIE JOHN

Little Willie John (born William Edgar John, November 15, 1937, Cullendale [now Camden], Arkansas, U.S.—died May 26, 1968, Walla Walla, Washington) grew up in Detroit, sang gospel music, and at age 16 began recording rhythm and blues for King Records. He introduced "Fever" (1956), which became a standard; "Talk to Me, Talk to Me" (1958) and "Sleep" (1960) were his other major hits. Just over five feet tall, with a resonant tenor voice and smooth delivery, he was best at blues ballads and a favourite performer on the rhythm-and-blues theatre circuit. He stabbed a man to death in a drunken brawl, was convicted of manslaughter in 1966, and died in Washington State Penitentiary. He was the brother of soul singer Mable John. Little Willie John was inducted into the Rock and Roll Hall of Fame in 1996.

## HUEY "PIANO" SMITH

Huey "Piano" Smith (born January 26, 1934, New Orleans, Louisiana, U.S.) contributed vocals and his aggressive, boogie-based piano style to the rhythm-and-blues recordings of others before forming his own band. For a time Huey Smith and the Clowns, which featured singer-comedian Bobby Marchan and outstanding New Orleans instrumentalists, toured widely as a result of their 1957–58 novelty hits "Rockin' Pneumonia and the Boogie Woogie Flu" and "Don't You Just Know It." The latter, with its "Koobo, kooba, kooba, kooba" chorus, was a favourite of American teenagers. The band's final hit was the 1959 Smith song "Sea Cruise," sung by a young white singer, Frankie Ford.

## RAY CHARLES

When Ray Charles (born Ray Charles Robinson, September 23, 1930, Albany, Georgia, U.S.—died June 10, 2004, Beverly Hills, California) was an infant his family moved to Greenville, Florida, and he began his musical career at age five on a piano in a neighbourhood café. He began to go blind at six, possibly from glaucoma, and had completely lost his sight by age seven. He attended the St. Augustine School for the Deaf and Blind, where he concentrated on musical studies, but left school at age 15 to play the piano professionally after his mother died from cancer (his father had died when the boy was 10).

Charles built a remarkable career based on the immediacy of emotion in his performances. After emerging as a blues and jazz pianist indebted to Nat King Cole's style in the late 1940s, Charles recorded the boogie-woogie classic "Mess Around" and the novelty song "It Should've Been Me" in 1952–53. His arrangement for Guitar Slim's "The Things That I Used

*Ray Charles in concert, c. 1970.* Tony Evans/Timelapse Library Ltd./Hulton Archive/Getty Images

to Do" became a blues million-seller in 1953. By 1954 Charles had created a successful combination of blues and gospel influences and signed on with Atlantic Records. Propelled by Charles's distinctive raspy voice, "I've Got a Woman" and "Hallelujah I Love You So" became hit records. "What'd I Say" led the rhythm-and-blues sales charts in 1959 and was Charles's own first million-seller.

Charles's rhythmic piano playing and band arranging revived the "funky" quality of jazz, but he also recorded in many other musical genres. He entered the pop market with the best-sellers "Georgia on My Mind" (1960) and "Hit the Road, Jack" (1961). His album *Modern Sounds in Country and Western Music* (1962) sold more than a million copies, as did its single "I Can't Stop Loving You." Thereafter his music emphasized jazz standards and renditions of pop and show tunes.

From 1955 Charles toured extensively in the United States and elsewhere with his own big band and a gospel-style female backup quartet called the Raeletts. He also appeared on television and worked in films such as *Ballad in Blue* (1964) and *The Blues Brothers* (1980) as a featured act and soundtrack composer. He formed his own custom recording labels, Tangerine in 1962 and Crossover Records in 1973. The recipient of many national and international awards, he received 13 Grammy Awards, including a lifetime achievement award in 1987. In 1986 Charles (billed for much of his career as "the Genius") was inducted into the Rock and Roll Hall of Fame and received a Kennedy Center Honor.

## SAM COOKE

Along with Ray Charles, Sam Cooke (born January 22, 1931, Clarksdale, Mississippi, U.S.—died December 11, 1964, Los Angeles, California) was one of the most influential African American vocalists of the post-World War II period. If Charles represented raw soul, Cooke symbolized sweet soul. To his many celebrated disciples—Smokey Robinson, James Taylor, and Michael Jackson among them—he was an icon of unrivaled stature.

Cooke's career came in two phases. As a member of the groundbreaking Soul Stirrers, a premier gospel group of the 1950s, he electrified the African American church community nation-wide with a light, lilting vocal style that soared rather than thundered. "Nearer to Thee" (1955), "Touch the Hem of His Garment" (1956), and "Jesus, Wash Away My Troubles" (1956) were major gospel hits and, in the words of Aretha Franklin, "perfectly chiseled jewels."

Cooke's decision to turn his attention to pop music in 1957 had tremendous implications in the black musical community. There long had been a taboo against such a move, but Cooke broke the mold. He reinvented himself as a romantic crooner in the manner of Nat King Cole. His strength was in his smoothness. He wrote many of his best songs himself, including his first hit, the ethereal "You Send Me," which shot to number one on all charts in 1957 and established Cooke as a superstar.

While other rhythm-and-blues artists stressed visceral sexuality, Cooke was essentially a spiritualist, even in the domain of romantic love. When he did sing dance songs—"Twistin' the Night Away" (1962), "Shake" (1965)— he did so with a delicacy theretofore unknown in rock music. Cooke also distinguished himself as an independent businessman, heading his own publishing, recording, and management firms. He broke new ground by playing nightclubs, such as the Copacabana in New York City, previously off-limits to rhythm-and-blues acts.

The tragedy of his demise in 1964—he was shot to death at age 33 by a motel manager—is shrouded in mystery. But the mystery has done nothing to damage the strength of his legacy. "A Change Is Gonna Come" (1965) remains his signature song, an anthem of hope and boundless optimism that expresses the genius of his poetry and sweetness of his soul. Cooke was inducted into the Rock and Roll Hall of Fame in 1986.

## BOBBY "BLUE" BLAND

Bobby "Blue" Bland (born Robert Calvin Bland, January 27, 1930, Rosemark, Tennessee, U.S.) began his career in Memphis with bluesman B.B. King and ballad singer Johnny Ace (all three were part of a loose aggregation of musicians known as the Beale Streeters). Influenced by gospel and by pop singers such as Tony Bennett and Andy Williams, as well as by rhythm and blues, Bland became famous with early 1960s hits for Duke Records such as "Cry Cry Cry," "I Pity the Fool," "Turn on Your Lovelight," and "That's the Way Love Is." Joe Scott's arrangements were pivotal to these successes in which Bland alternated between smooth, expertly modulated phrases and fiercely shouted, gospel-style ones. Long a particular favourite of female listeners, Bland for a time sang some disco material along with his blues ballads, and in later years he developed the curious habit of snorting between lines. While his recording output slowed in the early 2000s, Bland maintained an active touring schedule, and he was a guest performer with B.B. King and singer-songwriter Van Morrison. Bland was inducted into the Rock and Roll Hall of Fame in 1992, and he was awarded a Grammy Award for lifetime achievement in 1997.

## JACKIE WILSON

Jackie Wilson (born Jack Wilson, June 9, 1934, Detroit, Michigan, U.S.—died January 21, 1984, Mount Holly, New Jersey) was one of the most distinctively dynamic soul performers of the 1960s. Few singers could match his vocal range or his pure physicality onstage. He was a genuine original, and his stylistic innovations in the 1950s were as important in the evolution of American pop, rock, and soul as those of James Brown, Nat King Cole, or Sam Cooke, despite the fact that his recordings seldom enjoyed the commercial impact that theirs did.

Wilson—who possessed a dynamic multioctave tenor—started singing professionally while still a teenager, and in 1953 he replaced Clyde McPhatter as the lead singer of the vocal group the Dominoes, led by Billy Ward, with whom he sang until he became a solo performer in 1957. Wilson had to deal with the routine forms of racial segregation that made it difficult for African American male artists to secure mainstream success. The commercial and stylistic barriers between so-called "race music" and the predominantly white pop Top 40 forced singers such as Wilson to agonize over their choice of material

# REPRESENTATIVE WORKS

- ► "Reet Petite" (1957)
- ► "Lonely Teardrops" (1958)
- ► "Night"/"Doggin' Around" (1960)
- ► *A Woman, a Lover, a Friend* (1960)
- ► "Baby Workout" (1963)
- ► "Shake a Hand" (1963)
- ► "(Your Love Keeps Lifting Me) Higher and Higher" (1967)
- ► "Chain Gang" (1968)
- ► "For Your Precious Love" (1968)

as they sought to display their talents to the fullest without provoking racially motivated marginalization. This was the challenge songwriter and fellow Detroiter Berry Gordy, Jr., took on when he and Roquel ("Billy") Davis (also known as Tyran Carlo) wrote Wilson's first solo single, "Reet Petite," in 1957. Two years later Gordy formed Motown Records, where his goal was crossover success—that is, to take black performers from the rhythm-and-blues chart onto the pop chart. Both Gordy and Wilson had earlier pursued careers as boxers, possibly the source of Wilson's phenomenal stamina and breath control onstage. Gordy's affinity for Wilson's masculine, highly physical persona led him to cowrite (with his sister Gwendolyn and Davis) several of the singer's most successful singles, including "Lonely Teardrops" (1958), "To Be Loved" (1958), and "That's Why (I Love You So)" (1959), the first of which topped the rhythm-and-blues chart and reached number seven on the pop chart.

Once Wilson's solo career was launched, he toured constantly, creating a reputation as a consummate showman. In 1963 he scored a Top Five pop record with the deep-soul rave-up "Baby Workout," but he did not have another big hit until 1967, when—at the peak of Beatlemania—Wilson's soaring rendition of "(Your Love Keeps Lifting Me) Higher and Higher" reached number six on the pop chart. Unlike other stars at Stax and Motown, Wilson was not always backed by first-rate session musicians or provided with quality arrangements; however, Chicago-based producer Carl Davis hired the Motown rhythm section for "Higher and Higher," investing the record with a trendy, contemporary beat. Yet, despite Davis's imaginative contributions, Wilson's later records had limited commercial success, largely because Brunswick Records did not give them the necessary promotional push to secure radio play. Wilson resorted to touring to reignite public interest in his career. In September 1975, as he was about to mount a major comeback with the just-completed album *Nobody but You*, Wilson suffered a heart attack during a live performance that left him semicomatose for almost eight years until his death in 1984. He was inducted into the Rock and Roll Hall of Fame in 1987.

# CHAPTER 7

# Doo-wop

**O**ne of the most popular musical genres in the 1950s and early '60s was the style of rhythm-and-blues and rock-and-roll music known as doo-wop. The structure of doo-wop music generally featured a tenor lead vocalist singing the melody of the song with a trio or quartet singing background harmony. The term *doo-wop* is derived from the sounds made by the group as they provided harmonic background for the lead singer.

## THE MILLS BROTHERS

The roots of the doo-wop style can be found as early as the records of the Mills Brothers and the Ink Spots in the 1930s and '40s. The Mills Brothers turned small-group harmony into an art form when, in many of their recordings, they used their vocal harmony to simulate the sound of string or reed sections.

The Mills Brothers—John Charles (born October 19, 1910, Piqua, Ohio, U.S.—died January 24, 1936, Bellefontaine, Ohio), Herbert (born April 2, 1912, Piqua—died April 12, 1989, Las Vegas, Nevada), Harry (born August 19, 1913, Piqua—died June 28, 1982, Los Angeles, California), and Donald (b. April 29, 1915, Piqua—died November 13, 1999, Los Angeles)—began as a barbershop quartet, which was perhaps only natural, as their father, John H. Mills (1882–1967),

The Mills Brothers c. 1936 (left to right): Herbert, Donald, John C., and Harry. General Photographic Agency/Hulton Archive/Getty Images

owned a barbershop. They gave their first public performances in variety shows on the radio in Cincinnati, Ohio. In about 1930 they moved to New York City, where they became the first African American singers to have their own national radio show. Billed as "Four Boys and a Guitar" and accompanied only by brother John's guitar, they could sound like a full jazz band, particularly on such numbers as "Tiger Rag," "St. Louis Blues," and "Bugle Call Rag." Each brother specialized in an "instrument": they imitated two trumpets, a trombone, and a tuba. They were also a hit on records and in live performances, and they appeared in several films, including *The Big Broadcast* (1932) and *Broadway Gondolier* (1935).

John C. Mills's sudden death in 1936 was a blow to the close-knit siblings, and they almost dissolved the act. Fortunately, their father took over his son's role, and the group continued without any loss in popularity (although it was necessary to employ an outside guitarist). They continued mostly in the hot-jazz style, with a strong emphasis on scat singing and instrumental imitations, and made records with such artists as Louis Armstrong, Duke Ellington, Ella Fitzgerald, and the Boswell Sisters. The Mills Brothers had their biggest hit in 1943 with "Paper Doll," which sold more than six million records and was also a best seller as sheet music. In the mid-1940s they dropped the instrumental imitations and became a more-conventional vocal group, backed by a regular rhythm section or an orchestra. Their later hits included "You Always Hurt the One You Love" (1944), "Glow Worm" (1952), and "Opus One" (1952).

John H. Mills retired in 1956, and the brothers continued as a trio, recording and performing regularly into the 1970s. The act came to an end after Harry's death in 1982, but Donald Mills in his last years performed the group's hits with his son, John H. Mills II. Their sound became identified with an era, and many of their recordings were later used on the soundtracks of movies, including *Raging Bull* (1980), *Pearl Harbor* (2001), and *Being Julia* (2004).

## THE INK SPOTS

The Ink Spots established the preeminence of the tenor and bass singer as members of the pop vocal ensemble, and their influence can be heard in rhythm-and-blues music beginning in the 1940s (in records by the Ravens), throughout the '50s, and well into the '70s. One of the first African American groups, along with the Mills Brothers, to reach both black and white audiences, the Ink Spots exerted great influence on the development of the doo-wop vocal style. The principal members were Orville ("Hoppy") Jones (born February 17, 1905, Chicago, Illinois, U.S.—died October 18, 1944, New York, New York), Charles Fuqua (died 1971), Ivory ("Deek") Watson (born 1913, Indianapolis, Indiana—died November 4, 1969), Bill Kenny (born 1915, Philadelphia, Pennsylvania—died March 23, 1978), Jerry Daniels (born 1916, Indianapolis—died November 7, 1995, Indianapolis), Herb Kenny (born 1915, Philadelphia—died July 11, 1992, Columbia, Maryland), and Billy Bowen (born 1912, Birmingham, Alabama—died 1982).

Formed in 1932 as the King, Jack and the Jesters, the group became the Ink Spots when they relocated to New York City. After Herb Kenny replaced original member Daniels, the group began a slow evolution toward its distinctive sound. In 1939 the Ink Spots scored a huge hit with "If I Didn't Care," on which Bill Kenny's tenor lead contrasted with Jones's deep bass. In establishing the prominence of the high tenor lead and adding

The Ink Spots. Frank Ramage/Hulton Archive/Getty Images

spoken bass choruses to the backing harmonies, the Ink Spots laid the groundwork for countless doo-wop and rhythm-and-blues vocal groups, from the Ravens and the Orioles to Motown's Temptations. Among their many hits in the 1940s were "Address Unknown," "My Prayer" (later rerecorded by the Platters), "Into Each Life Some Rain Must Fall" (a collaboration with Ella Fitzgerald), "We Three," "To Each His Own," and "The Gypsy." In the early 1950s the group split into two, and multiple incarnations of the Ink Spots continued to perform through the 1990s. The Ink Spots were inducted into the Rock and Roll Hall of Fame in 1989.

The Ink Spots' influence is best exhibited in the remakes of their hit records "My Prayer" (1956) by the Platters and "If I Didn't Care" (1970) by the Moments. In fact, Motown's premier male group of the 1960s and '70s, the Temptations, had a vocal sound that was based in this classic doo-wop style, with the Ink Spots' tenor lead singer, Bill Kenny, and bass singer, Hoppy Jones, serving as inspiration for the Temptations' lead singers, Eddie Kendricks and David Ruffin, and their bass singer, Melvin Franklin. There also was a school of female doo-wop, best exemplified by the Chantels, the Shirelles, and Patti LaBelle and the Bluebelles.

## A CAPELLA AND ECHO

The popularity of doo-wop music among young singers in urban American communities of the 1950s such as New York City, Chicago, and Baltimore, Maryland, was due in large part to the fact that the music could be performed effectively a cappella (without instrumental accompaniment). Many young enthusiasts in these communities had little access to musical instruments, so the vocal ensemble was the most popular musical performing unit. Doo-wop groups tended to rehearse in locations that provided echoes—where their harmonies could best be heard. They often rehearsed in hallways and high school bathrooms and under bridges; when they were ready for public performance, they sang on stoops and street corners, in community centre talent shows, and in the hallways of the Brill Building. As a result many doo-wop records had such remarkably rich vocal harmonies that they virtually overwhelmed their minimalist instrumental accompaniment.

Doo-wop's appeal for much of the public lay in its artistically powerful simplicity, but this "uncomplicated" type of record also was an ideal, low-budget investment for a small record company to produce. The absence of strings and horns ("sweetening") in their production gave many of the doo-wop records of the early 1950s an almost haunting sparseness. The Orioles' "What Are You Doing New Year's Eve?" (1949) and "Crying in the Chapel" (1953), the Harptones' "A Sunday Kind of Love" (1953), and the Penguins' "Earth Angel" (1954) are excellent examples of this effect.

## THE ORIOLES

Formed in Baltimore in 1947, the Orioles are often cited as the first vocal group to sing in the rhythm-and-blues style, which they accomplished by taking the prevailing vocal pop style of the Ink Spots and adding a more rhythmic and rocking approach. The members of the Orioles were Sonny Til (born Earlington Carl Tilghman, August 18, 1925, Baltimore, Maryland, U.S.—died December 9, 1981, Washington, D.C.), Alexander Sharp (born December 1919, Baltimore—died January 1970), George Nelson (born 1925, Baltimore—died 1959), Johnny Reed (born c. 1929, Baltimore), and Tommy Gaither (born c. 1919, Baltimore—died November 5, 1950,

Baltimore). Following their success, vocal groups with ornithological names became a staple of rhythm and blues.

An appearance on *Arthur Godfrey's Talent Scouts* television show in 1948 led to a recording contract for the Orioles. Their first recording, "It's Too Soon to Know," a slow romantic ballad, launched their career spectacularly by going to number one on the rhythm-and-blues chart. Most of the group's records also were quiet ballads that featured Til's heartfelt lead vocal supported by soft choruses sung by the rest of the group and almost imperceptible instrumental accompaniment. Their most notable records were "Tell Me So" (1949), "Crying in the Chapel" (1953), and "In the Mission of St. Augustine" (1953). The group disbanded in 1955, by which time they had been all but forgotten as pioneers. Later generations, however, would recognize the group not only as pioneers in rhythm and blues but also as roots artists of rock and roll whose influence on the doo-wop vocal groups of the 1950s and '60s was considerable. The Orioles were inducted into the Rock and Roll Hall of Fame in 1995.

## THE PLATTERS

The Platters were managed by songwriter Buck Ram, who was taken with Tony Williams's dramatic, soaring voice and had the singer form a group around himself in 1953 in Los Angeles. The principal members were Williams (born Samuel Anthony Williams, April 5, 1928, Elizabeth, New Jersey, U.S.—died August 14, 1992, New York, New York), Zola Taylor (born March 17, 1934/38, Los Angeles, California—died April 30, 2007, Riverside, California), David Lynch (born July 3, 1929, St. Louis, Missouri—died January 2, 1981, Long Beach, California), Paul Robi (born August 30, 1931, New Orleans, Louisiana—died February 1, 1989, Los Angeles), Herb Reed (born August 7, 1931, Kansas City, Missouri), and Sonny Turner (born 1939, Fairmont, West Virginia). Ram wrote or cowrote some of the Platters' biggest hits, including "Only You (and You Alone)" (1955), "The Great Pretender" (which topped the pop and rhythm-and-blues charts in 1956), and "(You've Got) The Magic Touch" (1956). The Platters sustained their career by specializing in rock-and-roll renditions of old big-band hits, notably "My Prayer" (1956) and "Twilight Time" and "Smoke Gets in Your Eyes" (both 1958). The group also appeared in two rock-and-roll movies, *The Girl Can't Help It* and *Rock Around the Clock* (both 1956).

Williams left the Platters in 1961, but during the late 1960s, with Turner as the lead vocalist, the group achieved moderate success with soul-style hits. The history of the Platters, however, is primarily associated with the early days of rock and roll. The group was inducted into the Rock and Roll Hall of Fame in 1990.

## THE FLAMINGOS

The Flamingos were formed in Chicago in 1951. The principal members were Zeke Carey (born January 24, 1933, Bluefield, Virginia, U.S.), Jake Carey (born September 9, 1926, Pulaski, Virginia—died December 10, 1997, Lanham, Maryland), Paul Wilson (born January 6, 1935, Chicago, Illinois—died May 6, 1988, Chicago), Johnny Carter (born June 2, 1934, Chicago—died August 21, 2009, Harvey, Illinois), Sollie McElroy (born July 16, 1933, Gulfport, Mississippi—died January 14, 1994, Chicago), and Nate Nelson (b. April 10, 1932, Chicago—died June 1, 1984, Boston, Massachusetts). Later members included Tommy Hunt (born June 18, 1933, Pittsburgh, Pennsylvania) and Terry Johnson (born November 12, 1935, Baltimore, Maryland). Cousins Zeke and Jake Carey sang tenor and bass, respectively; Carter also sang tenor; and Wilson was the group's baritone. Most prominent among a succession of lead singers were McElroy (1951–54) and Nelson (1954–60). The group had regional success with a number of rhythm-and-blues records before achieving national fame in 1956 with the ballad "I'll Be Home." They went on to help pioneer rock and roll with appearances in several stage shows sponsored by legendary disc jockey Alan Freed, and in the films *Rock, Rock, Rock* (1956) and *Go Johnny Go* (1958). After moving to New York City in 1957, the Flamingos lost Carter but added vocalist-keyboardist Hunt and guitarist Johnson. Working with producer George Goldner, they registered their biggest hits: "Lovers Never Say Goodbye" (1958), "I Only Have Eyes for You" (1959), and "Nobody Loves Me Like You" (1960). In the early 1960s, with the Careys the only remaining original members, the group achieved a few soul-style hits, but by the early 1970s they had become a revival act. The Flamingos were inducted into the Rock and Roll Hall of Fame in 2001.

## THE MOONGLOWS

The Moonglows were discovered in Cleveland, Ohio, in 1952 by Alan Freed. The principal members were Bobby Lester (born January 13, 1930, Louisville, Kentucky, U.S.—died October 15, 1980, Louisville), Harvey Fuqua (born July 27, 1929, Louisville—died July 6, 2010, Detroit, Michigan), Alexander ("Pete") Graves (born April 17, 1930, Alabama), and Prentiss Barnes (born April 12, 1925, Magnolia, Mississippi). Lester sang lead, Fuqua was the alternate lead,

# REPRESENTATIVE WORKS

▶ The Ink Spots, "If I Didn't Care" (1939)
▶ The Ravens, "Write Me a Letter" (1947)
▶ Sonny Til and the Orioles, "Crying in the Chapel" (1953)
▶ The Chords, "Sh-Boom" (1954)
▶ The Mills Brothers, *Meet the Mills Brothers* (1954)
▶ The Moonglows, "Sincerely" (1954)
▶ Frankie Lymon and the Teenagers, "Why Do Fools Fall in Love?" (1956)
▶ The Platters, *The Fabulous Platters* (1956)
▶ The Chantels, "Maybe" (1958)
▶ Dion and the Belmonts, "I Wonder Why" (1958)
▶ Little Anthony and the Imperials, "Tears on My Pillow" (1958)
▶ The Four Seasons, "Sherry" (1962)
▶ Patti LaBelle and the Bluebelles, *The Apollo Presents the Bluebelles* (1963)
▶ The Temptations, *Temptations Sing Smokey* (1965)

Graves the first tenor, and Barnes the bass. From 1953 to 1954 they had minor success in the rhythm-and-blues market but achieved national fame only after signing with Chess Records in 1954. On such successful records as "Sincerely" (1954), "Most of All" (1955), "We Go Together" (1956), and "Ten Commandments of Love" (1958), the Moonglows perfected the distinctive rhythm-and-blues vocal harmony technique called "blow harmony," through which blown breath becomes part of harmonies that resonate as if they originated deep in the singers' chests. Freed helped make the group one of the most significant early rock-and-roll acts, including them in many of his stage shows and in his motion pictures *Rock, Rock,*

# THE FOUR SEASONS

Best remembered for lead singer Frankie Valli's soaring falsetto, the Four Seasons had a string of more than 25 hits over a five-year period that began with "Sherry" in 1962. The principal members were Valli (born Francis Castelluccio, May 3, 1937, Newark, New Jersey, U.S.), Tommy DeVito (born June 19, 1936, Belleville, New Jersey), Bob Gaudio (born November 17, 1942, New York, New York), Nick Massi (born Nicholas Macioci, September 19, 1935, Newark—died December 24, 2000, West Orange, New Jersey), and Nick DeVito.

Evolved from a Newark vocal group called the Varietones and briefly known as the Four Lovers, the Four Seasons developed a harmony-based style that shared Italian-American doo-wop origins with Dion and the Belmonts. Bassist Gaudio, along with producer Bob Crewe, became the group's chief songwriter as the Four Seasons cranked out rhythm-and-blues and rock-and-roll hits, first for Vee Jay and then for Philips Records. Among the Top Ten hits from the group's golden period were "Big Girls Don't Cry" (1962), "Walk Like a Man" (1963), "Dawn (Go Away)" (1964), and "Let's Hang On!" (1965). Valli, who possessed a three-octave range, began a parallel solo career with the hit "Can't Take My Eyes Off of You." His popularity and that of the group declined in the late 1960s but rebounded in the mid-1970s when Valli had number one singles with "My Eyes Adored You" and "Grease," while the Four Seasons had hits with "Who Loves You" and "December 1963 (Oh What a Night)" before being relegated to the oldies circuit. The Four Seasons were inducted into the Rock and Roll Hall of Fame in 1990.

*Rock* (1956) and *Mr. Rock and Roll* (1957). Fuqua, the group's leader and songwriter (and later a producer, label owner, and promoter), broke up the ensemble in 1958 and formed a new Moonglows group, whose members included Marvin Gaye. The group disbanded in 1960 but reorganized in 1972. Later albums include *The Return of the Moonglows* (1972) and *Sincerely* (1991). The Moonglows were inducted into the Rock and Roll Hall of Fame in 2000.

## FRANKIE LYMON AND THE TEENAGERS

The broad-based success of Frankie Lymon and the Teenagers helped signal the emergence of rock and roll as a part of mainstream teenage culture. The members were Frankie Lymon (born September 30, 1942, New York, New York, U.S.—died February 28, 1968, New York), Herman Santiago (born February 18, 1941, New York), Jimmy Merchant (born February 10, 1940, New York), Joe Negroni (born September 9, 1940, New York—died September 5, 1978, New York), and Sherman Garnes (born June 8, 1940, New York—died February 26, 1977, New York). The prepubescent soprano of 13-year-old lead singer Lymon, sounding innocent and girlish, represented one of the most appealing sounds in early rock and roll, and many later pop groups would feature a preteen male lead, most notably the Jackson 5. The Teenagers' first successful record, "Why Do Fools Fall In Love" (1956), was followed by five more singles that appeared on the national survey lists of the most popular records in the United States. The Teenagers also appeared in two popular rock-and-roll movies starring disc jockey Alan Freed, *Rock, Rock, Rock* (1956) and *Mr. Rock and Roll* (1957).

In 1957 Lymon left the group to launch a solo career, which failed when his changed adult voice, an unremarkable tenor, proved to have diminished commercial appeal. Long afflicted by a substance abuse problem, Lymon died in 1968 from a drug overdose. He and the group were inducted into the Rock and Roll Hall of Fame in 1993.

## RACE AND COVER VERSIONS

An unfortunate by-product of the poetic simplicity of doo-wop records was that it was relatively easy for major labels to cover (re-record) those records with greater production values (including the addition of strings and horns) and with a different vocal group. Consistent with the racial segregation of much of American society in the 1950s, the practice of major record labels producing cover records usually involved doo-wop records that were originally performed by African American artists being re-created by white artists, the objective being to sell these covers to a broader, "pop" (that is, white) audience. Among the legion of doo-wop records that suffered this fate were the Chords' "Sh-Boom" (covered by the Crew-Cuts in 1954) and the Moonglows' "Sincerely" (covered by the McGuire Sisters in 1955). A number of white singing groups adopted the doo-wop style—particularly Italian-American ensembles who shared the same urban environment with the African Americans who originated doo-wop. Like the phenomenon of cover records, the advent of the "clean-cut" teen idols who prospered on *American Bandstand*, and the popularity of blue-eyed soul, this version of doo-wop further exemplified how black music was co-opted by the white recording industry. Prominent practitioners of the "white doo-wop" sound were the Elegants ("Little Star" [1958]), Dion and the Belmonts ("I Wonder Why" [1958]), and the Four Seasons ("Sherry" [1962]).

# CHAPTER 8

# Rock and Roll

Rock and roll has been described as a merger of country music and rhythm and blues, but, if it were that simple, it would have existed long before it burst into the national consciousness. The seeds of the music had been in place for decades, but they flowered in the mid-1950s when nourished by a volatile mix of black culture and white spending power. Black vocal groups such as the Dominoes and the Spaniels began combining gospel-style harmonies and call-and-response singing with earthy subject matter and more aggressive rhythm-and-blues rhythms. Heralding this new sound were disc jockeys such as Alan Freed of Cleveland, Ohio, Dewey Phillips of Memphis, Tennessee, and William ("Hoss") Allen of WLAC in Nashville, Tennessee—who created rock-and-roll radio by playing hard-driving rhythm-and-blues and raunchy blues records that introduced white suburban teenagers to a culture that sounded more exotic, thrilling, and illicit than anything they had ever known. In 1954 that sound coalesced around an image: that of a handsome white singer, Elvis Presley, who sounded like a black man.

## ROCKABILLIES TO ROCKERS

Presley's nondenominational taste in music incorporated everything from hillbilly rave-ups and blues wails to pop-crooner ballads. Yet his early recordings with producer Sam

# ROCKABILLY

In the late 1940s radio was broadcasting blues, rhythm and blues, and gospel music, exciting listeners across North America and inspiring young, white, working-class musicians—especially those in locales with African American populations—to mix black music styles with the country music styles with which they were already familiar (western swing, hillbilly boogie, bluegrass, and honky-tonk). The result was initially labeled country-and-western rhythm and blues, but it became known as rockabilly—literally, rock and roll played by hillbillies—despite the mostly derogatory connotation of the word *hillbilly.*

In July 1954, in his first session for Sam Phillips's Sun label of Memphis, Tennessee, Presley recorded two songs that would lay the foundation for rockabilly: "That's All Right," written by Mississippi bluesman Arthur "Big Boy" Crudup, and a hopped-up version of "Blue Moon of Kentucky," a mid-tempo waltz by Bill Monroe, the creator of bluegrass. Presley sang with African American inflections and more emotional intensity than country singers of the time. He accompanied himself on strummed acoustic guitar, Scotty Moore provided fills with electric guitar, and Bill Black added propulsive upright bass as the trio established rockabilly's quintessential instrumentation. Following this blueprint, rockabilly records typically featured a wildly expressive vocalist tearing into a bluesy song while flailing away on an acoustic guitar. Backing was provided by a bass played in the slapping style, frequently supported by a drummer; an electric guitarist filled the gaps and took an energetic solo; and the whole sound was enlarged by a studio effect called slapback, or "Sun echo," developed by Phillips.

Presley, Moore, and Black, along with drummer D.J. Fontana, toured the South almost continually in 1954 and 1955, igniting audiences. Moreover, they inspired numerous musicians to make the switch from country to rockabilly, among them Buddy Holly and Marty Robbins, the latter already an established star. Almost all the rockabilly recorded in these early years was produced by musicians who had seen Presley perform. In 1956 Presley, by then signed to RCA and recording in Nashville, Tennessee, captivated millions with his performances on prime-time television and sold millions of records. Labels scrambled for similar performers, finding singers like Gene Vincent, whose "Be-Bop-A-Lula" soon hit the charts.

Sun recorded rockabilly by Jerry Lee Lewis, Roy Orbison, Warren Smith, Billy Lee Riley, Sonny Burgess, and many others. Among the label's brightest stars was Carl Perkins, whose "Blue Suede Shoes," the genre's best-known song, was a hit for Presley, though Perkins's own version was much more characteristically rockabilly. Nashville country stars jumped on the bandwagon, as did young female performers such as Wanda Jackson, Brenda Lee, and Janis Martin. Other places developed strong rockabilly communities, including Texas (where Buddy Knox, Sleepy LaBeef, Ronnie Dawson, and future country star George Jones were based) and California (home of Ricky Nelson, Eddie Cochran, and the Collins Kids). Still, of the thousands of rockabilly songs recorded in the 1950s, few made the charts. As rockabilly evolved, more sounds entered—piano, saxophone, harmony singing, background vocal groups—thus diluting its sound. By the end of the 1950s, rockabilly was spent.

Several factors, including the death of Presley in 1977, led to a rockabilly revival in the late 1970s that began in Europe. Fans wore 1950s-style clothes, collected old records, and brought veteran rockabillies overseas to festivals. Some erstwhile rockabillies such as Charlie Feathers and Johnny Burnette's Rock and Roll Trio received more recognition in the revival than they had in the genre's heyday. Younger bands formed, notably the Stray Cats from Long Island, New York. Finding acceptance in England, they brought a hard, lean version of rockabilly back to the United States, where their caricature look made an impact during MTV's early days. As a result of the revival, rockabilly became popular in countries as different as Japan and Russia.

*Representative Works*

- ▶ Carl Perkins, "Blue Suede Shoes"/"Honey Don't" (1956)
- ▶ Gene Vincent, "Be-Bop-A-Lula"/"Woman Love" (1956)
- ▶ Jerry Lee Lewis, "Whole Lotta Shakin' Goin' On"/"It'll Be Me" (1957)
- ▶ The Crickets, "That'll Be the Day"/"I'm Looking for Someone to Love" (1957)
- ▶ Buddy Knox with the Rhythm Orchids, "Party Doll"/"My Baby's Gone" (1957)
- ▶ Eddie Cochran, "Summertime Blues"/"Love Again" (1958)
- ▶ Ricky Nelson, "Believe What You Say"/"My Bucket's Got a Hole in It" (1958)
- ▶ Wanda Jackson, "Let's Have a Party"/"Cool Love" (1960)
- ▶ The Stray Cats, "Rock This Town"/"Can't Hurry Love" (1983)

Phillips, guitarist Scotty Moore, and bassist Bill Black for Sun Records in Memphis were less about any one style than about a feeling. For decades African Americans had used the term *rock and roll* as a euphemism for sex, and Presley's music oozed sexuality. Presley was hardly the only artist who embodied this attitude, but he was clearly a catalyst in the merger of black and white culture into something far bigger and more complex than both.

In Presley's wake, the music of African American singers such as Fats Domino, Little Richard, Chuck Berry, and Bo Diddley, who might have been considered rhythm-and-blues artists only years before, fit alongside the rockabilly-flavoured tunes of white performers such as Buddy Holly, Eddie Cochran, and Jerry Lee Lewis, in part because they were all now addressing the same audience: teenagers. For young white America, this new music was a soundtrack for rebellion, however mild. When Bill Haley and His Comets kicked off the 1955 motion picture *Blackboard Jungle* with "Rock Around the Clock," teens in movie houses throughout the United States stomped on their seats.

# FRANKIE AVALON

A wunderkind trumpet player, Frankie Avalon (born Francis Thomas Avallone, September 18, 1939, Philadelphia, Pennsylvania, U.S.) was already an experienced performer when, as a Philadelphia teenager, he joined Rocco and the Saints (whose drummer was future pop star Bobby Rydell). Guided by manager Bob Marcucci, Avalon undertook a career as a singer and rose to fame on the Philadelphia-based Bandstand; capitalizing on youthful good looks and a squeaky-clean image, he became the prototype of the pop-music teen idol created on that program. Rydell and Fabian quickly followed in his footsteps. Between 1958—when his first charting single, "Dede Dinah," reached the Top Ten—and 1962 Avalon had more than 20 hits (written, for the most part, by Marcucci), including two number ones, "Venus" (1959) and "Why" (1960). As an actor Avalon teamed with actress and pop singer Annette Funicello as the romantic leads in the "Beach Party" film series popular in the 1960s.

Movie stars such as Marlon Brando in *The Wild One* (1953) and James Dean in *Rebel Without a Cause* (1955) oozed sullen, youthful defiance that was echoed by the music. This emerging rock-and-roll culture brought a wave of condemnations from religious leaders, government officials, and parents' groups, some of whom branded it the "devil's music."

The music industry's response was to sanitize the product: it had clean-cut, nonthreatening artists such as Pat Boone record tame versions of Little Richard songs, and it manufactured a legion of pretty-boy crooners such as Frankie Avalon and Fabian who thrived on *American Bandstand* and who would essentially serve as the Perry Comos and Bing Crosbys for a new generation of listeners.

## INSTRUMENTALS

Serving primarily as dance music, rock-and-roll and rhythm-and-blues

## DUANE EDDY

*Duane Eddy.* Charlie Gillett Collection/ Redferns/Getty Images

Having taken up the guitar at age 5, Eddy (born April 26, 1938, Corning, New York, U.S.) quit high school to pursue a career in music and came to the attention of Lee Hazlewood, a Phoenix, Arizona, disc jockey turned producer who helped pioneer the use of echo in rock recording. Under Hazlewood's tutelage, Eddy developed the simple but evocative twang sound from his own Chet Atkins-influenced guitar style. Together they recorded a long string of hit instrumentals, beginning with "Rebel-Rouser" (1958), which, like a number of those hits, featured the raunchy, honking tenor saxophone of Steve Douglas.

Among Eddy's other hits were "Ramrod," "The Lonely One," "Peter Gunn," and the theme for the film *Because They're Young* (1960), on which his twang was softened with strings. Although his popularity waned in the 1960s, Eddy's playing influenced a bevy of guitarists, including Hank Marvin of the Shadows, George Harrison, and Bruce Springsteen. Eddy was inducted into the Rock and Roll Hall of Fame in 1994.

## THE SHADOWS

In Britain the Shadows had their own run of hits beginning in 1960,

instrumentals began appearing on the pop charts in the mid-1950s, with Bill Doggett's organ- and saxophone-driven "Honky Tonk" (1956) leading the way. Thereafter instrumental records regularly reached number one. Link Wray's "Rumble" and the Champs' "Tequila" hit it big in 1958, the year Duane Eddy began a string of hits featuring his trademark twang guitar sound.

# LEE HAZLEWOOD

The inspired use of an empty silo helped put Phoenix on the rock-and-roll map during the late 1950s. Working at the tiny Audio Recorders studio, disc jockey-turned-producer Lee Hazlewood was obsessed with emulating the power and atmosphere of the then-current hits on Chess (of Chicago) and Sun (of Memphis), but he did not have access to performers with the energy of Howlin' Wolf and Elvis Presley or their backing musicians. A relentless perfectionist, Hazlewood experimented with the use of echo effects and found that, by placing an amplifier and a microphone in a nearby grain storage silo and then relaying the signal back to the studio, he could make any sound or instrument seem huge and atmospheric—shouts, hand claps, saxophone, or guitar. The immaculate sound of his series of hits with guitarist Duane Eddy was widely imitated at the time, and the young Phil Spector made a pilgrimage from Los Angeles to Phoenix to see how it was done. Hazlewood later moved to Los Angeles himself and masterminded an amusing and imaginative series of hits with Frank Sinatra's daughter Nancy, including some to which he contributed his own deadpan baritone as her duet partner.

though they failed to export their success to the United States (unlike the Tornadoes, who topped the American charts in 1962 with "Telstar"). Having come together in 1958 to form a quartert called the Drifters, Hank B. Marvin (born Brian Robson Rankin, October 28, 1941, Newcastle upon Tyne, Tyne and Wear, England), Bruce Welch (born Bruce Cripps, November 2, 1941, Bognor Regis, Sussex), Jet Harris (born Terence Harris, July 6, 1939, London—died March 18, 2011, Winchester, Hampshire), and Tony Meehan (born Daniel Meehan, born March 2, 1943, London—died

November 28, 2005, London) became the backing group for Cliff Richard, the British answer to Elvis Presley. A name change to avoid conflict with the American vocal group the Drifters prefaced the release of the first of the Shadows' singles. The group's trademark was the smooth, twangy sound produced by lead guitarist Marvin's lavish use of the tremolo arm of his Fender Stratocaster, an effect that could be made to sound either lyrical or sinister.

As the primitive charm of the skiffle era faded, the Shadows showed a generation of embryonic British rockers what to do. Thousands learned to play guitar by imitating the Shadows' hits, which included "Apache," "F.B.I.," and "Wonderful Land"; many went on to buy their own Stratocasters as the British "beat boom" took off. The era of the Beatles and the Rolling Stones made the Shadows' music obsolete, and, after parting company with Richard in 1968, the group went on to become a well-loved oldies act. Later members of the Shadows included Brian Bennett (born February 9, 1940, London) and John Rostill (born June 16, 1942, Birmingham, West Midlands—died November 26, 1973, England).

## THE VENTURES

By the early 1960s the top American instrumental group was the Ventures, whose principal members were rhythm guitarist Don Wilson (born February 10, 1933, Tacoma, Washington, U.S.), bassist Bob Bogle (b. January 16, 1934, Portland, Oregon—died June 14, 2009, Vancouver, Washington), guitarist Nokie Edwards (born May 9, 1935), drummer Mel Taylor (born September 24, 1933, New York, New York—died August 11, 1996, Tarzana, California), and, later, drummers Howie Johnson and Skip Moore.

Most instrumental groups of the 1950s and '60s disappeared after one hit, but the longevity of the Ventures, the best-selling instrumental group of all time, demonstrated the enduring appeal of the genre as well as the band's skill in choosing recording material. Formed in the Seattle, Washington, area in 1958, the Ventures established their own label to market their recordings, and their efforts paid off in 1960 when the single "Walk Don't Run" became a hit. In 1964 the song was reworked with a more distinct "surf" sound and again was a success. Although the Ventures became identified as a surf band by featuring tremolo guitar and driving drums and bass, the band also adapted to musical trends and shifted its focus from the creation of singles to albums, which were often structured around themes and mixed cover versions with originals. One of their biggest hits, the theme for the television series *Hawaii Five-O,* came in 1969. In the

# LEO FENDER

Together with George Fullerton, Leo Fender (born Clarence Leo Fender, August 10, 1909, Anaheim, California, U.S.—died March 21, 1991, Fullerton, California) developed the first mass-produced solid-body electric guitar, in 1948. Called the Fender Broadcaster (renamed the Telecaster in 1950), it was produced under the auspices of the Fender Electric Instruments Company, which Fender had formed in 1946. In 1951 the Fender Precision Bass, the world's first electric bass guitar, was unveiled, and in 1954 the Fender Stratocaster was put on the market. More stylish and technically improved than the Telecaster, the Stratocaster was the first guitar to feature three electric pickups (instead of two) and the tremolo arm used for vibrato effects. Its clean, sharp sound earned it a loyal following among guitarists, rivaled only by that of Gibson's eponymous Les Paul, and it became the signature instrument of Jeff Beck, Eric Clapton, Jimi Hendrix, and others.

Fender, who never learned to play the instrument he revolutionized, sold his manufacturing and distribution companies to CBS Corporation in 1965, a concession to his failing health. When his physical condition improved a few years later, he returned to the company as a design consultant and continued to indulge his inventive and entrepreneurial inclinations well into the 1980s. Fender was inducted into the Rock and Roll Hall of Fame in 1992.

1970s the band became immensely popular in Japan. Despite numerous personnel changes, including the addition of Leon Taylor on drums after the death of his father Mel in 1996, the Ventures continued to produce records and perform in the 21st century. In 2008 the band was inducted into the Rock and Roll Hall of Fame.

## INSTRUMENTAL DEVELOPMENTS

Rhythm and blues also had its share of instrumental hits in the 1960s, ranging from Booker T. and the MG's' driving "Green Onions" (1962) to Hugh Masekela's lighter "Grazing in the Grass" (1968). As pop music became more sophisticated in the late 1960s, symphonically inspired songs such as Paul Mauriat's "Love is Blue" (1967) and Mason Williams's "Classical Gas" (1968) also were hits. In general, however, the heyday of instrumental rock ended in the early 1960s as the British Invasion bands shifted the focus back to vocalists.

The legacy of the golden era of instrumental rock, however, was its lasting influence on rock musicianship. Wray's rumble could be heard in the heavy electric guitar sound of the late 1960s; the Beach Boys took surf music to another level; and Johnny and the Hurricanes, best remembered for "Crossfire" (1959), left their mark on the Beatles, with whom they gigged on the Reeperbahn in Hamburg, West Germany (now Germany).

## SURF MUSIC

As the sport of surfing became increasingly popular on the West Coast of the United States, Dick Dale and the Del-Tones provided the soundtrack, beginning with "Let's Go Trippin" in 1961. Dale, a surfer himself, developed a distinctive style of electric-guitar playing that fused Middle Eastern influences, staccato picking, and skillful exploitation of the reverb amplifier (which he helped Leo Fender to develop) to create a pulsing, cascading sound that echoed the surfing experience, most notably on "Misirlou" (1962). He led a parade of mostly West Coast-based groups that gained local, then national, popularity with guitar-driven instrumental songs, among them the Chantays ("Pipeline"), the Ventures ("Walk Don't Run"), and the Surfaris (whose "Wipe Out" featured the most identifiable drum solo in rock history).

As Jan and Dean, Jan Berry (born April 3, 1941, Los Angeles, California, U.S.—died March 26, 2004, Los Angeles) and Dean Torrence (born March 10, 1941, Los Angeles) gave voice to surf music with distinctive falsetto harmonies, especially on "Surf City" (1963).

It was the Beach Boys whose complex vocal harmonies, skilled musicianship, inventive production, and evocative lyrics apotheosized surf music and culture with a remarkable string of hits such as "Surfin' U.S.A." (1963) and "California Girls" (1965). As the Beach Boys transcended surf music, the genre began to fade, but its influence could still be heard in the 1970s and '80s in the sound of

# SURFING CULTURE

Surfing's roots lie in premodern Hawaii and Polynesia, where the sport was practiced by both men and women from all social strata from royalty to commoners. Early European explorers and travelers praised the skills of Hawaiian surfers, but 19th-century missionaries assigned to the islands disapproved of the "constant intermingling, without any restraint, of persons of both sexes" and banned the pastime. Surfing was practiced only sporadically in Hawaii by the end of the 19th century.

In the early 20th century, however, concomitant with the development of Hawaii as a tourist destination, surfing underwent a revival, and the sport quickly spread to California and Australia. Key to its introduction in the Golden State were the American writer Jack London and the Hawaiian surfer George Freeth. After visiting Waikiki, London published several accounts of surfing in popular American magazines; in 1907 the American industrialist Henry Huntington hired Freeth, whom he billed as the "man who can walk on water," to help promote his new railway line to Redondo Beach. Surfing thus took hold in California.

In the 1930s American surfer Tom Blake developed a lighter board that proved much easier to ride in surf. New materials such as balsa wood, fibreglass, and polyurethane further revolutionized board design and manufacture in the 1940s, producing still more maneuverable wave-riding craft called "malibus," for the California beach on which they were introduced. Because they were lightweight, easy to transport, and easy to ride, malibus popularized surfing and sparked a unique, hedonistic subculture. This subculture originated in Southern California but was spread around the world, from South Africa to Australia, by surf-film cinematographers, surf magazines, and the travels of the peripatetic California surfers.

At the heart of this worldwide culture, which was loosely based on free-spirited beatnik philosophies of the 1950s, was the "surfari"—a wanderlust trip in search of perfect waves. This culture was reinforced by its own unique language: "like wow," "daddy-o," "strictly squaresville," "dude." "Surf's up!" meant the surf was high enough to ride; "Wipe out!" meant to fall off the board; and "Hang 10" meant surfing with all 10 toes over the nose of the board. There was also a "dress code" (T-shirts, striped Pendleton shirts, narrow white Levi's jeans, Ray-Ban sunglasses) and de rigueur bleached-blond hair and goatee. This surfing culture was predominantly male-oriented, with long-haired women in bikinis serving mostly as admirers on the periphery. The culture rapidly diffused into the mass consciousness of the baby-boomer generation, assisted by Hollywood surf films (romantic beach musicals and comedies: *Gidget* [1959], *Ride the Wild Surf* [1964]), surf music (a thundering guitar-based sound played as single-note riffs: Dick Dale's "Miserlou" [1962], the Chantays' "Pipeline" [1962], the Astronauts' "Baja" [1963]), "pure" surf films ("travelogs," with footage of surfers riding waves: *The Big Surf* [1957], *Slippery When Wet* [1958], *Surf Trek to Hawaii* [1961], *The Endless Summer* [1964]), and specialized surfing magazines (*Surfer*, *Surfing*, *Surfing World*). The nonconformism of surfers did not endear them to the public, and social commentators branded these youths as itinerants, nomads, and wanderers and characterized surfing as an indolent, wasteful, selfish, and institutionally unanchored pastime.

punk and new wave bands such as the Ramones and the Go-Go's.

## THE BEACH BOYS

Initially perceived as a potent pop act—celebrants of the surfing and hot rod culture of the Los Angeles Basin during the 1960s—the Beach Boys and lead singer-bassist-producer Brian Wilson later gained greater respect as muses of post-World War II American suburban angst. Notwithstanding sales of 70 million albums, their greatest achievement was their ability to express the bittersweet middle-class aspirations of those who had participated in

America's great internal westward movement in the 1920s. The Beach Boys extolled the promise of a fragile California dream that their parents had had to struggle to sustain.

The original members of the group were Brian Wilson (born June 20, 1942, Inglewood, California, U.S.), Dennis Wilson (born December 4, 1944, Inglewood—died December 28, 1983, Marina del Rey, California), Carl Wilson (born December 21, 1946, Los Angeles, California—died February 6, 1998, Los Angeles), Michael Love (born March 15, 1941, Los Angeles), and Alan Jardine (born September 3, 1942, Lima, Ohio). Significant later members included David Marks (born 1948, Newcastle, Pennsylvania) and Bruce Johnston (born William Baldwin, June 24, 1944, Chicago, Illinois).

Growing up in suburban Los Angeles (Hawthorne), the Wilson brothers were encouraged by their parents to explore music. Their father, Murry, who operated a small machinery shop, was also a songwriter. While still teenagers, Brian, drummer Dennis, and guitarist Carl joined with cousin Love and friends Jardine and Marks to write and perform pop music in the alloyed spirit of Chuck Berry and the harmonies-driven Four Freshmen and Four Preps.

Dennis, a novice surfer and adolescent habitué of the Manhattan Beach surfing scene, goaded Brian and the rest of the group (then called the Pendletons) into writing songs that glorified the emerging sport. The regional success in 1961 of the Beach Boys' first single, "Surfin'," led in 1962 to their signing as Capitol Records' first rock act. Brian's latent ambitions as a pop composer were unleashed; for years he would write almost all the group's songs, often with collaborators (most frequently Love). The Beach Boys soon appeared on *Billboard*'s U.S. singles charts with such odes to cars and surfing as "409" and "Surfin' Safari," while their debut album reached number 14. After the commercial triumph of the follow-up album and single, "Surfin' U.S.A.," in 1963 (the year in which Jardine, back from school, replaced his replacement, Marks), Brian assumed complete artistic control. Their next album, *Surfer Girl*, was a landmark for the unheard-of studio autonomy he secured from Capitol as writer, arranger, and producer. Redolent of the Four Freshmen but actually inspired by "When You Wish Upon a Star" from Walt Disney's film *Pinocchio* (1940), the title track combined a childlike yearning with sophisticated pop poignance. Like his hero, pioneering producer Phil Spector, the eccentric Brian proved gifted at crafting eclectic arrangements with crisply evocative rock

A 2005 reunion of Beach Boys members (left to right) *Mike Love, Glen Campbell, and Bruce Johnston.* PRNewsFoto/Mohegan Sun/AP Images

power (e.g., "Little Deuce Coupe," "Fun, Fun, Fun," "I Get Around," and "Don't Worry Baby").

After the first of a series of stress- and drug-related breakdowns in 1964, Brian withdrew from touring and was replaced first by singer-guitarist Glen Campbell, then by veteran surf singer-musician Johnston. Brian focused thereafter on the Beach Boys' studio output, surpassing all his role models with his band's masterwork, *Pet Sounds* (1966). A bittersweet pastiche of songs recalling the pangs of unrequited love and other coming-of-age trials, *Pet Sounds* was acknowledged by Paul McCartney as the catalyst for the Beatles' *Sgt. Pepper's Lonely Hearts Club Band* (1967). Brian soon eclipsed himself again with "Good Vibrations," a startlingly prismatic "pocket symphony" that reached number one in the autumn of 1966. His self-confidence stalled, however, when an even more ambitious project called *Dumb Angel*, then *Smile*, failed to meet its appointed completion date in December 1966.

Exhausted and depressed, Brian went into seclusion as the rest of the band cobbled remains of the abortive album into a tuneful but tentative release titled *Smiley Smile* (1967).

For the remainder of the decade, the Beach Boys issued records of increasing commercial and musical inconsistency. They departed Capitol amid a legal battle over back royalties and signed with Warner Brothers in 1970. When the splendid *Sunflower* sold poorly, Brian became a recluse, experimenting with hallucinogens and toiling fitfully while the rest of the group produced several strong but modest-selling albums in the early 1970s. Meanwhile, *Endless Summer,* a greatest hits compilation, reached number one in the charts in 1974. In 1976 an uneven but commercially successful album, *15 Big Ones,* signaled the reemergence of the still drug-plagued Brian. In 1977 Dennis released a critically acclaimed solo album, *Pacific Ocean Blue.* Despite personal turmoil, the reunited Beach Boys seemed destined for a new artistic peak when Dennis drowned in 1983. The excellent *The Beach Boys* was released in 1985. In 1988 Brian released a critically acclaimed self-titled solo album, the other

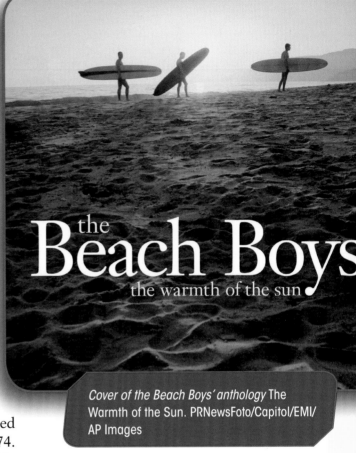

Cover of the Beach Boys' anthology The Warmth of the Sun. PRNewsFoto/Capitol/EMI/AP Images

Beach Boys had a number one hit with "Kokomo," and the group was inducted into the Rock and Roll Hall of Fame. In the 1990s the Beach Boys continued to tour and record, with Love continuing his longtime role as the band's business mind. Brian released another solo album (*Imagination*) and collaborated on albums with Van Dyke Parks (*Orange Crate Art*) and with his daughters Carnie and Wendy (*The Wilsons*), who were successful performers in their own right. Carl, who was considered the group's artistic anchor during the turbulent 1970s and '80s, died of cancer in 1998. Later that year the Beach Boys released *Endless Harmony*, a rarities collection culled from an acclaimed television documentary on the group.

In 2004 Brian released *Gettin' In Over My Head*, with contributions from Paul McCartney, Eric Clapton, and Elton John. The landmark work of this period in Brian's career, however, was *Smile*, finally offered to the world as a completed solo album after Brian had spent nearly four decades fine-tuning its sound. In 2008 he released *That Lucky Old Sun*, a nostalgic celebration of southern California made in collaboration with Scott Bennett and Parks.

# CHAPTER 9

# Rock and Rollers

The first generation of rock and rollers were weird—definitely out of the mainstream—and they liked it that way. But that they did not want their music to sound like the popular music with which they had grown up did not mean that they disliked that music. On the contrary, they loved blues, country, gospel, and pop; they just were ready to mix it up into something completely different and new. Perhaps just as important, they were also ready to discover a different way to live.

## ELVIS PRESLEY

Elvis Presley (born January 8, 1935, Tupelo, Mississippi, U.S.—died August 16, 1977, Memphis, Tennessee) grew up dirt-poor in Tupelo, moved to Memphis as a teenager, and, with his family, was off welfare only a few weeks when Sam Phillips responded to his "audition" tape with a phone call. Several weeks worth of recording sessions at Sun Studios ensued with a band consisting of Presley, guitarist Scotty Moore, and bassist Bill Black. Their repertoire consisted of the kind of material for which Presley would become famous: blues and country songs, Tin Pan Alley ballads, and gospel hymns. Presley knew some of this music from the radio, some of it from his parents' Pentecostal church and the group sings he attended at the Reverend H.W. Brewster's black Memphis church, and some of it from the Beale Street blues clubs he began frequenting as a teenager.

Presley was already a flamboyant personality, with relatively long greased-back hair and wild-coloured clothing combinations, but his full musical personality did not emerge until he and the band began playing with "Big Boy" Crudup's song "That's All Right Mama" in July 1954. They arrived at a startling synthesis, eventually dubbed rockabilly, retaining many of the original's blues inflections but with Presley's high tenor voice adding a lighter touch and with the basic rhythm striking a much more supple groove. This sound was the hallmark of the five singles Presley released on Sun over the next year. Although none of them became a national hit, by August 1955, when he released the fifth, "Mystery Train," arguably his greatest record ever, he had attracted a substantial Southern following for his recordings, his live appearances in regional roadhouses and clubs, and his radio performances on the nationally aired *Louisiana Hayride*. (A key musical change came when drummer D.J. Fontana was added, first for the *Hayride* shows but also on records beginning with "Mystery Train.")

Presley's management was then turned over to Colonel Tom Parker, a country music hustler who had made stars of Eddy Arnold and Hank Snow.

Parker arranged for Presley's song catalog and recording contract to be sold to major New York City-based enterprises, Hill and Range and RCA Victor, respectively. Sun received a total of $35,000; Elvis got $5,000. He began recording at RCA's studios in Nashville, Tennessee, with a somewhat larger group of musicians but still including Moore, Black, and Fontana and began to create a national sensation with a series of hits: "Heartbreak Hotel," "Don't Be Cruel," "Love Me Tender" (all 1956), "All Shook Up"(1957), and more.

From 1956 through 1958 he completely dominated the best-seller charts and ushered in the age of rock and roll, opening doors for both white and black rock artists. His television appearances, especially those on Ed Sullivan's Sunday night variety show, set records for the size of the audiences. Even his films, a few slight vehicles, were box office smashes.

Presley became the teen idol of his decade, greeted everywhere by screaming hordes of young women, and, when it was announced in early 1958 that he had been drafted and would enter the U.S. Army, there was that rarest of all pop culture events, a moment of true grief. More important, he served as the great cultural catalyst of his period. Elvis projected a mixed vision of humility and self-confidence, of intense commitment and comic disbelief in his ability to

*Elvis Presley and Joan Blackman in* Blue Hawaii *(1961).* © 1961 by Hal B. Wallis and Joseph H. Hazen, Paramount Pictures Corporation; photograph from a private collection

inspire frenzy. He inspired literally thousands of musicians—initially those more or less like-minded Southerners, from Jerry Lee Lewis and Carl Perkins on down, who were the first generation of rockabillies, and, later, people who had far different combinations of musical and cultural influences and ambitions. From John Lennon to Bruce Springsteen, Bob Dylan to Prince, it was impossible to think of a rock star of any importance who did not owe an explicit debt to Presley.

Beyond even that, Presley inspired his audience. "It was like he whispered his dream in all our ears and then *we* dreamed it," said Springsteen at the time of Presley's death. You did not have to want to be a rock-and-roll star or even a musician to want to be like Elvis—which meant, ultimately, to be free and uninhibited and yet still a part of the everyday. Literally millions of people—an entire generation or two—defined their sense of personal style and ambition in terms that Elvis first personified.

As a result, he was anything but universally adored. Those who did not worship him found him despicable (no one found him ignorable). Preachers and pundits declared him an anathema, his Pentecostally derived hip-swinging stage style and breathy vocal asides obscene. Racists denounced him for mingling black music with white (and Presley was always scrupulous in crediting his black sources, one of the things that made him different from the Tin Pan Alley writers and singers who had for decades lifted black styles without credit). He was pronounced responsible for all teenage hooliganism and juvenile delinquency. Yet, in every appearance on television, he appeared affable, polite, and soft-spoken, almost shy. It was only with a band at his back and a beat in his ear that he became "Elvis the Pelvis."

In 1960 Presley returned from the army, where he had served as a soldier in Germany rather than joining the Special Services entertainment division. Those who regarded him as commercial hype without talent expected him to fade away. Instead, he continued to have hits from recordings stockpiled just before he entered the army. Upon his return to the States, he picked up pretty much where he had left off, churning out a series of more than 30 movies (from *Blue Hawaii* to *Change of Habit*) over the next eight years, almost none of which fit any genre other than "Elvis movie," which meant a light comedic romance with musical interludes. Most had accompanying soundtrack albums, and together the movies and the records made him a rich man, although they nearly ruined him as any kind of artist. Presley did his best work in the 1960s on singles either unconnected to the films or only marginally stuck into them, recordings such as "It's Now or Never ('O Sole Mio')" (1960), "Are You Lonesome Tonight?," "Little Sister" (both 1961), "Can't Help Falling in Love," "Return to Sender" (both 1962), and "Viva Las Vegas" (1964). Presley was no longer a controversial figure; he had become one more predictable mass entertainer, a personage of virtually no interest to the rock audience that had expanded so much with the advent of the new sounds of the Beatles, the Rolling Stones, and Dylan.

By 1968 the changes in the music world had overtaken Presley—both movie grosses and record sales had fallen. In December his one-man Christmas TV special aired; a tour de force of rock and roll and rhythm and blues, it restored much of his dissipated credibility. In 1969 he released a single having nothing to do with a film, "Suspicious Minds"; it went to number one. He also began doing concerts again and quickly won back a sizable following, although it was not nearly as universal as his

*Ann-Margret and Elvis Presley in* Viva Las Vegas *(1964).* © 1964
Metro-Goldwyn-Mayer Inc.; photograph from a private collection

audience in the 1950s—in the main, it was Southern and Midwestern, working-class and unsophisticated, and overwhelmingly female. For much of the next decade, he was again one of the top live attractions in the United States. (For a variety of reasons, he never performed outside North America.) Presley was now a mainstream American entertainer, an icon but not so much an idol. He had married in 1967 without much furor, became a parent with the birth of his daughter, Lisa Marie, in 1968, and got divorced in 1973. He made no more movies, although there was a good concert film, *Elvis on Tour*. His recordings were of uneven quality, but on each album he included a song or two that had focus and energy. Hits were harder to come by—"Suspicious Minds" was his last number one and "Burning Love" (1972) his final Top Ten entry. But, thanks to the concerts, spectaculars best described by critic Jon Landau as an apotheosis of American musical comedy, he remained a big money earner. He now lacked the ambition and power of his early work, but that may have been a good thing— he never seemed a dated relic of the 1950s trying to catch up to trends but was just a performer, unrelentingly himself.

However, Presley had also developed a lethal lifestyle. Spending almost all his time when not on the road in Graceland, his Memphis estate (actually just a big Southern colonial house decorated somewhere between banal modernity and garish faux-Vegas opulence), he lived nocturnally, surrounded by sycophants and stuffed with greasy foods and a variety of prescription drugs. His shows deteriorated in the final two years of his life, and his recording career came to a virtual standstill. Presley never seemed confident in his status, never entirely certain that he would not collapse back into sharecropper poverty, and, as a result, he seems to have become immobilized; the man who had risked everything, including potential ridicule, to make himself a success now lived in the lockstep regimen of an addict and recluse. Finally, in the summer of 1977, the night before he was to begin yet another concert tour, he died of a heart attack brought on largely by drug abuse. He was 42 years old.

Almost immediately upon hearing of his death, mourners from around the world gathered at Graceland to say farewell to the poor boy who had lived out the American dream. In a way, that mourning has never ceased: Graceland remains one of the country's top tourist attractions more than 30 years later, and Presley's albums and other artifacts continue to sell briskly. Each August crowds flock to Graceland to honour him on the anniversary not of his birth but of his death. From time to time rumours have cropped up that he did not really die, that his death was a fake designed to free him from fame. Elvis impersonators are legion. His biggest fans—working-class white women, almost exclusively—have passed their fanaticism on to their children, or at least to a surprising number of daughters. "Elvis has left the building," but those who are still inside have decided to carry on regardless. Presley was inducted into the Rock and Roll Hall of Fame in 1986; Scotty Moore was inducted as a sideman in 2000, and Bill Black and D.J. Fontana were inducted as sidemen in 2009.

## BILL HALEY AND HIS COMETS

If not the father of rock and roll, Bill Haley (born William John Clifton Haley, Jr., July 6, 1925, Highland Park, Michigan, U.S.—died February 9, 1981, Harlingen, Texas) is certainly one of its fathers. He cut his first record in 1948 and the next year settled into a job as a disc jockey in Chester, Pennsylvania. At the time, his groups played a small-band version of western swing, and Haley continued recording country songs until 1951, when he covered Jackie Brenston's stomping rhythm-and-blues hit "Rocket 88." Although his version sold poorly, Haley was intrigued with the possibility of selling big-beat

music to teenagers, so he dropped his cowboy image and changed the band's name from the Saddlemen to Bill Haley and His Comets. In a conscious effort to capture the growing teen audience, he also incorporated the music of jump-blues stars into his sound (and later speculated that through them he was probably influenced by Louis Jordan). It worked, and Haley's self-written "Crazy Man Crazy" (1953) is often considered the first rock-and-roll record to hit the *Billboard* pop charts. Haley's original Comets were arguably the first self-contained rock-and-roll band and featured the booming slapped bass of Al Rex (born July 15, 1921, New York, New York, U.S.—died March 3, 1985, New York, New York), John Grande (born January 14, 1930, Philadelphia, Pennsylvania, U.S.—died June 2, 2006, Clarkesville, Tennessee) on the boogie piano, the screaming saxophone of Rudy Pompilli (b. April 16, 1924, Chester, Pennsylvania—died February 5, 1976, Brookhaven, Pennsylvania), and the guitar interplay between Danny Cedrone (born June 20, 1920, Jamesville, New York—died June 17, 1954, Philadelphia) and Billy Williamson (born February 9, 1925, Conshohocken, Pennsylvania—died March 22, 1996, Swarthmore, Pennsylvania).

In 1954 Haley signed with his first major label, Decca. "Rock Around the Clock" sold disappointingly that

*Bill Haley* (right) *and His Comets performing* c. mid-'50s. John Franks/
Hulton Archive/Getty Images

year, but in 1955 it was reissued as part of the soundtrack to *Blackboard Jungle,* one of the most popular juvenile delinquent movies of the 1950s, which was accompanied by teen rioting in many theatres. Haley rode the controversy to number one on the charts. Through the end of 1956 he tallied eight more Top 40 hits.

His tour of Britain in 1957 caused pandemonium.

By the end of 1958 (the year of his last significant hit), however, Haley was sinking. A balding, overweight, middle-aged man in a plaid suit (with a spit curl, to boot), he did not serve teen rebellion nearly as well as Elvis Presley, Little Richard, and many others did. Haley was on the nostalgia circuit just five years after his first hit, and—while it served him well, especially in Britain—he started growing bitter and unpredictable. He spent much of the 1960s in Mexico City. In the weeks before his death, he was seen wandering around the South Texas brush country mumbling to himself, a tragic and lonely end for a once-articulate singer who had sold some 60 million records. Haley was inducted into the Rock and Roll Hall of Fame in 1987, and in 2012 the Comets were selected for induction as well.

## LITTLE RICHARD

One of 12 children, the future Little Richard (born Richard Wayne Penniman, December 5, 1932, Macon, Georgia, U.S.) learned gospel music in Pentecostal churches of the Deep South. As a teenager he left home to perform rhythm and blues in medicine shows and nightclubs, where he took the name "Little Richard," achieving notoriety for high-energy onstage antics. His first recordings in the early 1950s, produced in the soothing jump-blues style of R&B singer and songwriter Roy Brown, showed none of the soaring vocal reach that would mark his later singing. His breakthrough came in September 1955 at a recording session at J & M Studio in New Orleans,

Louisiana, where Little Richard, backed by a solid rhythm-and-blues band, howled "Tutti Frutti," with its unforgettable exhortation, "A wop bop a loo bop, a lop bam boom!" In the year and a half that followed, he released a string of songs on Specialty Records that sold well among both black and white audiences: "Rip It Up," "Long Tall Sally," "Ready Teddy," "Good Golly, Miss Molly," and "Send Me Some Lovin'," among others. Blessed with a phenomenal voice able to generate croons, wails, and screams unprecedented in popular music, Little Richard scored hits that combined childishly amusing lyrics with sexually suggestive undertones. Along with Elvis Presley's records for the Sun label in the mid-1950s, Little Richard's sessions from the same period offer models of singing and musicianship that have inspired rock musicians ever since.

As his success grew, Little Richard appeared in some of the earliest rock-and-roll movies: *Don't Knock the Rock* and *The Girl Can't Help It* (both 1956) and *Mr. Rock and Roll* (1957). In the latter he stands at the piano belting out songs with an intensity that, in the bland Eisenhower years, seemed excessive, an impression amplified by his bizarre six-inch pompadour, eyeliner, and pancake makeup. At the very peak of his fame, however, he concluded that rock and roll was the devil's work; he abandoned the music business, enrolled in Bible college, and became a traveling Evangelical preacher. When the Beatles skyrocketed onto the music scene in 1964, they sang several of his classic songs and openly acknowledged their debt to their great forebear. This renewed attention inspired Little Richard to return to the stage and the recording studio for another shot at stardom. Although a new song, "Bama Lama Bama Loo" (1964), invoked the fun and vitality of his heyday, record-buying youngsters were not impressed. A major recording contract in the early 1970s produced three albums for Reprise Records— *The Rill Thing, King of Rock 'n' Roll,* and *Second Coming*—collections that showed Little Richard in fine voice but somewhat out of his element in the hard rock styles of the period.

In the late 1990s Little Richard continued to appear at concerts and festivals, performing songs that had become cherished international standards. He remained a frequent guest on television talk shows and children's programs; his madcap mannerisms, so threatening to parents in the 1950s, had come to seem amusingly safe. Having weathered a career marked by extraordinary changes in direction, Little Richard (who was inducted into the Rock and Roll Hall of Fame in 1986) survived not only as the self-proclaimed "architect of rock

and roll" but also as a living treasure of 20th-century American culture.

## CARL PERKINS

A "triple threat" performer—a strong singer, a prolific and imaginative songwriter, and an excellent and influential lead guitarist—Carl Perkins (born April 9, 1932, Tiptonville, Tennessee, U.S.—died January 19, 1998, Jackson, Tennessee) rose from sharecropping poverty to international fame. He was taught to play the guitar by an African American neighbour with whom he picked cotton. Grounded in gospel music and influenced by bluegrass and Hank Williams, Perkins developed his style on the bar circuit in Jackson, Tennessee, playing from age 14 in a band that was rounded out by his brothers Clayton (on upright bass) and Jay (on acoustic rhythm guitar). After hearing Elvis Presley on the radio and being excited by the similarities between his music and their own beat-driven approach to country music, the Perkins brothers went to Memphis, Tennessee, to audition for Sun Records, the label for which Presley recorded. Perkins's big break came in 1956 with "Blue Suede Shoes," which he wrote after observing a dancer taking pains to preserve his new footwear. The song made the Top Five on the pop, country, and rhythm-and-blues charts, an unprecedented feat. En route to New York City to perform on national television, Carl and Jay were seriously injured in a car accident, temporarily halting the band's momentum. In the meantime, Presley, by then recording for RCA, had a hit with his cover version of "Blue Suede Shoes."

Perkins produced two moderate hits for Sun before leaving Sam Phillips's label in 1958 to record for Columbia, where he managed only two minor chart entries; and Jay died that year of a malignant brain tumour. Dispirited by these events, Perkins fell victim to low morale and alcoholism. In 1964 and 1965, at the height of Beatlemania, he toured in Britain. George Harrison had been particularly influenced by his guitar playing, and the Beatles recorded several of his songs, including "Matchbox" (based on a blues standard) and "Honey Don't," raising Perkins's profile and providing him with royalty earnings. From 1965 to 1976 he performed with Johnny Cash as part of Cash's touring ensemble and on his television show. In their first year together the former Sun labelmates became born-again Christians and renounced their addictions. Cash also had a big hit with Perkins's composition "Daddy Sang Bass." Indeed, many other country acts found similar success with his songs. Subsequently, Perkins again played with a family band, this time with sons Greg (on bass) and Stan (on drums). Unquestionably one of rock music's pioneers, Perkins was inducted into the Rock and Roll Hall of Fame in 1987.

## JERRY LEE LEWIS

A child of poverty, Jerry Lee Lewis (born September 29, 1935, Ferriday, Louisiana, U.S.) began playing the piano at age nine at the home of an aunt. His father, a carpenter and bootlegger, saw his passion and talent and mortgaged their house to buy a piano. Lewis emulated the playing styles of a local preacher and black musicians, whom he surreptitiously observed during their appearances at local clubs, and was soon performing at school assemblies, talent shows, and tent revivals, as well as on the radio. He tried to break into the music business in New Orleans and Shreveport, Louisiana (on radio's *Louisiana Hayride*), and in Nashville, Tennessee. Drawn by the success of Elvis Presley, he landed at the Sun label in Memphis, Tennessee.

Nicknamed "the Killer," Lewis established himself as a major rockabilly star on Sun Records with "Whole Lotta Shakin' Goin' On," "Great Balls of Fire," and "Breathless," all Top Ten hits in 1957 and 1958. His rhythmically assured and versatile "pumping" piano style (the left hand maintaining a driving boogie pattern while the right added flashy ornamentation) was influenced by church music and country musicians such as Moon Mullican, who played western swing and honky-tonk. Other early influences included Al Jolson, Jimmie Rodgers, Hank Williams, zealous Pentecostal preachers, and African American rhythm-and-blues musicians whom the young Southerner stole away to observe.

A highly skilled instrumentalist and vocalist, Lewis wrote few songs; his was the art of the stylist, the interpreter able to put a personal stamp on a vast and diverse repertoire. A man of tremendous contradictions, he was tormented by conflicts between the hedonism of rock and roll and his strict religious upbringing. Like his cousin, television evangelist Jimmy Swaggart, with whom he grew up, Lewis was torn between flesh and spirit. He captivated legions of fans with his flamboyant attitude and unpredictable, charismatic showmanship in stage, television, and film appearances. His blond hair falling in his face, he exhibited seemingly boundless energy and a menacing sexuality while carrying out various stage antics: standing on the piano, playing it with arms and feet, kicking over the stool, even lighting the instrument on fire.

In 1958 scandal nearly ended his career. While on tour in England, Lewis was scorned by the press when it was learned that he had married his 13-year-old cousin (the daughter of his bassist). That Lewis's previous marriage was still valid only made matters worse. Despite the ensuing boycott, Lewis continued recording and performing wherever he could. In 1961 his version of Ray Charles's "What'd I Say" was a hit. Lewis soon returned to England, this time greeted as a star. Nevertheless, his comeback was complete only in the late 1960s, after he had shifted his musical focus and had a series of hits on the country charts; his success in that genre extended into the early 1980s. As Lewis entered middle age, his recordings became more sporadic, though he won positive notice later in his life for *Last Man Standing* (2006), an album of duets with a panoply of rock, blues, and country legends. A similarly conceived record, *Mean Old Man*, was released in 2010.

The subject of biographies, documentaries, and a major Hollywood film, Lewis's life was punctuated by erratic behaviour, alcohol and drug problems, bouts of ill health, tax debts, wild escapades, and six marriages. His talent, persistence, longevity, and huge legacy of recordings, however, guarantee his place among rock music's royalty. Lewis was inducted into the Rock and Roll Hall of Fame in 1986.

## FATS DOMINO

Singer and pianist Fats Domino helped define the New Orleans sound and was one of the first rock-and-roll stars. In the process he sold more than 65 million albums. From a musical family, Domino (born Antoine Domino, Jr., February 26, 1928, New Orleans, Louisiana, U.S.) received early training from his brother-in-law, guitarist Harrison Verrett. He began performing in clubs in his teens and in 1949 was discovered by Dave Bartholomew—the bandleader, songwriter, and record producer who helped bring New Orleans's J & M Studio to prominence and who became Domino's exclusive arranger. Domino's first recording, "The Fat Man" (1950), became the first of a series of rhythm-and-blues hits that sold 500,000 to 1,000,000 copies. His piano playing consisted of simple rhythmic figures, often only triad chords over a boogie pattern, forcefully played and joined by simple saxophone riffs and drum afterbeats (accents in a measure of music that follow the downbeat). These accompanied the smooth, gently swinging vocals he delivered in a small, middle baritone range, with even dynamics and a slight New Orleans accent, all of which made Domino one of the most distinctive rock-and-roll stylists.

With "Ain't That a Shame" (1955) Domino became a favourite of white as well as black audiences. "Blueberry Hill" (1956), his most popular recording, was one of several rock-and-roll adaptations of standard songs. The piano-oriented Domino-Bartholomew style was modified somewhat in hits such as "I'm Walkin'" (1957) and "Walking to New Orleans" (1960). He appeared in the 1956 film *The Girl Can't Help It*. One of his last hits was a version of the Beatles' "Lady Madonna" (1968). Domino was inducted into the Rock and Roll Hall of Fame in 1986.

## CHUCK BERRY

Raised in a working-class African American neighbourhood on the north side of the highly segregated city of St. Louis, Chuck Berry (born Charles Edward Anderson Berry, October 18, 1926, St. Louis, Missouri, U.S.) grew up in a family proud of its African American and Native American ancestry. He gained early exposure to music through his family's participation in the choir of the Antioch Baptist Church, through the blues and country and western music he heard on the radio, and through music classes, especially at Sumner High School. Berry was still attending high school when he was sent to serve three years for armed robbery at a Missouri prison for young offenders. After his release and return to St. Louis, he worked at an auto plant, studied hairdressing, and played music in small nightclubs. Berry traveled to Chicago in search of a recording contract; Muddy

*Chuck Berry.* GAB Archive/Redferns/Getty Images

Waters directed him to the Chess brothers. Leonard and Phil Chess signed him for their Chess label, and in 1955 his first recording session produced "Maybellene" (a country-and-western-influenced song that Berry had originally titled "Ida Red"), which stayed on the pop charts for 11 weeks, cresting at number five. Berry followed this success with extensive tours and hit after hit, including "Roll Over Beethoven" (1956), "School Day" (1957), "Rock and Roll Music" (1957), "Sweet Little Sixteen" (1958), "Johnny B. Goode" (1958), and "Reelin' and Rockin'" (1958). His vivid descriptions of teenage life, the distinctive sounds he coaxed from his guitar, and the rhythmic and melodic virtuosity of his piano player (Johnny Johnson) made Berry's songs staples in the repertoire of almost every rock-and-roll band.

At the peak of his popularity, federal authorities prosecuted Berry for violating the Mann Act, alleging that he transported an underage female across state lines "for immoral purposes." After two trials tainted by racist overtones, Berry was convicted and remanded to prison. Upon his release he placed new hits on the pop charts, including "No Particular Place to Go" in 1964, at the height of the British Invasion, whose prime movers, the Beatles and the Rolling Stones, were hugely influenced by Berry (as were the Beach Boys). In 1972 Berry achieved his first number one hit, "My Ding-A-Ling." Although he recorded more sporadically in the 1970s and '80s, he continued to appear in concert, most often performing with backing bands comprising local musicians. Berry's public visibility increased in 1987 with the publication of his book *Chuck Berry: The Autobiography* and the release of the documentary film *Hail! Hail! Rock 'n' Roll*, featuring footage from his 60th birthday concert and guest appearances by Keith Richards and Bruce Springsteen.

Berry is undeniably one of the most influential figures in the history of rock music. In helping to create rock and roll from the crucible of rhythm and blues, he combined clever lyrics, distinctive guitar sounds, boogie-woogie rhythms, precise diction, an astounding stage show, and musical devices characteristic of country and western music and the blues in his many best-selling single records and albums. A distinctive if not technically dazzling guitarist, Berry used electronic effects to replicate the ringing sounds of bottleneck blues guitarists in his recordings. He drew upon a broad range of musical genres in his compositions, displaying an especially strong interest in Caribbean music on "Havana Moon" (1957) and "Man and the Donkey" (1963), among others. Influenced by a wide variety of artists—including guitar players Carl Hogan, Charlie Christian, and T-Bone Walker and vocalists Nat King Cole, Louis Jordan, and Charles Brown—Berry played a major role in broadening the appeal of rhythm-and-blues music during the 1950s. He fashioned his lyrics to appeal to the growing teenage market by presenting vivid and humorous descriptions of high-school life, teen dances, and consumer culture. His recordings serve as a rich repository of the core lyrical and musical building blocks of rock and roll. In addition to the Beatles and the Rolling Stones, Elvis Presley, Buddy Holly, Linda Ronstadt, and a multitude of significant popular-music performers have recorded Berry's songs.

An appropriate tribute to Berry's centrality to rock and roll came when his song "Johnny B. Goode" was among the pieces of music placed on a copper phonograph record attached to the side of the Voyager 1 satellite, hurtling through outer space, in order to give distant or future civilizations a chance to acquaint themselves with the culture of the planet Earth in the 20th century. In 1984 he was presented with a Grammy Award for lifetime achievement. He was inducted into the Rock and Roll Hall of Fame in 1986.

## BO DIDDLEY

Raised mostly in Chicago by his adoptive family, Ellas McDaniel (born Ellas Bates, December 30, 1928, McComb, Mississippi, U.S.—died June 2, 2008, Archer, Florida) recorded for Chess Records as Bo Diddley (a name most likely derived from the diddley bow, a one-stringed African guitar popular in the Mississippi Delta region). Diddley scored few hit records but was one of rock's most influential artists nonetheless, because he had something nobody else could claim, his own beat: chink-a-chink-chink, ca-chink-chink. That syncopated beat (also known as "hambone" or "shave-and-a-haircut—two-bits") had surfaced in a few big-band rhythm-and-blues charts of the 1940s, but Diddley stripped it down and beefed it up. He made it, with its obvious African roots, one of the irresistible dance sounds in rock and roll. It was appropriated by fellow 1950s rockers (Johnny Otis's "Willie and the Hand Jive" [1958]), 1960s garage bands (the Strangeloves' "I Want Candy" [1965]), and budding superstars (the Rolling Stones' version of Buddy Holly's Diddley-influenced "Not Fade Away" [1964]). For all that, Diddley hit the pop charts just five times and the Top 20 only once (even though his 1955 debut single, "Bo Diddley," backed with "I'm a Man," was number one on the rhythm-and-blues charts).

After playing for several years on Chicago's legendary Maxwell Street, Diddley signed with Chess subsidiary Checker in 1955. The lyrics to his songs were rife with African American street talk, bluesy imagery, and raunchy humour (e.g., "Who Do You Love" [1957]). He used tremolo, fuzz, and feedback effects to create a guitar sound on which only Jimi Hendrix has expanded (consider sonic outbursts like "Bo Diddley"). His stage shows—featuring his half sister the Duchess on vocals and rhythm guitar and Jerome Green on bass and maracas—made an art out of bad taste. Commonly dressed in a huge black Stetson and loud shirts, Diddley no doubt influenced the dress of British Invasion groups such as the Rolling Stones. The odd-shaped guitars that he played reinforced his arresting look.

In the 1960s he recorded everything from surf music to straight-ahead blues with equal aplomb. But his last conquest was the sublime "You Can't Judge a Book by the Cover" (1962), until the British Invasion put him back on the map long enough for a minor 1967 hit, "Ooh Baby." Always outspoken about how black musicians have been underpaid, he toured only sporadically after the 1970s, appeared in a few movies, and made occasional albums. He was inducted into the Rock and Roll Hall of Fame in 1987.

## BUDDY HOLLY

Buddy Holly (born Charles Hardin Holley, September 7, 1936, Lubbock, Texas, U.S.—died February 3, 1959, near Clear Lake, Iowa) was the youngest of four children in a family of devout Baptists in the West Texas town of Lubbock, and gospel music was an important part of his life from an early age. A good student possessed of infectious personal charm, Holly (the *e* was dropped from his last name—probably accidentally— on his first record contract) was declared "King of the Sixth Grade" by his classmates. He became seriously interested in music at about age 12 and pursued it with remarkable natural ability.

The African American rhythm and blues that Holly heard on the radio had a tremendous impact on him, as it did on countless other white teenagers in the racially segregated United States of the 1950s. Among the rhythm-and-blues records that seem to have influenced Holly most were "Work with Me, Annie" by Hank Ballard and the Midnighters, "Bo Diddley" by Bo Diddley, and "Love Is Strange" by Mickey and Sylvia. Guitar riffs and rhythmic ideas from these three records crop up repeatedly in his work.

Already well versed in country music, bluegrass, and gospel and a seasoned performer by age 16, Holly became a rhythm-and-blues devotee. By 1955, after hearing Elvis Presley, Holly was a full-time rock and roller. Late that year he bought a Fender

*Buddy Holly.* Michael Ochs Archives/Getty Images

Stratocaster electric guitar and developed a style of playing featuring ringing major chords that became his trademark. (It is most recognizable in the solo break in "Peggy Sue.") In 1956 he signed with Decca Records's Nashville, Tennessee, division, but the records he made for them sold poorly and were uneven in quality (notwithstanding several outstanding efforts, among them his first single, "Blue Days, Black Nights," and the rockabilly classic "Midnight Shift"). His first break came and went quickly.

In 1957 Holly and his new group, the Crickets—Niki Sullivan (born June 23, 1937—died April 6, 2004) on second guitar and background vocals, Joe B. Mauldin (born July 8, 1940) on bass, and the great Jerry Allison (born August 31, 1939, Hillsboro, Texas) on drums—began their association with independent producer Norman Petty at his studio in Clovis, New Mexico. This was when the magic began. Together they created a series of recordings that display an emotional intimacy and sense of detail that set them apart from other 1950s rock and roll. As a team, they threw away the rule book and let their imaginations loose.

Unlike most independent rock-and-roll producers of the time, Petty, a cocktail lounge organist whose trio had had a couple of minor hits in 1954, did not own any cheap equipment. He wanted his recordings to sound classy and expensive, but he also loved to experiment and had a deep bag of sonic tricks. Some 10 years before George Martin provided a similar context for the Beatles, Petty encouraged Holly and drummer Jerry Allison to use the studio as a workshop, exploring unorthodox rhythms, instruments, and sounds on a series of 30 tracks recorded over a 12-month period (1957–58) that became a bedrock for future

# BUDDY HOLLY'S RECORD COLLECTION

When he went on performance tours, Buddy Holly brought a collection of 45-rpm records with him in two carrying cases. The 48 records that comprise this collection reveal Holly's eclectic musical influences—from blues (Jimmy Reed, Little Walter), rhythm and blues (Hank Ballard and the Midnighters, Ray Charles), and gospel (Mahalia Jackson) to pop (Doris Day, Peggy Lee), rockabilly (Buddy Knox), and rock and roll (Bo Diddley, Little Richard, Ritchie Valens).

▶ Angelic Gospel Singers, "Jesus Never Fails Me" and "I'll Be Alright" (unknown date)
▶ Toni Arden, "Padre and All at Once" (1958)
▶ Ray Campi with Johnny Maddox, Henry Hill, and the Debs, "With You" and "My Screamin' Screamin' Mimi!" (unknown)
▶ Valerie Carr with Hugo Peretti and His Orchestra, "Look Forward" and "Bad Girl" (1958)
▶ Wynona Carr, "Should I Ever Love Again?" and "Till the Well Runs Dry" (1956?)
▶ The Channels, "Stay as You Are" and "That's My Desire" (1957)
▶ Ray Charles, "Mary Ann" and "Drown in My Tears" (1956)
▶ Ray Charles, "What Would I Do Without You" and "Hallelujah I Love Her So" (1956)
▶ Ray Charles, "Swanee River Rock" and "I Want a Little Girl" (1957)
▶ Ray Charles, "You Be My Baby" and "My Bonnie" (1958)
▶ Ray Charles, "I Want to Know" and "Ain't That Love" (1957)
▶ Ray Charles, "Come Back" and "I've Got a Woman" (1955)
▶ Nat "King" Cole, "Bend a Little My Way" and "Non Dimenticar" (1958)
▶ Doris Day with Frank De Vol and his Orchestra, "Everybody Loves a Lover" and "Instant Love" (1958)

Doris Day with Frank De Vol and his Orchestra, "A Very Precious Love" and "Teacher's Pet" (1958)

Doris Day with Frank De Vol and his Orchestra, "Heart Full of Love" and "The Sound of Music" (1958?)

De John Sisters, "(My Baby Don't Love Me) No More" and "Theresa (The Little Flower)" (1955)

Bo Diddley, "Hey! Bo Diddley" and "Mona" (1957)

Bo Diddley, "Before You Accuse Me (Take a Look at Yourself)" and "Say (Boss Man)" (1957)

The Everly Brothers, "Bird Dog" and "Devoted to You" (1958)

The Everly Brothers, "Problems" and "Love of My Life" (1958)

Eddie Fontaine, "Nothin' Shakin'" and "Don't Ya Know" (1958)

Johnny Fuller and Band, "All Night Long" and "You Got Me Whistling" (1958)

Hugo and Luigi, "Honolulu Lu" and "La Plume de Ma Tante" (1959)

Mahalia Jackson, "Have You Any Rivers" and "For My Good Fortune" (1958?)

Roland Johnson, "I Traded Her Love" and "I'll Be With You" (1959)

The Jones Boys, "No One Home" and "Mary Smith" (unknown)

Kitty Kallen, "Come Live with Me" and "Be True to Me" (unknown)

Buddy Knox with the Orchids/Jim Bowen with the Orchids, "Party Doll" and "I'm Stickin' with You" (1956/1957?)

Peggy Lee, "You Don't Know" and "Fever" (1958)

Little Richard, "Good Golly, Miss Molly" and "Hey-Hey-Hey-Hey!" (1958)

Little Walter and His Jukes, "Thunder Bird" and "My Babe" (1955)

Little Walter and His Jukes, "I Got to Go" and "Roller Coaster" (1955)

Skeets McDonald, "I Can't Stand It Any Longer" and "Number One in Your Heart" (unknown)

- ▶ The McGuire Sisters, "Banana Split" and "Sugartime" (1957)
- ▶ Mantovani, "Love Song from 'Houseboat' (Almost in Your Arms) and Almost in Your Arms (Love Song from 'Houseboat')" (1958)
- ▶ The Midnighters, "Work with Me, Annie" and "Until I Die" (1954)
- ▶ The Midnighters, "Don't Say Your Last Goodbye" and "Sexy Ways" (1954)
- ▶ The Midnighters, "Annie Had a Baby" and "She's the One" (1954)
- ▶ Jimmy Reed, "Honey, Don't Let Me Go" and "You've Got Me Dizzy" (1956)
- ▶ Jimmy Reed, "You've Got Me Crying" and "Go on to School" (1958)
- ▶ Shirley and Lee, "Now That It's Over" and "I Feel Good" (1956)
- ▶ The Slades, "You Gambled" and "No Time" (1956)
- ▶ Ritchie Valens, "La Bamba" and "Donna" (1958)
- ▶ Larry Williams, "Dizzy, Miss Lizzy" and "Slow Down" (1957/1958?)
- ▶ Roger Williams, "Take Care" and "Autumn Leaves" (1955)
- ▶ Chuck Willis, "Thunder and Lightning" and "My Life" (1958)
- ▶ Peanuts Wilson, "Cast Iron Arm" and "You've Got Love" (1958?)

Source: From the collection of the Buddy Holly Center, Lubbock, Texas

generations. The Crickets' records feature unusual microphone placement techniques, imaginative echo chamber effects, and overdubbing, a process that in the 1950s meant superimposing one recording on another. While crafting tracks such as "Not Fade Away," "Peggy Sue," "Listen to Me," and "Everyday," Holly and the Crickets camped out at Petty's studio for days at a time, using it as a combination laboratory and playground. They were the first rock and rollers to approach the recording process in this manner. Holly was arguably the best all-around musician of the first generation of rockers—an inventive guitarist, songwriter, and singer—but he manifested these attributes only under the supervision of Petty, whose successes included "Party Doll" by college boy Buddy Knox in 1957 and several hits by the Fireballs, including "Sugar Shack," a chart topper in 1963.

When the Crickets' first single, "That'll Be the Day," was released in 1957, their label, Brunswick, did nothing to promote it. Nevertheless, the record had an irrepressible spirit, and by year's end it became an international multimillion-seller. Soon after, Holly became a star and an icon. Holly and the Crickets' association with Petty (who also served as their manager, songwriting partner, and publisher and owned their recordings) was far from all beneficial, however. He advised the group to "carry a Bible and READ IT!"; yet, according to virtually all accounts, he collected the Crickets' royalty checks and kept the money. By 1959 the hit records tapered off, and Holly was living in New York with his new bride. Estranged from the Crickets and broke, he was also contemplating legal action against Petty. This left him little choice but to participate in the doomed "Winter Dance Party of 1959" tour through the frozen Midwest, during which he and coheadliners Ritchie Valens and the Big Bopper (J.P. Richardson) were killed in a plane crash.

The music of Holly and the Crickets, their innovative use of the studio, and the fact that they wrote most of their songs themselves made them the single most important influence on the Beatles, who knew every Holly record backward and forward. In 1986 Holly was inducted into the Rock and Roll Hall of Fame, and the Crickets followed in 2012.

In 1996 Holly was honoured by the National Academy of Recording Arts and Sciences with a lifetime achievement award. His records, conveying a sense of the wide-open spaces of West Texas and unstoppable joie de vivre, remain vital today.

## GENE VINCENT

Rockabilly singer Gene Vincent (born Vincent Eugene Craddock, February 11, 1935, Norfolk, Virginia, U.S.—died October 12, 1971, Newhall, California) went a long way toward defining the look of the rock rebel with his swaggering, black-leather-clad image. Discharged from the U.S. Navy in 1955 following a motorcycle accident in which his leg was seriously injured, Vincent tried his hand at country music. In 1956, with record companies frantically seeking their own answers to Elvis Presley, Vincent recorded "Be-Bop-A-Lula." When the record sold 200,000 copies in June alone, Capitol Records seemed to have found its Presley. "Be-Bop-A-Lula" became a rockabilly classic, driven by Vincent's assured vocals and a rollicking performance by his backing band, the Blue Caps. The principal members of the Blue Caps included Cliff Gallup (born June 17, 1930—died October 9, 1988, Norfolk), whose stellar guitar work gave the band much of its exuberant sound, rhythm guitarist Ervin ("Wee

Willie") Williams (born December 1935, Millinocket, Maine—died August 28, 1999, Bradenton, Florida), drummer Dickie "Be-Bop" Harrell (born August 27, 1940, Portsmouth, Virginia), and bassist Jack Neal (born November 7, 1930, Norfolk County, Virginia—died September 22, 2011, Virginia Beach, Virginia).

Although Vincent would subsequently score minor hits (notably "Race with the Devil" and "Lotta Lovin'"), he never equaled the success of his first. He continued to record and tour and remained popular in Britain, where in 1960 he reinjured his leg in the automobile accident in which fellow rockabilly singer Eddie Cochran was killed. Touring and drug and alcohol abuse eventually took their toll; Vincent died at age 36. He was inducted into the Rock and Roll Hall of Fame in 1998; the Blue Caps were selected for induction in 2012.

## EDDIE COCHRAN

Singer, guitarist, and songwriter Eddie Cochran (born Ray Edward Cockran, October 3, 1938, Albert Lea, Minnesota, U.S.—died April 17, 1960, near Chippenham, Wiltshire, England) lived at least relatively fast and died young, at age 21, in a car crash while on tour in England. Cochran's family lived in Oklahoma and Minnesota before settling in California in 1950, and the young Cochran sang and played country music—touring and recording as part of the Cochran Brothers, with the unrelated Hank Cochran—until the arrival of Elvis Presley persuaded him to change his style. His good looks made him a perfect swivel-hipped rock-and-roll idol, which is evident in his appearances in a series of exploitation movies: *The Girl Can't Help It* (1956), *Untamed Youth* (1957), and *Go Johnny Go* (1959).

The echo-laden "Sittin' in the Balcony" gave him his first hit in 1957, but nothing about it suggested that the singer was anything other than just another handsome kid who had gotten lucky. It was his inherent talent, however, that turned "Summertime Blues" (1958) and "C'mon Everybody" (1958) into perfect examples of early rock, blending the driving, riffing rhythms of Cochran's own acoustic guitar with witty lyrics devoted to the pleasures (sun, girls, parties) and tribulations (parents, school) of being a teenager in the California of the 1950s. He had cowritten both songs, the first with Jerry Capehart, his producer, and the second with Sharon Sheeley, his girlfriend. Sheeley, a successful professional songwriter, was another passenger in the car taking Cochran and Gene Vincent back to London after a concert in Bristol on the fateful night in 1960; the crash killed Cochran, put Sheeley into the hospital, and left Vincent partially disabled. Cochran's "Three Steps to Heaven" was issued shortly after his death, reaching number one in the United Kingdom, where the intensity of the mourning was greater and more enduring than in his homeland, whose citizens have always mysteriously undervalued his contribution to rock music. Nevertheless, Cochran's handful of great records continue to evoke a mood of teenage abandon with rare humour, precision, and vitality. He was inducted into the Rock and Roll Hall of Fame in 1987.

## THE EVERLY BROTHERS

Born into a musical family, Don Everly (born February 1, 1937, Brownie, Kentucky, U.S.) and Phil Everly (born January 19, 1939, Brownie) first performed as part of their parents' country music act, then moved to Nashville, Tennessee, to work as songwriters. In 1957, as the Everly Brothers, the duo signed with Cadence Records and had their first big success later that year with "Bye Bye Love." Unlike the vocal harmonies in most early rock-and-roll recordings, which supported a moving vocal line with block harmonies, the Everly Brothers' vocal approach was based on the high, lonesome sound of bluegrass and Appalachian music, supporting the lead vocal with a moving secondary line to create the effect of intertwined melodies. When contrasted with the brusque insistence of a rock-and-roll rhythm, the duo's sweet, sad sound was almost as perfect a blend of rhythm and country as Elvis Presley's and fueled a string of chart-topping hits, including "Wake Up Little Susie" (1957), "All I Have to Do Is Dream" (1958), and "Cathy's Clown" (1960).

As vocal stylists, the Everlys were major inspirations for other rock groups such as the Beatles and the Hollies. Likewise, the Everlys' interlocking harmonies provided an aural template for folk rockers Simon and Garfunkel, as well as inspiring country rock pioneers Gram Parsons and Emmylou Harris. But, even as their influence grew, the Everlys' popularity waned. Sales in America slowed to a trickle after 1962, and, although the duo maintained a large and loyal audience in Britain, their reign on the charts all but ended after 1965. Moreover, personal problems (including an addiction to amphetamines) began wearing away on the pair, and in 1973 the Everlys broke up during a concert at Knott's Berry Farm in Buena Park, California. Both thereafter pursued solo careers.

In June 1983 Don and Phil reunited and released the album *EB 84,* which included the minor hit "On the Wings of a Nightingale." The Everly Brothers were inducted into the Rock and Roll Hall of Fame in 1986.

## SIR CLIFF RICHARD

Having played in skiffle bands during his youth in northern London, Cliff Richard (born Richard Harry Roger Webb, October 14, 1940, Lucknow, India), backed by a band that eventually became known as the Shadows, moved on to rock and roll and released the first great British rock-and-roll record, "Move It," in 1958. Dubbed the British Elvis Presley, he quickly found greater success as an all-around entertainer with pop hits such as Living Doll (1959) and as an actor in "clean teen" films such as *The Young Ones* (1961) and *Summer Holiday* (1962). Supplanted by the Beatles as British pop's prime mover, Richard became a born-again Christian in 1965. Eternally youthful, he went on to produce more than 100 hits en route to becoming a national figure in Britain and earning a knighthood in 1995, though he remained little known in the United States.

## RITCHIE VALENS

Singer and songwriter Ritchie Valens (born Richard Stephen Valenzuela, May 13, 1941, Pacoima, California, U.S.—died February 3, 1959, near Clear Lake, Iowa) was the first Latino rock and roller. His short career ended when he died at age 17 in the 1959 plane crash in which Buddy Holly and the Big Bopper also perished.

Valens grew up in suburban Los Angeles in a family of Mexican-Indian extraction. While in high school, he used an electric guitar made in shop class to front a band and came to the attention of Bob Keane, owner of Del-Fi records, who produced the sessions at Gold Star Studios that resulted in Valens's hits. His first hit, "Come On, Let's Go" (1958), was followed later that year by "Donna," a ballad written for an ex-girlfriend, and "La Bamba," Valens's best-remembered recording, a rock-and-roll reworking of a traditional Mexican wedding song, sung in Spanish (though Valens hardly spoke the language). He performed the Little Richard-inspired "Ooh! My Head" in the film *Go Johnny Go* (1959). Valens left a small legacy of recordings, but his compositions (often based on only three or four chords), exciting guitar style, emotional singing, and stylistic versatility influenced generations of rock musicians. His story is told in the film *La Bamba* (1987). In 2001 Valens was inducted into the Rock and Roll Hall of Fame.

## ROY ORBISON

Singer-songwriter Roy Orbison is best remembered for his soaring operatic voice and his carefully crafted ballads of loneliness and heartache. Orbison (born April 23,

1936, Vernon, Texas, U.S.—died December 6, 1988, Hendersonville, Tennessee) was raised in West Texas and formed his first musical group at age 13. He dropped out of college to pursue music, and as a member of the Teen-Kings he recorded "Ooby Dooby" in 1955 at Norman Petty's Clovis, New Mexico, studio. When he rerecorded the song at Sun Records, it became his first hit. Sam Phillips's efforts to make Orbison a rockabilly star were unsuccessful, however, and the shy Texan (whose trademark sunglasses masked eyes the singer feared looked beady) moved to Nashville, where he concentrated on writing songs for others, notably "Claudette" for the Everly Brothers.

At Monument Records, Orbison, no longer limited to up-tempo rockabilly numbers, recorded a series of unforgettable ballads beginning in 1960. His distinctive style flourished as he applied his incredible vocal range to lushly orchestrated three-minute romances filled with yearning and despair. "Running Scared" (1961), a delirious fantasy of romantic paranoia, epitomizes Orbison's artistry: tension mounts in the accompaniment and in the singer's voice as he frets that a chance encounter with his rival for his lover's affections will cause her to leave him. The rival appears, but the woman chooses the singer, and the song ends in a crescendo of relief.

"Only the Lonely" (1960), "Crying" (1961), "It's Over" (1964), and "Oh, Pretty Woman" (1964) were all hits, and Orbison was one of the few American rockers to maintain a place high on the pop charts during the British Invasion. After a series of personal tragedies and professional setbacks that derailed his career in the mid-1960s, Orbison made a stunning comeback in the late 1980s, partly as a result of the use of his song "In Dreams" in the film *Blue Velvet*. He became a member of the Traveling Wilburys, which boasted a lineup of Orbison, George Harrison, Bob Dylan, Tom Petty, and Jeff Lynne, and their debut album in 1988 landed Orbison in the Top Ten for the first time since 1964. He also recorded a new solo album, *Mystery Girl*, his finest work in decades. Tragically, Orbison died of a heart attack only a few weeks after the release of the Wilburys' album. *Mystery Girl*, released posthumously in 1989, featured the single "You Got It," which remained in the Top Ten for 18 weeks. In his speech for Orbison's induction into the Rock and Roll Hall of Fame in 1987, Bruce Springsteen said, "Roy's ballads were always best when you were alone in the dark....They were scary. His voice was unearthly."

## WANDA JACKSON

The "Queen of Rockabilly," Wanda Jackson (born October 20, 1937,

Maud, Oklahoma, U.S.) began singing on a daily Oklahoma City radio show in 1952, when she was still in high school. In 1954 country singer Hank Thompson invited her to record with his band, the Brazos Valley Boys, a collaboration that produced the country hit You Can't Have My Love. After finishing school, Jackson joined a concert tour that also featured Elvis Presley, who encouraged her to branch out into the fast-developing rockabilly genre. In 1956 she signed with Capitol Records, with whom she demonstrated her stylistic versatility by recording a number of singles that featured a country track on one side of the record and a rockabilly track on the other. On her debut 45, I Gotta Know (1956), she even alternated between both genres on the same song.

With a series of hits such as Let's Have a Party (1960), Right or Wrong (1961), and In the Middle of a Heartache (1961), Jackson quickly made a name for herself as a rare and powerful female voice in the rockabilly world. She also achieved international success with Fujiyama Mama (1957) in Japan and with a German-language rendition of Santo Domingo (1965).

As the commercial appetite for rockabilly waned in the 1960s, Jackson's recordings increasingly focused on country. A religious conversion in the early 1970s turned her attention toward gospel music, beginning with the album *Praise the Lord* (1972). In the 1980s Jackson began touring in Europe, where rockabilly was undergoing a revival, and she released several records there. The following decade she returned to touring the United States, performing secular material. At age 73, Jackson mounted a comeback with the album *The Party Ain't Over* (2011), which was produced by Jack White of the White Stripes. She was inducted into the Rock and Roll Hall of Fame in 2009.

## GENE PITNEY

A master of the dramatic pop ballad, singer and songwriter Gene Pitney (born February 17, 1941, Hartford, Connecticut, U.S.—died April 5, 2006, Cardiff, Wales) first gained success as a composer with hits such as Hello Mary Lou (recorded by Rick Nelson in 1961) and He's a Rebel (recorded by the Crystals in 1962). In 1961 Pitney began recording his compositions, with I Wanna Love My Life Away demonstrating a passionate vocal style. However, he sold more records with songs by other writers, such as Town Without Pity and Burt Bacharach and Hal David's The Man Who Shot Liberty Valance; the latter rendition rose to number four in the American pop charts in 1962. Pitney also reached the Top Ten with

Only Love Can Break a Heart (1962), It Hurts to Be in Love (1964), and I'm Gonna Be Strong (1964). As his career waned in the United States, Pitney enjoyed continued popularity in Europe. An Italian-language country album sold well in 1966, and he appeared regularly on the British pop charts through 1970. In 1989 a rerecording of Something's Gotten Hold of My Heart (duet with Marc Almond) became his first number one song in England. Pitney was inducted into the Rock and Roll Hall of Fame in 2002. A tireless performer, he died while on tour in 2006.

## DEL SHANNON

One of the first white rock and rollers to write his own songs, Del Shannon (born Charles Weedon Westover, December 30, 1934, Coopersville, Michigan, U.S.—died February 8, 1990, Santa Clarita, California) is best known for the pop music classic "Runaway" (1961). After playing in bands as a teenager in Grand Rapids, Michigan, Shannon released his first single, "Runaway," in 1961. Punctuated by his trademark falsetto cries, this ode to lost love (a common theme in Shannon's songs)

topped the charts. A series of hits quickly followed: "Hats Off to Larry," "So Long Baby," "Hey! Little Girl" (all 1961), "Little Town Flirt" (1963), "Keep Searchin' (We'll Follow the Sun)" (1964), and "Stranger in Town" (1965). All were marked by simple, ringing chord changes and Shannon's gravelly, vibrant baritone, always ready to ascend into higher registers of longing and hurt. Shannon also wrote "I Go to Pieces," a 1965 hit for the British duo Peter and Gordon, and endured a misguided attempt by producer Snuff Garrett and arranger Leon Russell to make him into a teen idol. Between battles with alcoholism in the 1970s, he recorded with Electric Light Orchestra and Dave Edmunds. *Drop Down and Get Me* (1982), a strong album and a modest chart success, was produced by Tom Petty and featured his band, the Heartbreakers.

Following the death of Roy Orbison in 1988, it was rumoured that Shannon would be asked to replace Orbison in the Traveling Wilburys; however, Shannon—always something of a haunted figure—committed suicide in 1990. He was inducted into the Rock and Roll Hall of Fame in 1999.

# CHAPTER 10

# Buildings and Walls of Sound

**M**any accounts of the history of popular music identify the period from the end of the 1950s until the mid-1960s as a time when rock and roll lost its excitement and edge. Elvis Presley had begun military service in 1958, and when he was discharged from the army in 1960—despite the release of backlogged recordings that kept him in the charts—he seemed somehow tamer. By 1960 both Buddy Holly and Eddie Cochran had died, in a plane and automobile crash, respectively. Moreover, at the beginning of 1962 Chuck Berry began a two-year prison term after being convicted of violating the Mann Act. But their absence did not mean that popular music was reduced to the bland posturing of Frankie Avalon and Fabian on *American Bandstand* and in beach movies. Music of considerable merit, much of it producer-driven rhythm and blues, resulted from the efforts of Brill Building tunesmiths, girl groups, and Phil Spector's "wall of sound" studio wizardry.

## THE BRILL BUILDING: ASSEMBLY-LINE POP

Located at 1619 Broadway in New York City, the Brill Building was the hub of professionally written rock and roll. As the 1960s equivalent of Tin Pan Alley, it reemphasized a specialized division of labour in which professional songwriters worked closely with producers and artists-and-repertoire

# LEIBER AND STOLLER

Jerry Leiber (born Jerome Leiber, April 25, 1933, Baltimore, Maryland, U.S.—died August 22, 2011, Los Angeles, California) and Mike Stoller (born Michael Stoller, March 13, 1933, Belle Harbor, New York) became partners as teenagers in Los Angeles; when their "Hound Dog" was recorded by Big Mama Thornton in 1952, they also became producers. Major success followed with their series of novelty story-songs—including "Black Denim Trousers and Motorcycle Boots" (performed by the Cheers), "Young Blood" and "Yakety Yak" (by the Coasters), and "Love Potion Number Nine" (by the Clovers)—and with their songs for Elvis Presley movies, including *Jailhouse Rock* and *Love Me Tender*. Their early 1960s productions of Ben E. King and the Drifters, including "Stand By Me" and "On Broadway," were especially influential. In 1964 they established their own label, Red Bird, on which the Shangri-Las recorded. They went on to write for films and theatre; among their last hits, in 1969, was the world-weary "Is That All There Is?" (by Peggy Lee). Leiber and Stoller were inducted into the Rock and Roll Hall of Fame in 1987.

personnel to match selected artists with appropriate songs.

The professionalization of rock and roll was anticipated in the late 1950s by the team of Jerry Leiber and Mike Stoller, who wrote and produced their biggest hits with the Coasters and the Drifters. While their successors sometimes filled the roles of producer and writer, the Brill Building professionals tended to focus more narrowly on elevating the craft of songwriting.

The flagship company of Brill Building pop music (actually located across the street at 1650 Broadway) was Aldon Music, founded by Al Nevins and Don Kirshner. Brill

# BOBBY DARIN

At age 8, Bobby Darin (born Walden Robert Cassotto, May 14, 1936, New York, New York, U.S.—died December 20, 1973, Los Angeles, California) was diagnosed with a heart defect and was not expected to reach age 16, but this death sentence became the anvil on which he forged his ambition. Moving from performing in New York City coffeehouses into recording in the late 1950s, Darin flopped with his early singles, but in 1958 "Splish Splash," a novelty song he reputedly wrote in 12 minutes, became an international hit. Other hit singles followed, but, not content to remain a teenage sensation, Darin changed tack in 1959 and

*American pop singer Bobby Darin sitting next to his wife, actress Sandra Dee.* Darlene Hammond/ Archive Photos/Getty Images

began recording adult standards à la Frank Sinatra, whom Darin famously aspired to surpass. The first was a reworking of Bertolt Brecht and Kurt Weill's ominous "Moritat" from *The Threepenny Opera* into the finger-popping amoral swagger of "Mack the Knife" (1959). Though other adult hits followed, including "Beyond the Sea" (1960), it was "Mack" that became Darin's signature song and earned him two Grammy Awards.

In the 1960s, while pursuing a film career (which included an Oscar nomination in 1964), Darin explored a variety of styles before embracing the folk rock movement. In 1966 he had a hit with Tim Hardin's "If I Were a Carpenter," but Darin's musical fortunes subsequently slipped, and in 1973 his heart failed. Darin was inducted into the Rock and Roll Hall of Fame in 1990.

Building-era songwriting teams such as Gerry Goffin and Carole King, Barry Mann and Cynthia Weil, Jeff Barry and Ellie Greenwich, and Doc Pomus and Mort Shuman were to rock and roll what Richard Rodgers and Lorenz Hart and George and Ira Gershwin were to Tin Pan Alley. The difference was that the writers of Brill Building pop understood the teenage idiom and wrote almost exclusively for a youth audience. Teen idols Paul Anka, Neil Sedaka (who teamed with Howard Greenfield), Gene Pitney, and Bobby Darin also had careers composing Brill Building pop. On the other hand, Aldon writer King went on to achieve stardom as a singer-songwriter in the 1970s.

Working in assembly-line fashion in the Brill Building's small rooms containing upright pianos, these writers turned out their share of teen drivel—Connie Francis's "Stupid Cupid" (Sedaka and Greenfield) and James Darren's "Her Royal Majesty" (Goffin and King)—but at their best they married the excitement and urgency of rhythm and blues to the brightness of mainstream pop—Goffin and King's "Up on the Roof" for the Drifters and "A Natural Woman" for Aretha Franklin. Nowhere was this union stronger than in the classic hits of the girl groups of the early 1960s: Goffin and King's "Will You Love Me Tomorrow" for the Shirelles and "One Fine Day" for the Chiffons

and Mann and Weil's "Uptown" and Pitney's "He's a Rebel" for the Crystals. Producer Phil Spector was perhaps the Brill Building's biggest customer as well as a frequent collaborator. He worked variously with Greenwich and Barry, Goffin and King, and Mann and Weil to cowrite material for the Crystals, the Ronettes, the Dixie Cups, and the Righteous Brothers.

Brill Building professionals often wrote with intelligence and wit but less frequently with substance. As Bob Dylan and the Beatles ushered in an era of artists who wrote more personal and topical material, the Brill Building declined as a force in popular music.

## PHIL SPECTOR

Writer Tom Wolfe described producer Phil Spector as the "First Tycoon of Teen." There had been producers since the beginning of the record industry, but none had assumed the degree of control first demanded by Spector in the early 1960s. At age nine, Spector (born Harvey Phillip Spector, December 26, 1940, New York, New York, U.S.) lost his father when the elder Spector, an ironworker, committed suicide. In 1952 the family left the Bronx and moved to West Hollywood, California. Several years later, an 18-year-old Spector and two of his school friends recorded "To Know

# DON KIRSHNER

Don Kirshner managed singers Bobby Darin and Connie Francis before forming Aldon Music in 1958 with veteran publisher Al Nevins. Setting up office in the heart of Tin Pan Alley they cultivated prolific songwriting partnerships including those of Neil Sedaka and Howard Greenfield and of Gerry Goffin and Carole King, whose well-honed songs for Francis, Bobby Vee, the Drifters, and the Shirelles helped New York City pop wrench the teenage market away from the spontaneous rock-and-roll artists who had unearthed it.

With song-plugger and producer Lou Adler among Kirshner's lieutenants, Aldon merged with the film company Screen Gems Columbia. Kirshner channeled his songs through the company's Colpix, Dimension, and Colgems subsidiary labels and masterminded a television project in which four young men were to become "America's answer to the Beatles." The Monkees had six Top Three singles and two of the best-selling albums of the decade, mostly written by in-house songwriters—including Tommy Boyce and Bobby Hart, Neil Diamond, and Goffin and King. Setting up a West Coast office under music business veteran Lester Sill (previously the business partner of Jerry Leiber and Mike Stoller, Lee Hazlewood, and Phil Spector), Kirshner was involved in such other network TV ventures as the Archies cartoon project, *The Partridge Family* (which launched David Cassidy), and *Don Kirshner's Rock Concert* (a live rock show).

Him Is to Love Him," a simple teenage ballad written by Spector, its title taken from his father's gravestone. Released under the name of the Teddy Bears, it was one of the biggest hits of 1958. But the group was never to be heard from again, because Spector had other ideas. He moved back to

# GOLD STAR STUDIOS

Opened in 1950 at 6252 Santa Monica Boulevard in Hollywood, Gold Star Studios took its name from its founders, David S. Gold and Stan Ross (*STAn Ross*). It was there, from 1962 through 1965, that Phil Spector produced a string of hits by the Ronettes, the Crystals, and the Righteous Brothers featuring his signature wall of sound. Spector used far more instruments than was customary—three or four pianos with several guitars playing more or less the same chords amid a welter of percussion—and he encouraged engineer Larry Levine to swamp everything in echo, seeking to convey intense emotion through texture, atmosphere, and rhythm.

Because the studio was not particularly big and had no air-conditioning, Spector sessions were not comfortable, but they were as unforgettable to the participants as the results were to those who heard them on the radio. Learning not to resist Spector's unorthodox requests, Levine became part of a team that also included arranger Jack Nitzche and a number of first-choice session musicians who were to become the core of the West Coast recording scene for the next 10 years—drummers Earl Palmer and Hal Blaine, bass players Carole Kaye and Larry Knechtal, guitarists Barney Kessel, Tommy Tedesco, and Bill Strange, pianist Leon Russell, and countless percussionists.

According to legend, Sonny and Cher met while performing backing vocals on a Spector session at Gold Star. Once Brian Wilson heard Spector's records, the Beach Boys' composer-producer made many of his group's records at Gold Star, and the rest of the industry followed, vainly hoping to capture that magic sound by using the same ingredients.

New York City and served an apprenticeship with the writer-producer team of Jerry Leiber and Mike Stoller before branching out to supervise the recordings of Curtis Lee ("Pretty Little Angel Eyes"), the Paris Sisters ("I Love How You Love Me"), and others. In 1961, needing to escape the restraining influence of older and more conservative opinion, he formed his own label, Philles Records, and, moving back west, worked at Gold Star Recording Studios in Los Angeles, where he began to release a string of records that demonstrated his unique vision of what pop music could achieve in its age of innocence.

With the Crystals' "Da Doo Ron Ron" and "Then He Kissed Me" and the Ronettes' "Be My Baby" and "Baby I Love You," Spector blended conventional teen romance sentiments with orchestral arrangements of immense scale and power in what he described as "little symphonies for the kids." Others called it the wall of sound. The style reached a peak in 1965 with the blue-eyed soul of the Righteous Brothers' epic You've Lost That Lovin' Feelin', a huge worldwide hit.

Spector threatened to top "Lovin' Feelin'" with Ike and Tina Turner's majestic "River Deep—Mountain High" the following year, but some sectors of the music industry, jealous of his success and irritated by his arrogance, ensured its commercial failure. A wounded Spector went into a retirement from which he briefly emerged in 1969 to work on the solo records of John Lennon and George Harrison, at whose behest (and to Paul McCartney's lasting displeasure) he completed the postproduction of *Let It Be*, the Beatles' final album. Later collaborations with Leonard Cohen and the Ramones were no more successful than his attempts to reestablish his own label. His time had gone. Spector was inducted into the Rock and Roll Hall of Fame in 1989. In 2009, after two trials, Spector was sentenced to 19 years to life in prison for the murder of actress Lana Clarkson, who had been fatally shot at Spector's home in 2003.

## GIRL GROUPS

From the early to the mid-1960s—the period between the heyday of early rock and roll and the British Invasion—was the girl group era, which produced a clearly identifiable hybrid of gospel, rhythm and blues, doo-wop, and quirky pop. The high-pitched, husky, teen-girl sound of acts such as the Ronettes and the Supremes epitomized the ebullient hopes of early 1960s culture and feminized rock music, providing a model for male beat groups such as the Beatles.

The scene centred around a cluster of fiercely competitive, specialist independent labels such as Philles,

# CAROLE KING

Carole King (born Carol Klein, February 9, 1940, Brooklyn, New York, U.S.) began playing piano at age 4. In high school she formed a band called the Co-sines. While attending New York's Queens College in 1958 King met Paul Simon and began writing songs professionally. She also met Gerry Goffin, her musical collaborator, lyricist, and future husband. King wrote several singles in the late 1950s and even had one written for her ("Oh! Carol") by Neil Sedaka, but her career actually took off when she and Goffin penned "Will You Love Me Tomorrow?" for the Shirelles.

Among the approximately 100 hits cowritten by King and Goffin and performed by others were "Wasn't Born to Follow" (the Byrds); "Chains" (the Cookies); "Don't Bring Me Down" (the Animals); "I'm Into Something Good" (Herman's Hermits); "Up on the Roof" and "When My Little Girl is Smiling" (the Drifters); "Take Good Care of My Baby" (Bobby Vee); "One Fine Day" (the Chiffons); "Halfway to Paradise" (Tony Orlando and Bill Fury); "Every Breath I Take" (Gene Pitney); and "The Locomotion" (Little Eva).

Persuaded to record her own songs, King released her solo debut album *It Might As Well Rain Until September* in 1962. The album was an international hit, though it would be another decade before King would follow up her success as a performer. In 1967 King and Goffin separated, and they later divorced. The following year, King formed a new band with bass player Charles Larkey (who would become her second husband) and guitarist Danny Kortchmar, who became part of James Taylor's band. The band dissolved a year later. King and Taylor became good friends and collaborators; she played piano on Taylor's *Sweet Baby James* (1969) album, and he recorded a number of her songs on his hit albums.

In 1970 King released *Writer*. While not a huge success, the album set the stage for her next release, *Tapestry* (1971), which eventually sold more than 15 million copies and featured such hits as "It's Too Late," "So Far Away," "I Feel The Earth Move," "You've Got a Friend," "Will You Still Love Me Tomorrow?," "Natural Woman," and the title track. The album swept the Grammy awards. King's greatest subsequent hits were the singles "Jazzman" (1974), "Nightingale" (1975), and "One Fine Day" (1980). Over the years King continued to collaborate with her ex-husband Goffin, with whom she was inducted into the Rock and Roll Hall of Fame in 1990. King's memoir, *A Natural Woman*, was published in 2012.

*Carole King from the* Tapestry *LP cover photo session, 1971.* Jim McCrary/Redferns/Getty Images

Scepter, Red Bird, Dimension, and Motown. The material for many of the genre's biggest acts came mainly from three successful husband-and-wife songwriting teams with Brill Building connections: Gerry Goffin and Carole King, Ellie Greenwich and Jeff Barry, and Barry Mann and Cynthia Weil. Meanwhile, the Motown girl groups benefited from the songwriting talents of the Holland-Dozier-Holland team and Smokey Robinson.

The girl group sound was a mixture of black doo-wop, rock and roll, and white pop. In attempting to sweeten rock and roll for the teen pop market, songwriters and producers in the early 1960s created an original sound characterized by a raw-edged lead vocal, echoing harmonies from the backing vocalists, fulsome string arrangements, and a driving beat. Groups sang of teen concerns such as romance, sexual etiquette, and marriage, as well as love, loss, and abandonment. The sound exploded in 1961, following the release in late 1960 of the Shirelles' "Will You Love Me Tomorrow," the first girl group single to reach number one.

## THE SHIRELLES

The Shirelles began singing together at high school functions in Passaic, New Jersey. The original members of the quartet were Addie ("Micki") Harris (born January 22, 1940, Passaic—died June 10, 1982, Los Angeles, California), Doris Coley (born August 2, 1941, Goldsboro, North Carolina—died February 4, 2000, Sacramento, California), Shirley Owens Alston (born June 10, 1941, Passaic), and Beverly Lee (born August 3, 1941, Passaic). Florence Greenberg, the mother of one of their classmates, signed them to her own small Tiara label and later to her more ambitious Scepter Records (for which Dionne Warwick also recorded). Unlike most girl groups, the Shirelles wrote some of their own songs, but their biggest hits were written by others—including Goffin and King, who wrote "Will You Love Me Tomorrow."

"Dedicated to the One I Love," "Mama Said," and "Baby It's You" were all Top Ten hits for the Shirelles. Following their most successful song, "Soldier Boy" (1962), cowritten by their principal collaborator, producer Luther Dixon, the Shirelles' popularity waned—partly because of Dixon's departure and partly because of the onset of the British Invasion. Ironically, the Beatles recorded two Shirelles songs—"Baby It's You" and "Boys"—on their debut album. The Shirelles broke up in the late 1960s but re-formed later for "oldies" shows. Remembered for their sweet, gospel-tinged harmonies, they were inducted into the Rock and Roll Hall of Fame in 1996.

## THE CRYSTALS

Over the next five years hundreds of girl group records were released, including "Chapel of Love" (1964) by the Dixie Cups, a trio from New Orleans, Louisiana, and "Leader of the Pack" (1964) by the Shangri-Las, two pairs of sisters from New York City. Phil Spector, in particular, dominated the genre with his inventive production for the Crystals and Ronettes.

Formed in 1960, the Crystals were made up of Barbara Alston (born 1943, Brooklyn, New York, U.S.), Merna Girard (born 1943, Brooklyn), Delores ("Dee Dee") Kenniebrew (born 1945, Brooklyn), Mary Thomas (born 1946, Brooklyn), and Pattie Wright (born 1945, Brooklyn). Girard was replaced by Delores ("Lala") Brooks (born 1946, Brooklyn) in 1962. The group was created by Alston's uncle, Benny Wells, when he recruited the singers to record a series of pop singles. Wells enlisted the aid of a series of songwriters, a quest that led him to the Manhattan headquarters of publishers Hill and Range. It was there, while rehearsing the single "There's No Other (Like My Baby)," that the group met Spector. In the recording studio, Spector gave the song a rhythm-and-blues feel and added the layered instrumentation that would later characterize his production style. Released on Spector's Philles label in late 1961, "There's No Other (Like My Baby)" reached the Billboard Top 20. The group followed with "Uptown," a modest hit that allowed Spector to experiment with nontraditional pop instruments such as castinets and Spanish guitars. The single "He's a Rebel" (1962) reached number one on the pop charts, and although the song was credited to the Crystals, Spector brought in singer Darlene Love of the Blossoms to record the lead vocals. The following year, with Brooks as their lead vocalist, the Crystals reclaimed their name with the smash singles "Da Do Ron Ron" and "Then He Kissed Me." The latter song represented one of the finest achievements of Spector's wall of sound technique, and it was the

band's biggest international hit. Later releases failed to reach that level of success, however, and the group disbanded in 1967.

## THE RONETTES

The trio that became the Ronettes started as a song-and-dance act at the Peppermint Lounge in New York City in 1959, with Ronnie Bennett (born Veronica Bennett, August 10, 1943, New York, New York, U.S.) taking lead vocals and her sister Estelle (born July 22, 1941, New York, New York—died February 11, 2009, Englewood, New Jersey) and their cousin Nedra Talley (born January 27, 1946, New York, New York) singing backup. They were discovered by Don Kirshner, who signed them to his Colpix label. As Ronnie and the Relatives, they recorded a number of singles, but none of them reached the national charts. In 1963 the group, now called the Ronettes, teamed with Spector, who reshaped their image (incorporating the beehive hairdos that soon became characteristic of the girl-group genre) and applied his dense production style to the trio's music. The first single produced by Spector, "Be My Baby," was a wall-of-sound masterpiece, and it was the first of five Ronettes songs to reach the Top 40, charting in 1963–64. This marked the peak of the group's success, however, and the Ronettes disbanded in 1966.

The disbandment notwithstanding, Ronnie became romantically involved with Spector and married him in 1968. The couple divorced in 1974, but she retained his name and forged a solo career as Ronnie Spector. Her biggest solo hit, "Take Me Home Tonight," a duet with Eddie Money, reached number four on the Billboard chart in 1986. The Ronettes were inducted into the Rock and Roll Hall of Fame in 2007.

While Spector made huge financial profits for his Philles label, many of his acts did not. Girl groups were treated like factory production line fodder—the Crystals, for instance, were cheated out of royalties when Spector paid a session singer, Darlene Love, a flat studio fee to record songs like "He's a Rebel" that were credited to the group. The Crystals then found themselves fronting songs they had not recorded. Although royalty disputes were endemic in the industry at the time, girl groups were often treated the worst.

## THE SHANGRI-LAS

The Shangri-Las, who all attended the same high school in Queens, New York, began performing at area nightclubs in 1963 and had achieved some local success when they were noticed by producer George ("Shadow") Morton. The group had been formed by two pairs of sisters: Mary Weiss (born 1946, Queens) and Betty Weiss (born Elizabeth Weiss, 1948, Queens), and twins Margie Ganser (born Marguerite Ganser, February 4, 1948, Queens—died July 28, 1996, Valley Stream, New York) and Mary-Ann Ganser (born February 4, 1948, Queens—died March 14, 1970, Queens). Morton, who was auditioning for work with the newly formed Red Bird label, recruited the Shangri-Las to perform his song "Remember (Walking in the Sand)." The label promptly hired Morton and signed the Shangri-Las to a recording contract. With Mary in the lead, and the others providing backing vocals, a reworked version of "Remember (Walking in the Sand)" reached the Top Five in the summer of 1964. Morton then enlisted songwriting veterans at the Brill Building to provide the group with material. The Shangri-Las' next single proved to be their defining hit. "Leader of the Pack," which topped the charts in 1964, was a tale of rebellion punctuated by the crack of a motorcycle engine. Around that time, Betty left the band, but the Shangri-Las continued as a trio, touring throughout 1965–66 and scoring a Top Ten hit with "I Can Never Go Home Anymore" (1965). Red Bird folded in 1966, and the Shangri-Las, unable to find success at another label, disbanded two years later.

## LEGACY

Although the 1960s were the golden age of girl groups, the style endured. In the 1980s it was combined with rock and punk music by such bands as the Go-Go's and the Bangles, and in the 1990s a new generation of vocal acts interpreted the style with added funkiness. Moreover, latter-day performers such as En Vogue, Janet Jackson, and the British act the Spice Girls (whose success sparked another explosion of girl groups, especially in Asia) received the recognition and financial rewards they deserved.

# CHAPTER 11

# Independent Record Labels and Producers

From 1946 to 1958 the American music business was turned upside down by a group of mavericks who knew little about music but were fast learners about business. What they discovered was an expanding "market" of clubs and bars in each of which stood a jukebox that needed stocking with an ever-changing stack of 78-rpm records. These records had to have either a beat heavy enough to cut through the raucous clamour of a bar or a message desolate enough to haunt late-night drinkers not yet ready to go home. The common thread was that these clubs were in the sections of town where African Americans lived, and the established record business had almost abandoned this market during World War II, when a shortage of shellac (then the principal raw material of record manufacture) caused them to economize. Only Decca among the major companies had maintained a strong roster of black performers, headed by the phenomenally successful Louis Jordan and the Tympany Five. The other majors stuck faithfully to the novelty songs and Tin Pan Alley ballads that had been the staple of popular music, while also tapping the burgeoning country market. Perry Como, Bing Crosby, and Eddy Arnold ruled the airwaves.

# WILLIE DIXON

Producer, bassist, and prolific songwriter Willie Dixon (born William James Dixon, July 1, 1915, Vicksburg, Mississippi, U.S.—died January 29, 1992, Burbank, California) exerted a major influence on post-World War II electric blues. Dixon's mother wrote religious poetry, and he sang in a gospel quartet before moving to Chicago in 1936. The following year he won the Illinois Golden Glove amateur heavyweight boxing championship. He began playing the double bass in 1939 and worked extensively with the Big Three Trio (1946–52). When that group dissolved, he began working full-time for Chess Records, serving as a house bassist and arranger on recording sessions. Dixon's upbeat blues compositions, which he sold for as little as $30, helped usher in the Chicago blues sound of the 1950s.

Among his best-known songs are "I'm Your Hoochie Coochie Man" and "I'm Ready," written for Muddy Waters; "Little Red Rooster" and "Back Door Man," for Howlin' Wolf; "My Babe," for Little Walter; "Bring It on Home," for the second Sonny Boy Williamson (Alex "Rice" Miller); and "The Seventh Son" and "Wang Dang Doodle." In the late 1950s he worked with the short-lived Cobra label; in the 1960s he toured Europe with the American Folk Blues Festival and formed the Chicago Blues All-Stars, which traveled widely throughout the United States and Europe. Rock performers such as the Rolling Stones, Jimi Hendrix, Elvis Presley, and Led Zeppelin recorded his songs. He was the founder of the Blues Heaven Foundation, a nonprofit organization designed to benefit destitute blues performers and provide scholarships to young musicians. (1989). Dixon was inducted into the Rock and Roll Hall of Fame as an early influence in 1994.

## ENTREPRENEURS WITH EARS

While the major companies ignored the so-called "race" market, a new wave of entrepreneurs moved in. Most of them were already involved with music in one way or another: owning a record shop (Syd Nathan of King Records in Cincinnati, Ohio) or a nightclub (the Chess brothers in Chicago), working in the jukebox business (the Bihari brothers of Modern Records in Los Angeles) or in radio (Lew Chudd of Imperial Records in Los Angeles, Sam Phillips of Sun Records in Memphis, Tennessee), or, in one case, turning a hobby into a living (Ahmet Ertegun of Atlantic Records in New York City).

Several companies set up studios in their office buildings, and label owners efficiently doubled as producers in an era when recording sessions lasted only three hours (according to union requirements). With the notable exception of Phillips, they had no experience in the studio. Some bluffed, telling the musicians to play the next take harder or faster or with more feeling. Others preferred to delegate studio supervision to experienced arrangers or engineers while dealing themselves with the logistics of pressing, distributing, and promoting their records and trying to collect money from sales.

Although the term *producer* did not come into currency until the mid-1950s, several arrangers had been performing that function for 10 years by then, most notably Maxwell Davis in Los Angeles, Dave Bartholomew in New Orleans, Louisiana, Willie Dixon in Chicago, Henry Glover in Cincinnati, and Jesse Stone in New York City. Veterans of the big-band era who created rhythm-based arrangements for rhythm and blues, they acted as midwives for what we now call rock and roll.

For all concerned, the experience was a crash course in economics, and practices ranged from the honourable (Art Rupe at Specialty Records in Los Angeles was tough but principled in his negotiations and royalty payments) to the disreputable. When label bosses discovered that whoever published the song was legally entitled to receive two cents per title on each record sold, they soon became song publishers, too. But some bought out the writers' share for a few dollars, thereafter taking all the proceeds from both sales and airplay.

## THE LITTLE LABELS THAT COULD

By the early 1950s, radio play had become even more important than getting stocked on jukeboxes, and the market now included the white teenagers who tuned in to stations that were nominally aimed at black listeners. Of the first generation of successful rock-and-roll singers, almost all recorded for labels that initially supplied rhythm-and-blues records: Fats Domino for Imperial, Chuck Berry for Chess, Little Richard for Specialty, and Elvis Presley and Carl Perkins for Sun. The notable exception was Bill Haley, who recorded for Decca, the only major company to have taken the race market seriously.

## ATLANTIC RECORDS: "THE HOUSE THAT RUTH BUILT"

Formed in 1947 by jazz fans Ahmet Ertegun, son of a Turkish diplomat, and Herb Abramson, formerly the artists-and-repertoire director for National Records, Atlantic became the most consistently successful New York City-based independent label of the 1950s, with an incomparable roster including Joe Turner, Ruth Brown, the Clovers, Ray Charles, Clyde McPhatter and the Drifters, and LaVern Baker. Apart from Charles none of these singers regularly wrote their own songs, which were provided by freelance writers including Jesse Stone, Rudolph Toombs, and Winfield Scott. Stone was also a vital part of the production team in

*Record executive Ahmet Ertegun, c. 1970.* Michael Ochs Archives/Getty Images

his capacity as rehearsal coach and session arranger. Former music journalist Jerry Wexler (who was inducted into the Rock and Roll Hall of Fame in 1987) joined the company in 1953. He was just in time to take part in a golden era when many of the label's classic records were recorded at evening sessions in the 56th Street office after the desks had been stacked on top of each other to make room for engineer Tom Dowd to set up his recording equipment. As the roster expanded, Atlantic set a precedent by hiring Jerry Leiber and Mike Stoller as producers of records by the Coasters and the Drifters, while Ertegun (who was inducted into the Rock and Roll Hall of Fame in 1987) himself helped launch Bobby Darin as a teen star.

## DECCA RECORDS: SHAKING, RATTLING, AND ROLLING

Formed as an American division by its British parent company in 1934, Decca was the only major company to stand by its black roster during the 1940s, although most of its artists—including vocal groups (the Mills Brothers and the Ink Spots) and big bands (led by Lionel Hampton and Buddy Johnson)—worked in pre-war idioms. Decca's black roster was supervised by Milt Gabler, a jazz fan who had previously run his own Commodore label. At Decca, Gabler

(who was inducted into the Rock and Roll Hall of Fame in 1993) formed a close relationship with Louis Jordan, whose hugely popular and influential jump-blues combo topped the black music market's best-seller chart for an unrivaled total of 118 weeks during the 1940s.

When Jordan left Decca to join the independent Aladdin label in 1954, Gabler signed a white group with a comparable style: Bill Haley and His Comets. The first sessions with Haley, recorded at Manhattan's Pythian Temple, resulted in two extremely influential hits—a cover version of Joe Turner's recent rhythm-and-blues hit "Shake Rattle and Roll" and the record that was to become one of the best-selling rock-and-roll hits of all time, "Rock Around the Clock." In an attempt to take advantage of the more flexible procedures of the independent sector (notably in radio promotion), Decca set up two independently distributed subsidiary labels, Brunswick and Coral, whose rosters included Buddy Holly, the Crickets, and Jackie Wilson.

## CHESS RECORDS: FROM MUDDY TO "MAYBELLENE"

In 1947 brothers Leonard and Phil Chess became partners with Charles and Evelyn Aron in the Aristocrat Record Company. The Chesses had operated several taverns on Chicago's

South Side—the last and largest of which was the Mocamba Lounge—and their desire to record one of the singers who performed in their nightclub led them into the record business. In 1950, after buying out the Arons, they changed the name of their company to Chess and attracted an unparalleled roster of blues artists who had come to the city from the Mississippi Delta, including Muddy Waters, Howlin' Wolf, the second Sonny Boy Williamson (Alex ["Rice"] Miller), Little Walter, and Bo Diddley. Bassist-arranger Willie Dixon was a vital presence at these blues sessions. He also was versatile enough to help deliver Chuck Berry's version of rock and roll. As rhythm and blues began to infiltrate the pop market, Chess and its subsidiary label, Checker, recorded such vocal groups as the Moonglows and the Flamingos and administered the Arc and Jewel publishing companies through Maurice Levy. Levy managed disc jockey Alan Freed and assigned to him a share of the songwriting royalties for the Moonglows' "Sincerely" and Berry's "Maybellene." Leonard Chess was inducted into the Rock and Roll Hall of Fame in 1987.

## VEE JAY RECORDS

Record store owners Vivian Carter ("Vee") and James Bracken ("Jay"), later husband and wife, formed Vee Jay Records in 1953. (At various times the company's labels also read VJ or Vee-Jay.) With Carter's brother Calvin as producer and Ewart Abner in charge of promotion, Vee Jay became the most successful black-owned record company of its period. Jimmy Reed made more commercial blues records than Chess managed to produce; without ever sounding like rock and roll, his simple, hypnotic grooves were jukebox staples through the early 1960s, when both he and John Lee Hooker became bedrock influences on the emerging British blues movement.

Vee Jay reached the pop charts mostly through vocal groups, starting in 1954 with "Goodnite, Sweetheart, Goodnite" by the Spaniels, continuing with "For Your Precious Love" by Jerry Butler and the Impressions in 1958, and reaching a pinnacle with a string of hits by the Four Seasons in the early 1960s. When Capitol refused its option to release several Beatles singles—as well as their first American album, *Introducing…the Beatles* (1964)—Vee Jay jumped at the opportunity, taking the album to number two and four singles to the Top Five. Ironically, overexpansion in the wake of this success contributed to the bankruptcy that befell the company soon after.

## KING RECORDS IN THE QUEEN CITY

Record store owner Syd Nathan established King Records in Cincinnati,

Ohio, in 1943. Situated just across the Ohio River from more rural, Southern-oriented Kentucky, Nathan (who was inducted into the Rock and Roll Hall of Fame in 1997) recorded country acts who came to town to play on WLW's *Midwestern Hayride* and the touring black singers and bands who included Cincinnati on their itinerary. By reputation irascible and penny-pinching, the single-minded Nathan created a uniquely self-sufficient operation with not only a recording studio and publishing company but his own pressing plant, printing press (for labels and sleeves), and distribution system.

Despite being incapable of actually writing a song himself, Nathan regularly bought out the composer rights for nominal sums and claimed authorship under the name Lois Mann. To supervise recordings he hired Henry Glover and Ralph Bass, who pulled together an incomparable roster of performers that included country stars Cowboy Copas and the Delmore Brothers, big band refugees Earl Bostic (alto sax) and Bill Doggett (organ), blues shouters Wynonie Harris and Roy Brown, blues ballad singers Little Esther and Little Willie John, and vocal groups Billy Ward and the Dominoes (featuring first Clyde McPhatter and later Jackie Wilson) and Hank Ballard and the Midnighters. But by far the biggest artist to record for King was

the maverick James Brown, who succeeded despite Nathan's initial skepticism at Bass's decision to record and release Brown's first single, "Please, Please, Please" (1956), which launched his remarkable career.

## SUN RECORDS: SAM PHILLIPS'S MEMPHIS RECORDING SERVICE

Former radio engineer Sam Phillips opened the Memphis Recording Service at 706 Union Avenue in 1950. Among his first customers were out-of-town rhythm-and-blues labels Modern (based in Los Angeles) and Chess, who hired Phillips to find and record local artists on their behalf. Phillips (who was inducted into the Rock and Roll Hall of Fame in 1986) was a genius at making musicians feel at home in the studio, and over the next three years he recorded some classic performances by B.B. King, Howlin' Wolf, and teenage bandleader Ike Turner. Having delivered a couple of rhythm-and-blues number ones—"Rocket 88" by Jackie Brenston (1951) and "Booted" by Rosco Gordon (1952)—Phillips set up his own label, Sun Records, whose first rhythm-and-blues hit was "Bear Cat" by Rufus Thomas (1953), an answer record to "Hound Dog," the rhythm-and-blues hit from Houston, Texas, by Willie Mae Thornton.

The following year Phillips recorded his first white singer, Elvis

# ARTHUR "BIG BOY" CRUDUP

Arthur "Big Boy" Crudup (born August 24, 1905, Forest, Mississippi, U.S.—died March 28, 1974, Nassawadox, Virginia) moved to Chicago in 1939 and performed for spare change on street corners before becoming a favourite recording artist of the 1940s. He generated infectious charm and energy with his singing. One of the early electric guitarists in blues, Crudup provided himself with simple, rocking accompaniments. Among the songs written by him that became blues standards are "That's All Right," "Mean Old Frisco," "Rock Me Mama," and "So Glad You're Mine." Presley's recordings of three Crudup songs, including "That's All Right," sold millions of copies, but Crudup was not paid royalties. Disgusted with the recording business, he lived in Mississippi and Virginia and largely abandoned music apart from some blues revival appearances and the recording of at least three albums during a period from the late 1960s until his death.

Presley, whose version of Arthur "Big Boy" Crudup's "That's All Right" convinced Phillips he was on to something big. Presley's five singles for Sun are among the most notable pop records of the 20th century. Country, gospel, and blues came together and emerged as something entirely different, full of emotion, pride, and an irresistible sense of freedom.

Sun became a magnet for talented young artists throughout the South, including Carl Perkins, Johnny Cash, and Jerry Lee Lewis, all of whom Phillips recorded with patience, humour, and considerable inventiveness. His simple but ingenious use of echo helped to define the new sound of rock and roll.

## DUKE AND PEACOCK RECORDS

A decade before the ascendance of Motown, Houston's Duke and Peacock record labels flourished as an African American-owned company. Don Robey, a nightclub owner with reputed underworld connections, founded Peacock Records in 1949 and ran it with an iron hand. In 1952 Robey and James Mattias of Duke Records (founded in Memphis, Tennessee, earlier in the year) formed a partnership. A year later Robey became the outright owner of Duke and centralized its operation in Houston. The company's staples were gospel (the Five Blind Boys of Mississippi) and gospel-oriented blues (Bobby "Blue" Bland and Junior Parker, with arrangements by Joe Scott and Bill Harvey, respectively). In 1953 Willie Mae ("Big Mama") Thornton recorded the first version of "Hound Dog." In 1954 Duke's ballad singer Johnny Ace became the first martyr of the new teen era, losing at Russian roulette after a concert; his posthumous hit "Pledging My Love" became one of the most-played "oldies" in the decades that followed.

## MONUMENT RECORDS: ROY ORBISON'S MUSICAL LANDMARKS

Roy Orbison's sequence of nine Top Ten hits for Monument Records—from "Only the Lonely" in 1960 to "Oh, Pretty Woman" in 1964—placed him among the best-selling artists of his era. Yet his qualities had eluded three of the most accomplished producers of the period: Norman Petty, Sam Phillips, and Chet Atkins. Not until he teamed up with Fred Foster did Orbison find a kindred spirit who knew how to showcase his extraordinary talent.

Foster had launched Monument Records in 1958 from a base in Washington, D.C., but relocated the company to Nashville in 1960. He picked up his first artists from the unsigned hopefuls appearing on local television shows, one of whom, Billy Grammer, put the label in the national Top Five with its first release, "Gotta Travel On" (1958), a fusion of folk and pop. With cowriters Bill Dees and Joe Melson, Orbison wrote a series of spectacularly sombre ballads that plumbed the depths of teen misery; ignoring local prejudices, Foster framed Orbison's doleful vocals with variations of doo-wop backing vocals and soaring strings. Country stations ignored these majestic records, but the pop world did not, and Orbison was particularly revered in Britain. Orbison was signed to Acuff-Rose Publishing, though Foster also ran a strong publishing division—Combine Music—whose protégés included gravel-voiced baritones Tony Joe White and Kris Kristofferson.

# CHAPTER 12

# Rock and Radio

**R**adio and rock and roll needed each other, and it was their good fortune that they intersected at the exact moment when rock and roll was being born and radio was facing death. Radio had experienced a "Golden Age" since the 1930s, broadcasting popular swing bands and comedy, crime, and drama series. In the early 1950s, however, its standing as the electronic centre of family entertainment slipped. America had discovered television.

With a mass exodus of both the listeners and the stars of radio's staple programs, radio needed more than new shows if it was to survive. It needed something that would attract an entire new generation of listeners, something that would take advantage of technological advances. While television replaced radio in the living room, the invention of the transistor set the radio free. Teenagers no longer had to sit with their parents and siblings to hear radio entertainment. Now they could take radio into their bedrooms, into the night, and into their own private worlds. What they needed was a music to call their own. They got rock and roll.

They got it because radio, forced to invent new programming, turned to disc jockeys. The deejay concept had been around since Martin Block, in New York City, and Al Jarvis, in Los Angeles, began spinning records in the early 1930s. By the time the founders of Top 40 radio—Todd Storz and Bill Stewart in Omaha, Nebraska, and Gordon McLendon in

Dallas, Texas—came up with their formula of excitable deejays, contests, jingles, abbreviated news, and a playlist of 40 hit records, the deejay ranks had swelled and changed.

## RIGHT OF THE DIAL

At independent stations—those not affiliated with the networks that dominated the early years of radio—disc jockeys had played a wide range of music, and many of them discovered an audience that the larger stations had ignored: mostly younger people, many of them black. These were the disenfranchised, who felt that the popular music of the day spoke more to their parents than to them. What excited them was the music they could hear, usually late at night, coming from stations on the upper end of the radio dial, where signals tended to be weaker. Thus disadvantaged, owners of those stations had to take greater risks and to offer alternatives to the mainstream programming of their more powerful competitors. It was there that radio met rock and roll and sparked a revolution.

### WDIA: BLACK MUSIC MOTHER STATION

When WDIA went on the air in Memphis, Tennessee, in 1948, its white owners, Bert Ferguson and John R. Pepper, were anything but

blues aficionados; however, deejay Nat D. Williams was. A former high-school history teacher and journalist, Williams brought his own records and his familiarity with Memphis's blues hotbed Beale Street with him. But rather than aspiring to be a hipster, Williams acted as a cultural historian and gatekeeper, watching for lyrics that might be deemed offensive to WDIA's audience. The popularity of his show helped open WDIA to more black performers. B.B. King deejayed and sang commercial jingles at the station, and Rufus Thomas, a former student of Williams, joined the on-air staff in 1950. Together the three transformed WDIA into the South's first African American-oriented radio station, soon to be known throughout the region as the "Mother Station of the Negroes." Moreover, the station owners established several other successful rhythm-and-blues outlets, including KDIA in Oakland, California. Williams continued on the air until his health failed in the early 1970s. He died in 1983.

### WLAC: NASHVILLE'S LATE-NIGHT R&B BEACON

For many lovers of rock and roll, the station of choice was neither a local outlet nor a national network. It was something in between—WLAC, based in Nashville, Tennessee, which blasted 50,000 watts of varied programming, including plenty of rhythm and blues at night. In response to the contention that African Americans in rural areas of the South were still unserved by radio, the Federal Communications Commission granted WLAC permission to have one of the strongest signals in the country, provided that the station broadcast rhythm and blues.

Three white disc jockeys—John Richbourg, Gene Nobles, and Bill ("Hoss") Allen—brought fame to themselves and WLAC by playing rhythm and blues, at least partly in response to the requests of returning World War II veterans who had been exposed to the new music in other parts of the country. Nobles, who joined WLAC in 1943, was the host of *The Midnight Special*—just one of three programs he hosted on the station. A native of Arkansas and a former carnival barker, Nobles pushed the limits of deejay decorum, assaulting his listeners with insults and double entendres. Nobles retired in 1972 and died in 1989.

Hoss Allen, who began at WLAC as a utility deejay, is known for giving James Brown's "Please, Please, Please" its first airplay in 1956, spinning it, in fact, before it was an official release. The station had received a rough version of the song, and Allen, filling in one day for Nobles, tried it out and kept it on the air for two weeks. Nobles and Richbourg also played the record constantly, and the three shared credit for Brown's first chart success.

Richbourg, better known as John R., was loud and clear—mainly because he broadcast late at night, when there were fewer signals competing with that of WLAC, and because he worked hard at selling his music. Off the air, he also acted as a music promoter and manager. It was on the air, however, that he made his mark, as he invariably opened his show, "Yeah! It's the big John R., the blues man. Whoa! Have mercy, honey, have mercy, have mercy. John R., way down south in the middle of Dixie. I'm gonna spread a little joy. You stand still now and take it like a man, you hear me?"

## THE DEEJAYS

The first disc jockeys were both black and white; what they had in common was what they played: the hybrid of music that would evolve into rock. The first new formats were rhythm and blues and Top 40, with the latter exploding in popularity in the late 1950s.

### ALAN FREED

Alan Freed did not coin the phrase *rock and roll;* however, by way of his radio show, he popularized it and redefined it. Once slang for sex, it came to mean a new form of music. This music had

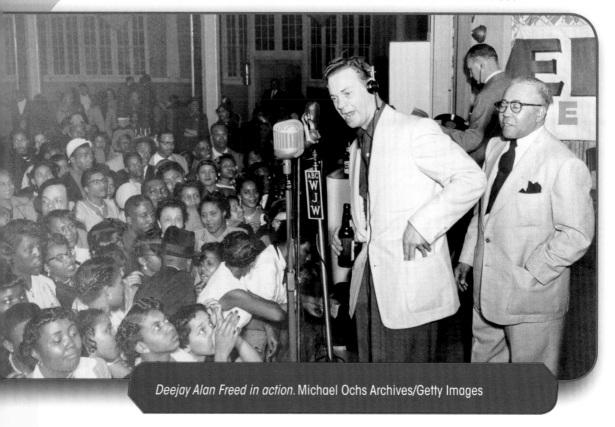

*Deejay Alan Freed in action.* Michael Ochs Archives/Getty Images

been around for several years, but Freed's primary accomplishment was the delivery of it to new—primarily young and white—listeners. Besides exposing his audience to blues, rhythm and blues, swing, and doo-wop, he brought black and white fans together at his dance concerts. He began staging his shows in Cleveland, Ohio, where he had joined WJW in 1951 and soon reigned as the "King of the Moon Doggers." Moving to New York City and WINS in 1954, he continued to produce lucrative concerts. For his efforts, he drew charges

of "race-mixing" and the attention of vigilant police. A disturbance at a concert in Boston in 1958 resulted in criminal charges against Freed and his departure from WINS. In 1960 he was enveloped in the congressional hearings on payola (money or gifts given to deejays by representatives of record companies in return for playing their records), and his career was in jeopardy. After relocating to Los Angeles, where he worked at KDAY for a short time, he was indicted on charges of tax evasion in 1964 and died in 1965. Freed was inducted into the Rock and Roll Hall of Fame in 1986.

## DEWEY PHILLIPS

Broadcasting on WHBQ in Memphis six nights a week from 9:00 PM until midnight, Dewey Phillips was tremendously popular with both black and white listeners in the 1950s. An excitable, flamboyant good old boy who seemed to have stepped from the pages of Al Capp's "Li'l Abner" comic strips but who played cutting-edge rhythm and blues, Phillips had an uncanny ability to pick hits and hit makers, including Jerry Lee Lewis and Memphis's own Elvis Presley.

When Sam Phillips (no relation) gave the deejay an advance copy of Presley's remake of "That's All Right" in July 1954, Dewey was floored. On his show the next night, he played the acetate some 30 times. He invited the singer to the studio for an interview, but Presley, aware his record might be played and anxious about it, had gone to the movies. Presley's parents hunted down their son and took him to the WHBQ studios. Phillips chatted with the shy, nervous Presley as if he were just getting him to relax. When Presley declared himself ready to begin the interview, Phillips told him that it was already over; he had left the microphone on during their warm-up conversation.

In 1956 Phillips hosted *Pop Shop,* a television dance program that was so popular locally that it kept *American Bandstand* off Memphis television screens for six months.

## GEORGE "HOUND DOG" LORENZ

Music lovers in more than a dozen states along the Eastern Seaboard in the 1950s tuned in to "the Sound of the Hound," George "Hound Dog" Lorenz, who broadcast on 50,000-watt WKBW in Buffalo, New York. Lorenz began in Buffalo radio in the late 1940s; in 1953 he moved to Cleveland, Ohio, where the Hound Dog went up against the King of the Moon Doggers, Alan Freed. Freed moved on to New York City, but Lorenz returned to Buffalo and became an institution on the "Big KB." He often did his show from the Club Zanzibar, a nightclub with a predominantly African American clientele; there he hosted visiting artists such as Little Richard, who credited Lorenz with being one of the first white deejays to carry black music all over the United States.

## AL BENSON

Critic and historian Nelson George called Al Benson, who worked at several Chicago radio stations beginning in the mid-1940s, one of the most influential black deejays of all time. While many of his African American peers were indistinguishable from white deejays over the airwaves, Benson, who was nicknamed "Yo' Ol' Swingmaster," never tried to mask what he called "native talk." By most accounts, however, Benson—who was known to drink while on the air—was often unintelligible. Yet for all the derision he drew, Benson attracted listeners—he was voted the most popular deejay in Chicago in a 1948 *Chicago Tribune* poll—and he wielded enormous power. In *The Death of Rhythm and Blues,* George quotes one of Benson's fellow announcers, who said of him, "He sounded black. They [the listeners] knew he was and most of us were proud of the fact. 'Here's a black voice coming out of my little radio and we know it's him.'"

## JACK THE RAPPER

Jack the Rapper (Jack Gibson) helped open the first African American-owned radio station in the United States, WERD in Atlanta, Georgia, in 1949. Gibson learned about radio while working as a gofer for deejay Al Benson in Chicago. He learned even more while at WERD, where he discovered that a white disc jockey received twice the amount of payola (in the form of "consulting fees") from record labels that he got.

After all, he was told, he was black and attracted black listeners, whereas the white deejay drew both black and white listeners. From Atlanta, Gibson moved on to Louisville, Kentucky, where he called himself Jockey Jack and wore jockey silks as a play on the name of his chosen profession. Later he became Jack the Rapper, a nickname he maintained through several stations and into his own business as publisher of *Jack the Rapper,* a radio industry publication, and as a producer of radio and music business conferences.

## WOLFMAN JACK

Possessed of one of the most distinctive voices and styles in radio, Wolfman Jack played rhythm and blues and partied wildly in the studios—or at least it sounded like he did. He told listeners that he was "nekkid" and urged them to disrobe as well. In a raspy voice that alternated from a purr to a roar, he sold his music, himself, and a myriad of patent medicines and oldies albums on powerful stations located in Mexico, just across the border from the United States. Armed with 250,000-watt signals, his nighttime shows on stations such as Ciudad Acuña's XERF reached most of North America beginning in the early 1960s. After a series of legal and political problems forced him to do his show

# THE SOUND OF LOS ANGELES

Capitol Records was launched in Los Angeles in 1942 in association with the British company EMI and soon became a serious rival to the major New York City-based companies, but no other major label appeared on the West Coast until Warner Brothers launched a record division in 1958. Among the independent labels that sprang up to record local artists and meet the tastes of the city's rapidly expanding population during the 1940s, Modern, Imperial, Aladdin, and Specialty survived long enough to enjoy pop success in the mid-1950s.

Art Rupe, a graduate of the University of California, Los Angeles, and the owner of Specialty Records, started out by recording local black artists for the jukebox market. He soon built a strong roster of small combos led by Roy Milton and brothers Jimmy and Joe Liggins as well as gospel groups such as the Soul Stirrers and the Pilgrim Travelers. Specialty scored three of the biggest rhythm-and-blues hits of the early 1950s with "Please Send Me Someone to Love" by Percy Mayfield (1950), "Lawdy Miss Clawdy" by Lloyd Price (1952), and "The Things That I Used to Do" by Guitar Slim (1954), the last two recorded in New Orleans, Louisiana, with musicians from Fats Domino's session band. When Rupe added Little Richard to his roster in 1955, newly appointed artists-and-repertoire man Robert ("Bumps") Blackwell went to New Orleans for the label's first session with Richard, which resulted in "Tutti Frutti." Richard turned out to be Specialty's biggest artist. Rupe missed a chance for even greater success with Sam Cooke. The young lead singer of the Soul Stirrers recorded "You Send Me" at Specialty's studio under the supervision of Blackwell, but an unconvinced Rupe (determined not to lose his gospel star to secular music) terminated the contracts of both singer and producer. Rupe then watched ruefully as the single topped the pop charts on another local label, Keen.

and Cooke emerged as one of the biggest artists of the era. The scrupulous Rupe stayed in business for several more years but was never comfortable with the practice of payola.

While some Los Angeles-based labels found the teen market almost by accident—simply by being there and having the rhythm-and-blues and rock-and-roll music that white kids suddenly wanted—several other labels were formed deliberately to meet this new market. Most were small fly-by-night operations, but two substantial independent companies emerged to rival the majors—Dot and Liberty.

Dot was founded in Gallatin, Tennessee, by record shop owner Randy Wood, who made a specialty of covering rhythm-and-blues hits with pop versions by white singers Pat Boone, Gale Storm, and the Fontane Sisters. The company became even more successful after Wood moved to a Hollywood base in 1956, notably with records by film star Tab Hunter. Liberty was driven by salesman Al Bennett, whose artists-and-repertoire man, "Snuff" Garrett, had a flair for matching songs and singers to meet the new teen market—making the most of the talents of Johnny Burnette, Bobby Vee, and the more authentic Eddie Cochran.

Radio was also a crucial element of the Los Angeles music scene, and no one was a more important on-air presence than Hunter Hancock, who is remembered as the first white disc jockey to play rhythm-and-blues records in southern California, where he went on the air on KFVD in 1943 playing his first love, jazz. On the advice of a friend, he began including a few "race" (rhythm-and-blues) records in his show, and his popularity soared. In the early 1950s he began moonlighting on another Los Angeles station, KGFJ, doing a show aimed at African American listeners. A Texan and product of the Old South, Hancock now found himself ostracized by some white listeners. Nevertheless, his show, *Huntin' with Hunter,* also known as *Harlem Matinee,* enjoyed great success into the mid-1960s.

by tape, the Wolfman took charge of XERB in Tijuana in 1966, hiring a mix of favourite disc jockeys and medicine men to fill the time. For his own show, he set up shop in a studio in Los Angeles and shipped his tapes to Mexico, where they were broadcast, reaching back to Hollywood and far beyond.

Before he became Wolfman Jack, Robert Weston Smith grew up in New York City and later became a country music deejay. It was as Wolfman Jack, however, that he became a cult figure and icon of rock-and-roll radio. George Lucas typecast him as a mysterious deejay in his coming-of-age film *American Graffiti* (1973), and the Wolfman went on to host television's *Midnight Special*—featuring popular rock, soul, folk, and country performers—and to achieve success in syndicated radio.

*Wolfman Jack.* Michael Ochs Archives/Getty Images

## GORDON MCLENDON AND KLIF

Gordon McLendon, the Texas broadcaster who is credited (along with Todd Storz and Bill Stewart) with the creation of Top 40 radio, owned KLIF in Dallas, Texas. In 1953 he switched from live music and magazine-style programming to records and disc jockeys. By then an in-house musical ensemble had been producing station jingles—an idea that quickly spread throughout radio—and McLendon added wild contests and promotions, along with an emphasis on local news, to the mix. At its peak KLIF drew some 40 percent of Dallas's listeners. Many of them tuned in to the nighttime shenanigans of Russ ("Weird Beard") Knight. Holder of a master's degree in journalism and the self-proclaimed "savior of Dallas radio," Knight had a larger-than-life personality, a way with rhymes, and a penchant for the sound effects of the day (horns, whistles, and echo machines).

# CHAPTER 13

# Motown

**M**oving from Georgia to Detroit, Michigan, Berry Gordy, Jr.,'s family was part of the massive migration of hundreds of thousands of African Americans from the South during and after World War I, lured largely by the promise of work in Northern manufacturing industries such as Detroit's auto plants. Gordy's parents, hardworking entrepreneurs, instilled in their children the gospel of hard work and religious faith. They also played a major role in financing Gordy in his early years in the music business.

Following an attempt at a professional boxing career and a stint in the army during the Korean War, Gordy (born November 28, 1929, Detroit) entered the music business. He briefly owned a jazz record store, but his true love was songwriting. Although he could not read music, he demonstrated an unerring ability to gauge whether a song had the elements of popular appeal. Before forming Motown, Gordy tried to make it as an independent songwriter and record producer, cowriting hit songs for Jackie Wilson, another former boxer and Detroiter, and Marv Johnson. Despite his success, Gordy remained on the fringes of the popular music business, making very little money, until he discovered William ("Smokey") Robinson, a Detroit high schooler with a soothing falsetto and an ear for sweet lyrics.

In 1959, not long after recording Robinson's group, the Miracles, for New York-based End Records and establishing

Having just sung a tribute to his Motown mentor at a 50th anniversary celebration of the legendary record company, Smokey Robinson warmly embraces Berry Gordy, Oct. 20, 2007, Detroit. Bill Pugliano/Getty Images

Jobete Publishing Company, Gordy began Motown Records (its name derived from Detroit's nickname, "Motor City"). Three major factors came together to make Motown's success possible at this time. First, after World War II, big-band swing, the dominant popular dance music in the United States during the Great Depression, became passé. Big musical units were no longer economically feasible. Jazz had been taken over by a new group of Young Turk stylists; calling themselves beboppers, they were inclined to play music for listening rather than dancing.

The second factor in Motown's success was the ascendance of a new urban dance music: rhythm and blues. Emerging primarily from inner-city ghettos and popularized by such bandleaders as Louis Jordan and Lionel Hampton, rhythm and blues was almost exclusively recorded by small independent labels. Of the three major recording companies—Columbia, Capitol, and Decca—only the last showed any interest in the

# THE MOTOR CITY

Even before Berry Gordy, Jr., brought Detroit to musical prominence in the 1960s with Motown Records, the Motor City had been the site of important recordings by John Lee Hooker and the base for rhythm-and-blues performers Hank Ballard and Jackie Wilson. It also was the home of the New Bethel Baptist Church, presided over by the Reverend C.L. Franklin, whose daughter Aretha's first gospel records were made in the church. The Flame Show Bar and Twenty Grand nightclub presented rhythm-and-blues greats such as Sam Cooke and LaVern Baker in the 1950s and later were showcases (and downtime haunts) for Motown artists. Not far from Detroit, in Idlewild, a predominantly African American resort community near the Manistee National Forest, musical acts performed in clubs where the traditions of black vaudeville became building blocks for Motown showmanship.

In the late 1960s Detroit was the breeding ground for the influential proto-punk bands Iggy and the Stooges and the MC5. They practiced their loud, hard-rocking style on the stage of the Grande (pronounced "Grandee") Ballroom, which had been created in the image of San Francisco's psychedelic rock ballrooms. Detroit also played an important role in the history of rock criticism. Founded in 1969, edited by Dave Marsh, and featuring the writing of Lester Bangs, *Creem* magazine offered an early alternative to *Rolling Stone*.

exciting new music that would spawn rock and roll. During the 1950s it was possible for a young entrepreneur with an ear for this music to start a moderately successful independent company producing a sound that appealed to young people and inner-city African Americans.

The final ingredient in Motown's rise was that Gordy was not going into completely uncharted territory as a black music entrepreneur. By the late 1950s, two other black-owned independent record companies that specialized in rhythm and blues and rock and roll had been enjoying considerable success for nearly a decade—Peacock Records, formed in Houston, Texas, by Don Robey, and Vee Jay Records, formed in Chicago by Vivian Carter Bracken, James Bracken, and Calvin Carter. Advancement for blacks was happening in other arenas, as well. In 1959, the year Gordy founded Motown, Harry Belafonte became the first black to produce a Hollywood film, *Odds Against Tomorrow,* through his own company. The social change promised by the 1954 *Brown* v. *Board of Education of Topeka* school desegregation decision and the new civil rights activism made this a heady time indeed to be an enterprising African American—anything seemed possible. Moreover, black radio had become a force in the marketing of popular music after World War II. This gave black listeners great clout as consumers and made it possible for black record company owners to market their wares directly to this growing audience.

## "HITSVILLE"

During the 1960s Motown became one of the reigning presences in American popular music, along with the Beatles. Gordy (who was inducted into the Rock and Roll Hall of Fame in 1988) assembled an array of talented local people (many of whom had benefited from the excellent music education program at Detroit public schools in the 1950s) at 2648 West Grand Boulevard, destined to become the most famous address in Detroit. Serving as both recording studio and administrative headquarters, this two-story house became the home of "Hitsville." Motown's roster included several successful solo acts, such as Marvin Gaye, Stevie Wonder (a star as both a child and an adult), and Mary Wells. In addition to the Miracles, who notched Motown's first million-selling single, "Shop Around" (1960), there were several young singing groups, including the Temptations, Martha and the Vandellas, and the Marvelettes. There also were a number of somewhat older groups that scored big, such as the Four Tops, the Contours, and Junior Walker and the All-Stars. A number of acts that were not developed by Motown wound up enjoying hit records during a stint with the company, including the Isley Brothers and Gladys Knight and the Pips.

Yet, despite the considerable acclaim these performers garnered, no Motown act of the 1960s matched the success of the Supremes, a girl group that scored number one hits with "Where Did Our Love Go," "Baby Love," "Come See About Me" (all

*The Jackson 5 at the 1970 NAACP Image Awards, Los Angeles, California. From left, Jackie, Tito, Michael, Jermaine, and Marlon Jackson.* Fotos International/Archive Photos/Getty Images

1964), "Stop! In the Name of Love," "Back in My Arms Again," "I Hear a Symphony" (all 1965), and "You Can't Hurry Love" (1966). Not only were they the second most successful singing group of the decade—surpassed only by the Beatles—but they remain the most successful female singing group of all time. The group's glamorous lead singer, Diana Ross, went on to a remarkable solo career as a singer and a moderately successful career as an actress.

Not only did Motown's acts become famous but its songwriters and producers also became household, or at least familiar, names. Brian Holland, Lamont Dozier, and Eddie Holland, who wrote and produced most of the Supremes' mid-1960s hits, were nearly as famous as the Supremes themselves, and their squabble with Gordy over money, which resulted in a nasty lawsuit and their departure from the company, was major industry news. Robinson was an important

# REPRESENTATIVE WORKS

- The Miracles, "Shop Around" (1960)
- The Marvelettes, "Please Mr. Postman" (1961)
- Mary Wells, "You Beat Me to the Punch" (1962)
- Martha and the Vandellas, "Heat Wave" (1963 )
- Stevie Wonder, "Fingertips (Part 2)" (1963)
- Martha and the Vandellas, "Dancing in the Street" (1964)
- The Supremes, "Baby Love" (1964)
- The Supremes, "Where Did Our Love Go" (1964)
- The Temptations, "My Girl" (1964)
- Mary Wells, "My Guy" (1964)
- The Four Tops, "I Can't Help Myself" (1965)
- The Miracles, "Ooo Baby Baby" (1965)
- The Miracles, "The Tracks of My Tears" (1965)
- The Supremes, "Stop! In the Name of Love" (1965)
- The Four Tops, "Standing in the Shadows of Love" (1966)
- The Marvelettes, "Don't Mess with Bill" (1966)
- Marvin Gaye, "I Heard It Through the Grapevine" (1968)
- The Jackson 5, "I Want You Back" (1969)
- The Jackson 5, "I'll Be There" (1970)
- Smokey Robinson and the Miracles, "The Tears of a Clown" (1970)
- Diana Ross, "Ain't No Mountain High Enough" (1970)
- Marvin Gaye, *What's Going On* (1971)
- Marvin Gaye, *Trouble Man* (1972)
- The Temptations, "Papa Was a Rollin' Stone" (1972)
- Stevie Wonder, *Music of My Mind* (1972)
- Marvin Gaye, *Let's Get It On* (1973)
- Diana Ross, "Touch Me in the Morning" (1973)
- Stevie Wonder, *Songs in the Key of Life* (1976)

songwriter at Motown, as were Sylvia Moy, Norman Whitfield, Mickey Stevenson, Ivy Joe Hunter, and Gordy himself. All these songwriters were also producers. Some were assigned by Gordy to work with specific acts. Such fame did some of Motown's writers achieve and such problems did their fame cause for Gordy that, when the Jackson 5 were signed by the company in 1969, the team that wrote the group's early hits was credited simply as the Corporation.

## THE MOTOWN SOUND

Motown had an extraordinary house band (known as the Funk Brothers) made up of some of the best nightclub and bar musicians in black Detroit, including Earl Van Dyke on keyboards, Benny Benjamin and Uriel Jones on drums, and James Jamerson on bass. They played a huge role in the development of the Motown sound, a branch of soul music that featured more sophisticated arrangements and orchestration than the grittier Southern soul that contemporaneously flourished at Stax Records as the Memphis Sound. Motown brought together rhythm-and-blues, gospel, and pop influences as it sought to "cross over" (i.e., move beyond single-genre listeners) to reach a wide audience that included white teenagers. Motown records were specifically mixed to sound good on car radios and were characterized by a thumping backbeat that made dancing easy for everyone. Motown sought to be and became the "Sound of Young America."

## QUALITY CONTROL

Despite its great number of hits, Motown was actually a small company, but it was run with unmatched efficiency. Gordy prided himself on having learned about producing a quality product from a brief stint on the assembly line at an auto plant. He had rigorous quality control meetings, and only records that could pass the harsh criticism of his assembled brain trust were released. As a result of Gordy's stringent measures, at the height of its popularity (in the mid- to late 1960s), Motown enjoyed the highest hit ratio for its released singles of any record company in history. In truth, Gordy had to employ these extraordinary means if a company as small as his was to survive against bigger companies in the popular music business.

Artist development at Motown was comprehensive. Equal parts finishing school and academy of popular arts, the company provided its acts with elaborate choreography under the tutelage of Cholly Atkins. Young women raised in public housing projects, like the Supremes, were schooled in the social graces, and chaperones accompanied the package-tour bus cavalcades that brought Motown to other parts of the United States during the company's early years.

## LATER YEARS

Motown enjoyed its greatest success between 1965 and 1968, when it dominated the *Billboard* charts. Although the company was never quite the force in the 1970s that it was in the '60s (having lost several key performers), it was still a formidable enterprise with the Jackson 5, the Commodores, Wonder, and Ross. In 1971 Motown released what became, arguably, the most influential soul record ever, Gaye's *What's Going On*. In the late 1960s Detroit was wracked with violent race riots, and in the early '70s the company relocated to Los Angeles, where its move into filmmaking was generally fruitful. Motown's most famous film, *Lady Sings the Blues* (1972), starred Ross and was loosely based on the career of jazz singer Billie Holiday.

In the 1980s Gordy found it difficult to prosper in a music industry increasingly dominated by multinational conglomerates, and in 1988 he sold Motown to MCA, which later sold the company to PolyGram. Motown remained a force in popular music—a vital, near-primal influence with stunning longevity. No one has quite been able to reproduce the classic Motown Sound.

# CHAPTER 14

# Motown Cavalcade

To consider the Motown Sound separately from the soul music that was created contemporaneously in other parts of the United States creates a divide that is not completely helpful. Motown music *was* soul music, but it also was polished and the most popular crossover music of its day. It billed itself not as the sound of young black Americans but as the "Sound of Young America." As such, it was accessible to many white Americans who were not yet ready to embrace the grittier, more Afrocentric soul of James Brown, Aretha Franklin and the stable of artists recording for Stax in Memphis. Proud and, as the '60s went on, increasingly politicized, Motown music was for most of the decade the soundtrack of integrationist aspiration and interracial solidarity.

## SMOKEY ROBINSON AND THE MIRACLES

Whether writing for fellow artists Mary Wells, the Temptations, or Marvin Gaye or performing with the Miracles, singer-lyricist-arranger-producer Smokey Robinson created songs that were supremely balanced between the joy and pain of love. At once playful and passionate, Robinson's graceful lyrics led Bob Dylan to call him "America's greatest living poet." In addition to Robinson (born William Robinson, February 19, 1940, Detroit, Michigan, U.S.), the principal members of the Miracles were Warren Moore (born November 19,

1939, Detroit), Bobby Rogers (born February 19, 1940, Detroit), Ronnie White (born April 5, 1939, Detroit), and Claudette Rogers (born 1942).

Coming of age in the doo-wop era and deeply influenced by jazz vocalist Sarah Vaughan, Robinson formed the Five Chimes with school friends in the mid-1950s. After some personnel changes, the group, as the Matadors, auditioned unsuccessfully for Jackie Wilson's manager. However, they greatly impressed Wilson's songwriter Berry Gordy, who soon became their manager and producer. Most importantly, Gordy became Robinson's mentor, harnessing his prodigious but unformed composing talents, and Robinson, assisted by the Miracles, became Gordy's inspiration for the creation of Motown Records.

With the arrival of Claudette Rogers, the group changed its name to the Miracles and released "Got a Job" on End Records in 1958. The Miracles struggled onstage in their first performance at the Apollo Theatre that year, but good fortune came their way in the form of Marv Tarplin (born June 13, 1941, Atlanta, Georgia—died September 30, 2011, Las Vegas, Nevada), guitarist for the Primettes, who were led by Robinson's friend Diana Ross. Tarplin became an honorary (but essential) Miracle, while Robinson introduced Gordy to the Primettes, who soon became the Supremes.

In 1959 Robinson and Claudette Rogers were married, and "Bad Girl," licensed to Chess Records, peaked nationally at number 93. The fiery "Way Over There" and the shimmering "(You Can) Depend on Me" were followed in 1960 by "Shop Around," the second version of which became an enormous hit, reaching number one on the rhythm-and-blues charts and number two on the pop charts.

While Robinson was writing such vital songs as "My Guy" for Mary Wells, "I'll Be Doggone" for Marvin Gaye, and "My Girl" for the Temptations, he and the Miracles proceeded to record stunning compositions, including "You've Really Got a Hold on Me" (1962), "I'll Try Something New" (1962), "Ooo Baby Baby" (1965), "Choosey Beggar" (1965), "The Tracks of My Tears" (1965), and "More Love" (1967, written following the premature birth and death of Robinson's twin daughters). The Miracles complemented their songs of aching romance and mature love with buoyant numbers such as "Mickey's Monkey" (1963), "Going to a Go-Go" (1965), "I Second That Emotion" (1967), and "The Tears of a Clown" (1970).

In 1972 Robinson left the Miracles to pursue a solo career. Without him the Miracles enjoyed moderate success in subsequent years—the disco-era "Love Machine (Part 1)" hit number one on the pop charts in 1975—while Robinson produced such solo hits as "Cruisin' " (1979) and "Being with You" (1981). He also unintentionally inspired the new soul radio format that took its name from the title track of his 1975 conceptual album *A Quiet Storm*. Robinson was inducted into the Rock and Roll Hall of Fame in 1987. The Miracles were selected for induction in 2012.

## MARTHA AND THE VANDELLAS

The group that became Martha and the Vandellas was founded in 1960 as the Del-Phis, which consisted of school friends from Detroit. The original members were Martha Reeves (born July 18, 1941, Eufaula, Alabama, U.S.), Annette Beard Sterling-Helton (born July 4, 1943, Detroit, Michigan), Rosalind Ashford (born September 2, 1943, Detroit), and Gloria Williams. Later members included Betty Kelly (born September 16, 1944, Attalla, Alabama), Lois Reeves (born April 12, 1948, Detroit), and Sandra Tilley (born May 6, 1946). Their big break came in 1962 when Reeves, then working as a secretary at Motown, landed them the chance to provide backing vocals for recording sessions by Marvin Gaye. So impressed was Motown head Berry Gordy, Jr., that he signed the group (a trio as a result of Williams's departure) to his label. The group's new

name, Martha and the Vandellas, was derived from the names of a Detroit street (Van Dyke) and one of Reeves's favourite singers (Della Reese). Their raw, soulful sound flourished under the guidance of the renowned songwriting-production team Holland-Dozier-Holland and produced a string of hits, including "Come and Get These Memories" (1963), "(Love Is Like a) Heat Wave" (1963), "Nowhere to Run" (1965), and "Jimmy Mack" (1967). Their biggest hit, "Dancing in the Street" (1964), was cowritten by Gaye. A shifting lineup of Vandellas had limited success into the 1970s, and Reeves embarked on a solo career in 1974. Martha and the Vandellas were inducted into the Rock and Roll Hall of Fame in 1995.

## THE SUPREMES

Not only were the Supremes the Motown label's primary crossover act, they also helped change the public image of African Americans during the civil rights era. With their sequined evening gowns and the sophisticated pop-soul swing given them by Brian Holland, Lamont Dozier, and Eddie Holland from 1964 to 1967, the Supremes were the idealized look and sound of the "integrated Negro." Indeed, the youth of America learned many of its first lessons about racial equality from teen magazines

*The Supremes. From left to right, Cindy Birdsong, Diana Ross, and Mary Wilson.* Michael Ochs Archives/Getty Images

that documented every hyperglamourized move the Supremes made as they went from topping the pop chart to appearances on "The Ed Sullivan Show" to sold-out Las Vegas, Nevada, bookings.

The principal members of the group were Diana Ross (born Diane Earle, March 26, 1944, Detroit, Michigan, U.S.), Florence Ballard (born June 30, 1943, Detroit—died February 22, 1976, Detroit), Mary Wilson (born March 6, 1944, Greenville, Mississippi), and Cindy Birdsong (born December 15, 1939, Camden, New Jersey). Their story began humbly enough when a group of working-class girls from Detroit's Brewster public housing project formed a singing group called the Primettes, their name derived from their sister-act association with the Primes, a forerunner of the Temptations. The details of the group's formation (namely, who came first) have been disputed, but, from a series of permutations of five principals (including, initially, Betty

McGlown), a quartet emerged that comprised Ballard, Barbara Martin, Ross, and Wilson. After recording briefly with Lupine Records, the quartet signed with Motown in 1960. They changed their name to the Supremes before releasing their first Motown single in 1961, and upon the subsequent departure of Martin the remaining trio went on to score five U.S. number one hits in a row between 1964 and 1965.

But the Supremes didn't catch on right away. It took a while to create the distinctive look and sound that ultimately made them famous. Berry Gordy, Jr., unsuccessfully paired the group with different musicians and songs for three years until he finally stumbled upon the right formula. In 1964 Holland-Dozier-Holland gave the Supremes their first number one single with "Where Did Our Love Go." Embellishing Ross's precise, breathy phrasing with chiming bells and a subdued rhythm section gave the Supremes an intentional lack of identifiable ethnicity. Not really sounding "white" or stereotypically "black," hit singles like "Baby Love" and "Come See About Me" (both 1964) sounded modern, upwardly mobile, and stylishly sensual in a way that appealed equally to adults and teens of all persuasions.

The group continued to rack up chart-topping hits but was ultimately pulled apart by conflicting individual and corporate ambitions. By the end of 1967, the Supremes had lost both Ballard (who was replaced by Birdsong) and producers Holland-Dozier-Holland. The group continued recording for two more years as Diana Ross and the Supremes, largely to prepare the public for Ross's solo career. Jean Terrell became the first of many new group members who helped Wilson keep the Supremes alive and recording for seven years after Ross departed in 1970.

Ross's solo career was greatly aided by starring roles in films financed by her longtime mentor, Gordy. *Lady Sings the Blues* (1972), *Mahogany* (1975), and *The Wiz* (1978) and their soundtrack albums kept Ross in the public eye and ear for most of the 1970s. *The Boss* (1979), produced by Nickolas Ashford and Valerie Simpson, and *Diana* (1980), produced by Chic's Nile Rodgers and Bernard Edwards, were both hits, but aside from a controversial concert in Central Park, New York City, in 1983 and some American television appearances, Ross spent the rest of the 1980s and '90s cultivating a foreign fan base that outstripped her popularity in the United States.

The Supremes were inducted into the Rock and Roll Hall of Fame in 1988.

# HOLLAND-DOZIER-HOLLAND

Prior to their formation as a songwriting and production team, Lamont Dozier (born June 16, 1941, Detroit, Michigan, U.S.) and Eddie Holland (born October 30, 1939, Detroit) had both pursued careers as singers, while Holland's brother Brian (born February 15, 1941, Detroit) had collaborated with other Motown producers and songwriters, including Dozier. In 1963 Berry Gordy, Jr., matched Holland-Dozier-Holland with the then hitless Supremes. Beginning with "Where Did Our Love Go" (1964) and continuing through "In and Out of Love" (1967), the trio wrote and produced more than a dozen U.S. Top Ten singles for the Supremes. Dozier's forte was melodies, Eddie Holland's was lyrics, and Brian Holland's was producing. Leaving Motown in 1968 after battling with Gordy over royalties, they began their own record company, Invictus/Hot Wax, for which Freda Payne, Honey Cone, and the Chairmen of the Board recorded. Holland-Dozier-Holland were inducted into the Rock and Roll Hall of Fame in 1990.

# THE TEMPTATIONS

The Temptations were among the most popular performers of soul music in the 1960s and '70s. The principal members of the group were Otis Williams (born Otis Miles, October 30, 1949, Texarkana, Texas, U.S.), Paul Williams (born 2, 1939, Birmingham, Alabama—died August 17, 1973, Detroit, Michigan), Melvin Franklin (born David English, October 12, 1942, Montgomery, Alabama—died February 23, 1995, Los Angeles, California), Eddie Kendricks (born December 17, 1939, Union Springs, Alabama—died October 5, 1992, Birmingham), David Ruffin (born Davis Eli Ruffin, January 18, 1941, Meridian, Mississippi—died June 1, 1991, Philadelphia, Pennsylvania), and Dennis Edwards (born February 3, 1943, Birmingham).

Originally called the Elgins, the Temptations were formed in 1961 from the coupling of two vocal groups based in Detroit—the Primes, originally from Alabama, and the Distants. That same year they signed with Motown. After a slow start—with the addition of Ruffin and largely under the direction of songwriter-producer Smokey Robinson—the Temptations turned out a string of romantic hits, beginning with "The Way You Do the Things You Do" (1964) and including "My Girl" (1964), "Get Ready" (1966), and "Beauty Is Only Skin Deep" (1966). Bass Franklin, baritone Otis Williams, and occasional lead Paul Williams provided complex

*The Temptations in 1965: David Ruffin* (front), *Paul Williams* (centre left), *Eddie Kendricks* (centre right), *Melvin Franklin* (back left), *and Otis Williams* (back right). Hulton Archive/Getty Images

harmonies, and the two regular lead singers, Ruffin and Kendricks, strikingly complemented each other. Ruffin had a remarkable sandpaper baritone and Kendricks a soaring tenor. Paragons of sleek fashion and practitioners of athletic choreography (provided by Paul Williams and Motown's house choreographer, Cholly Atkins), the "Tempts" epitomized sophisticated cool.

In the late 1960s they shifted to a more funk-oriented sound and to more socially conscious material when Norman Whitfield became the group's producer and principal songwriter (along with partner Barrett Strong). Influenced by psychedelic rock and with Edwards replacing Ruffin (who had embarked on a solo career), the Temptations produced hits such as "Cloud Nine" (1968), "Runaway Child, Running Wild" (1969), "Psychedelic Shack" (1970), "Ball of Confusion (That's What the World Is Today)" (1970), and the Grammy Award-winning "Papa Was a Rollin' Stone" (1972). In 1968–69 they were paired with Diana Ross and the Supremes for two television specials and recordings that included "I'm Gonna Make You Love Me" (1968) and "I'll Try Something New" (1969). In 1971 Kendricks left to pursue a solo career, notable for "Keep On Truckin'" (1973). From the mid-1970s the Temptations changed personnel frequently and produced occasional hits, but they never regained the form that earned them induction into the Rock and Roll Hall of Fame in 1989.

## THE FOUR TOPS

The Four Tops formed after singing together at a party in 1953, calling themselves until 1956 the Four Aims. The members were Renaldo ("Obie") Benson (born June 14, 1936, Detroit, Michigan, U.S.—died July 1, 2005, Detroit), Abdul ("Duke") Fakir (born December 26, 1935, Detroit), Lawrence Payton (born 1938, Detroit—died June 20, 1997, Southfield, Michigan), and Levi Stubbs (born Levi Stubbles, June 6, 1936, Detroit—died October 17, 2008, Detroit). They spent a decade performing primarily jazz-oriented material in clubs and releasing poorly received singles before signing with Motown Records. Under the stewardship of the Holland-Dozier-Holland team, the Four Tops became consistent hit makers, registering their first hit, "Baby I Need Your Loving," in 1964. "I Can't Help Myself" (number one on the pop and rhythm-and-blues charts in the United States) and "It's the Same Old Song" followed in 1965, establishing the group's signature sound: Stubbs's gruff, passionate lead vocals set against gentler background harmonies. The group reached a pinnacle of fame in 1966 with its second million-seller, "Reach Out I'll Be There." Splitting with Motown in 1972 when the label relocated to California but returning for another five-year stint with the company in the mid-1980s, the group's original lineup continued to tour and record together throughout the 1970s, '80s, and '90s. The Four Tops were inducted into the Rock and Roll Hall of Fame in 1990.

## STEVIE WONDER

Blind from birth and raised in inner-city Detroit, Stevie Wonder (born

*Stevie Wonder.* PRNewsFoto/BET Black Entertainment Television/AP Images

Steveland Judkins or Steveland Morris, May 13, 1950, Saginaw, Michigan, U.S.) was a skilled musician by age eight. Renamed Little Stevie Wonder by Berry Gordy, Jr.—to whom he was introduced by Ronnie White, a member of the Miracles—Wonder made his recording debut at age 12. The soulful quality of his high-pitched singing and the frantic harmonica playing that characterized his early recordings were evident in his first hit single, "Fingertips (Part 2)," recorded during a show at Chicago's Regal Theatre in 1963. But Wonder was much more than a freakish prepubescent imitation of Ray Charles, as audiences discovered when he demonstrated his prowess with piano, organ, harmonica, and drums. By 1964 he was no longer described as "Little," and two years later his fervent delivery of the pounding soul of "Uptight (Everything's Alright)," which he also had written, suggested the emergence of both an unusually compelling performer and a composer to rival Motown's stable of skilled songwriters. (He had already cowritten, with Smokey Robinson, "The Tears of a Clown.")

Over the next five years Wonder had hits with "I Was Made to Love Her," "My Cherie Amour" (both cowritten with producer Henry Cosby), and "For Once in My Life," songs that suited dancers as well as lovers. *Where I'm Coming From*, an album

released in 1971, hinted not merely at an expanded musical range but, in its lyrics and its mood, at a new introspection. *Music of My Mind* (1972) made his concerns even more plain. In the interim he had been strongly influenced by Marvin Gaye's *What's Going On*, the album in which Gaye moved away from the label's "hit factory" approach to confront the divisive social issues of the day. Any anxieties Gordy may have felt about his protégé's declaration of independence were amply calmed by the run of recordings with which Wonder obliterated the competition in the mid-1970s. Those albums produced a steady stream of classic hit songs, among them "Superstition," "You Are the Sunshine of My Life," "Higher Ground," "Living for the City," "Don't You Worry 'Bout a Thing," "Boogie On Reggae Woman," "I Wish," and "Sir Duke."

Although still only in his mid-20s, Wonder appeared to have mastered virtually every idiom of African American popular music and to have synthesized them all into a language of his own. His command of the new generation of electronic keyboard instruments made him a pioneer and an inspiration to rock musicians, the inventiveness of his vocal phrasing was reminiscent of the greatest jazz singers, and the depth and honesty of his emotional projection came straight from the black church music of his childhood. Such a fertile period was unlikely to last forever, and it came to an end in 1979 with a fey and overambitious extended work called *Stevie Wonder's Journey Through the Secret Life of Plants*. Thereafter his recordings became sporadic and often lacked focus, although his concerts were never less than rousing. The best of his work formed a vital link between the classic rhythm-and-blues and soul performers of the 1950s and '60s and their less commercially constrained successors. Yet, however sophisticated his music became, he was never too proud to write something as apparently slight as the romantic gem "I Just Called to Say I Love You" (1984). He was inducted into the Rock and Roll Hall of Fame in 1989 and received a Grammy Award for lifetime achievement in 2005. In 2008 the Library of Congress announced that Wonder was the recipient of its Gershwin Prize for Popular Song.

## MARVIN GAYE

To a large extent singer-songwriter-producer Marvin Gaye (born Marvin Pentz Gay, Jr., April 2, 1939, Washington, D.C., U.S.—died April 1, 1984, Los Angeles, California) ushered in the era of artist-controlled popular music of the 1970s. Gaye's father was a storefront preacher; his mother was a domestic worker. Gaye sang in his father's Evangelical church in Washington, D.C., and became a member of a nationally known doo-wop group, the Moonglows, under the direction of Harvey Fuqua, one of the genre's foremost maestros, who relocated the group to Chicago.

When doo-wop dissipated in the late 1950s, Gaye had already absorbed Fuqua's lessons in close harmony. After disbanding the Moonglows, Fuqua took the 20-year-old Gaye to Detroit, Michigan, where Berry Gordy, Jr., was forming Motown Records.

Gaye, who also played drums and piano, bucked the Motown system and its emphasis on teen hits. He was set on being a crooner in the Nat King Cole–Frank Sinatra vein, but his first efforts in that style failed. His break came with "Stubborn Kinda Fellow" (1962), the first of a long string of hits in the Motown mold—mainly songs written and produced by others, including "I'll Be Doggone" (1965), by Smokey Robinson, and "I Heard It Through the Grapevine" (1968), by Norman Whitfield. Gaye also enjoyed a series of successful duets, most notably with Tammi Terrell ("Ain't Nothing Like the Real Thing" [1968]).

Blessed with an exceptionally wide range that encompassed three distinct vocal styles—a piercing falsetto, a smooth mid-range tenor, and a deep gospel growl—Gaye combined great technical prowess with rare musical individuality. Rebellious by nature, he turned the tables on Motown's producer-driven hierarchy by becoming his own producer for *What's Going On* (1971), the most significant work of his career. A suite of jazz-influenced songs on the nature of America's political and social woes, this concept album—still a novel format at the time—painted a poignant landscape of America's black urban neighbourhoods. Gaye also displayed dazzling virtuosity by overdubbing (building sound track by track onto a single tape) his own voice three or four times to provide his own rich harmony, a technique he would employ for the rest of his career. *What's Going On* was a critical and commercial sensation in spite of the fact that Gordy, fearing its political content (and its stand against the Vietnam War), had argued against its release.

Other major artists—most importantly Stevie Wonder—followed Gaye's lead and acted as producer of their own efforts. In 1972 Gaye wrote the soundtrack for the film *Trouble Man*, with lyrics that mirrored his own sense of insecurity. *Let's Get It On*, released in 1973, displayed Gaye's sensuous side. *I Want You* (1976) was another meditation on libidinous liberation. *Here, My Dear* (1979) brilliantly dealt with Gaye's divorce from Gordy's sister Anna (the first of the singer's two tumultuous divorces).

Marvin Gaye posing in a portrait session for his 1971 album What's Going On. Michael Ochs Archives/Getty Images

Gaye's growing addiction to cocaine exacerbated his psychological struggles. Deeply indebted to the Internal Revenue Service, he fled the country, living in exile in England and Belgium, where he wrote "Sexual Healing" (1982), the song that signaled his comeback and led to his only Grammy Award.

Back in Los Angeles, his home from the 1970s, his essential conflict—

between the sacred and secular—grew more intense. His 1983 "Sexual Healing" tour, his last, was marked by chaos and confusion. On April 1, 1984, during a family dispute, Gaye initiated a violent fight with his father, who shot him to death. Those close to the singer theorized that it was a death wish come true. For months before, he had toyed with suicide. Gaye, who cited his chief influences as Ray Charles, Clyde McPhatter, Rudy West (lead singer for the doo-wop group the Five Keys), and Little Willie John, was inducted into the Rock and Roll Hall of Fame in 1987.

As an artist who employed urban soul music to express social and personal concerns, as well as a singer of exquisite sensitivity and romantic grace, Gaye left a legacy that has widened since his demise, and his music has become a permanent fixture in American pop.

## MICHAEL JACKSON

Reared in Gary, Indiana, in one of the most acclaimed musical families of the rock era, Michael Jackson (born August 29, 1958, Gary—died June 25, 2009, Los Angeles, California) was the youngest and most talented of five brothers whom his father, Joseph, shaped into a dazzling group of child stars known as the Jackson 5. In addition to Michael, the members of the Jackson 5 were Jackie Jackson (born Sigmund Jackson, May 4, 1951, Gary), Tito Jackson (born Toriano Jackson, October 15, 1953, Gary), Jermaine Jackson (born December 11, 1954, Gary), and Marlon Jackson (born March 12, 1957, Gary).

Berry Gordy, Jr., was impressed with the group and signed them to Motown in 1969. Sporting the loudest fashions, the largest Afros, the snappiest choreography, and a youthful, soulful exuberance, the Jackson 5 became an immediate success. They scored four consecutive number one pop hits with "I Want You Back," "ABC," "The Love You Save," and "I'll Be There" in 1970. With Michael topping the pop charts as a solo performer with "Ben" and reaching number two with "Rockin' Robin," and with the Jackson 5 producing trendsetting dance tracks such as "Dancing Machine," the family's string of hits for Motown lasted through 1975. As Michael matured, his voice changed, family tensions arose, and a contract standoff ensued. The group finally broke with Motown, moving to Epic Records as the Jacksons. Jermaine remained at Motown as a solo performer and was replaced by his youngest brother, Randy Jackson (born Steven Randall Jackson, October 29, 1961). As a recording act, the Jacksons enjoyed consistent success through 1984, and their sister Janet Jackson embarked on her own singing career in the early 1980s; however, Michael's solo albums took on an entirely different status.

Jackson's first solo effort for Epic, *Off the Wall* (1979), exceeded all expectations and was the best-selling album of the year (and has since sold more than 20 million copies). Produced by industry veteran Quincy Jones, *Off the Wall* yielded the massive international hit singles "Don't Stop 'til You Get Enough" and "Rock with You," both of which showcased Michael's energetic style and capitalized on the contemporary disco dance fad. Three years later he returned with another collaboration with Jones, *Thriller*, a tour de force that featured an array of guest stars and elevated him to a worldwide superstar. *Thriller* captured a slew of awards, including a record-setting eight Grammys; remained on the charts for more than two years; and sold more than 40 million copies, long holding the distinction of being the best-selling album in history. The first single on the album, "The Girl Is Mine," an easygoing duet with Paul McCartney, went to number one on the rhythm-and-blues charts and number two on the pop charts in the fall of 1982. The follow-up single, "Billie Jean," an electrifying dance track and the vehicle for Jackson's trademark "moonwalk" dance, topped the pop charts, as did "Beat It," which featured a raucous solo from famed guitarist Eddie Van Halen. Moreover, "Beat It" helped break down the artificial barriers between black and white artists on the radio and in the emerging format of music videos on television.

By 1984 Jackson was renowned worldwide as the "King of Pop." His much anticipated "Victory" reunion tour with his brothers was one of the most popular concert events of 1984. In 1985 Jackson and Lionel Richie cowrote "We Are the World," the signature single for USA for Africa, an all-star project aimed at famine relief. Further solo albums—*Bad* (1987), which produced five chart-topping hits, and *Dangerous* (1991), much of which was produced by New Jack Swing sensation Teddy Riley—solidified Jackson's dominance of pop music. In 2001 he was inducted into the Rock and Roll Hall of Fame; the Jackson 5 were inducted in 1997.

Jackson's eccentric, secluded lifestyle grew increasingly controversial in the early 1990s. His reputation was seriously damaged in 1993 when he was accused of child molestation by a 13-year-old boy he had befriended; a civil suit was settled out of court. In 1994 Jackson secretly married Lisa Marie Presley, daughter of Elvis Presley, but their marriage lasted less than two years. Shortly thereafter Jackson married again, this marriage producing children, though it, too, ended in divorce. While he remained an international celebrity, his image in the United States was slow to recover, and it suffered even more in November 2003 when he was arrested and charged with child molestation. After a 14-week trial that became something of a media circus, Jackson was acquitted in 2005.

In the wake of these events, Jackson suffered a financial collapse that resulted in the sale of many of his considerable assets, including, ultimately, his lavish Neverland ranch. He was preparing for a series of high-profile concerts he hoped would spark a comeback when he died suddenly of cardiac arrest on June 25, 2009—prompting a widespread outpouring of grief from his fans that culminated in a memorial celebration of his life and legacy on July 7 at the Staples Center in Los Angeles, featuring tributes by friends and luminaries such as Stevie Wonder, Berry Gordy, Jr., Brooke Shields, and Al Sharpton. In August 2009 the coroner ruled Jackson's death a homicide; the cause was a lethal combination of sedatives and propofol, an anesthetic. In November 2011 Jackson's personal physician was found guilty of involuntary manslaughter.

The documentary film *This Is It*, which drew from more than 100 hours of footage compiled during rehearsals for Jackson's scheduled 50-concert comeback engagement in London, premiered in October 2009. Also in 2009 Jackson's 14-minute music video "Thriller" (1983), directed by John Landis, was inducted into the National Film Registry of the Library of Congress—the first music video to be so honoured.

## THE ISLEY BROTHERS

The Isley Brothers began recording in the late 1950s and continued to have hit records in the '60s and '70s. The original members were Kelly Isley (born O'Kelly Isley, Jr., December 25, 1937, Cincinnati, Ohio, U.S.—died March 31, 1986), Rudolph Isley (born April 1, 1939, Cincinnati), and Ronald Isley (born May 21, 1941, Cincinnati). Later members included Ernie Isley (born March 7, 1952, Cincinnati), Marvin Isley (born August 18, 1953, Cincinnati—died June 6, 2010, Chicago, Illinois), and Chris Jasper.

After performing gospel music with their mother in and around their native Cincinnati, Kelly, Rudolph, and Ronald Isley gained pop recognition in 1959 with their composition "Shout." In 1962 the trio's rollicking cover version of the Top Notes' "Twist and Shout" remained on *Billboard*'s pop chart for 11 weeks. The Isleys began their own record company, T-Neck Records, in 1964, shortly thereafter recruiting budding guitarist Jimi Hendrix for their band. Abandoning T-Neck and signing with Motown in 1965, the group had a hit a year later with "This Old Heart of

Mine (Is Weak for You)." The Isleys' sound was rawer than standard-issue Motown, however, and they restarted T-Neck in 1969, developing an increasingly funky fusion of rock and soul, most notably on "It's Your Thing" (1969). Joined by younger brothers Ernie and Marvin and brother-in-law Chris Jasper in 1973, the Isleys scored hits with "That Lady (Part 1)" (1973), "Fight the Power (Part 1)" (1975), and "For the Love of You (Part 1 and 2)" (1975). In 1992 the Isley Brothers were inducted into the Rock and Roll Hall of Fame.

## GLADYS KNIGHT AND THE PIPS

Gladys Knight and the Pips were unique in having a female lead singer and male backup singers. The principal members were Gladys Knight (born May 28, 1944, Atlanta, Georgia, U.S.), Merald ("Bubba") Knight (born September 4, 1942, Atlanta), William Guest (born June 2, 1941, Atlanta), and Edward Patten (born August 2, 1939, Atlanta—died February 25, 2005, Livonia, Michigan). Initially composed of siblings and cousins, the group formed in Atlanta in 1952 at a family party (eight-year-old Gladys Knight had already won a nationally televised talent competition). Taking their name from their first manager, cousin James ("Pip") Woods, the group began performing

in local churches, in Atlanta clubs, and on the chitlin circuit. By the time they signed with Motown Records in 1966, they had scored hits on other labels, and their polished stagecraft, vocal harmonies, and dance routines had inspired a number of contemporary rhythm-and-blues acts. They produced 24 Top 40 hits between 1961 and 1977, including "I Heard It Through the Grapevine" (1967), "If I Were Your Woman" (1970), and the million-selling singles "Midnight Train to Georgia" and "Best Thing That Ever Happened to Me" from their million-selling 1973 album, *Imagination*. Contractual disputes slowed their output in the late 1970s, and eventually the Pips retired while Gladys Knight pursued a solo career. The group was inducted into the Rock and Roll Hall of Fame in 1996.

## NORMAN WHITFIELD

Norman Whitfield (born May 12, 1941, New York, New York, U.S.—died September 16, 2008, Los Angeles, California) helped shape the Motown Sound by cowriting (often with Barrett Strong), arranging, and producing many of the hits of the Temptations, notably "I Heard It Through the Grapevine"; he also produced that song for Gladys Knight and the Pips and for Marvin Gaye. Other of Whitfield's hits for the Temptations include "I Wish It Would

Rain" (1968), "Psychedelic Shack" and "Ball of Confusion" (both 1970), and "Just My Imagination" (1971), in addition to "Cloud Nine," which won a 1968 Grammy for best rhythm-and-blues performance by a duo or group, and "Papa Was a Rollin' Stone," which won a 1972 Grammy for best rhythm-and-blues song. In 1975 Whitfield left Motown and started his own label; the biggest success of Whitfield Records was the recording by the band Rose Royce of the soundtrack album *Car Wash,* which won Whitfield a 1976 Grammy as composer for Best Original Score written for a motion picture. Whitfield was inducted into the Songwriters Hall of Fame in 2004.

# CHAPTER 15

# Rock and Roll Onscreen in the 1950s

**F**or much of the 1950s teenagers in search of rhythm-and-blues and rock-and-roll thrills found them on record, on the radio, and occasionally at "race-mixing" concerts that hinted at the promise of a different kind of America. Yet as the decade progressed rock and roll became a presence on both the new mass media of television and the older one of film. Both the large and small screens began to offer opportunities for viewers not only to hear rock and roll and R&B but to know what it looked and felt like to try on rock-and-roll attitude and to empathetically experience teen angst and rebellion.

## ROCK AND TELEVISION

Think of rock and television as one of those couples plainly destined to get together but often at odds until the shotgun wedding arranged by MTV/Music Television finally got them to the altar in 1981. From the start, which in this case means Elvis Presley, TV in the United States and Britain functioned—or tried to—as a taming influence on the music's unruly streak. Famously, Presley's gyrations were obscured by waist-up shots during his TV debut on the Dorsey Brothers' *Stage Show* in 1956, an emasculation that proved emblematic of the relation between the two as rock fans long perceived it. Television was domesticated, family-oriented, and basically wholesome if not oppressively straitlaced; rock was freewheeling, youth-oriented, and basically insolent if not thrillingly dissolute. Tensions were inevitable, even if antagonism was commercially impractical.

As indeed it was. If only because they shared a market—the emerging baby boomer audience—rock and roll and TV were linked from the start. In the United States Presley's ascent to nationwide stardom in 1956 owed a great deal to his TV appearances, above all on *The Ed Sullivan Show*; the following year Ricky (later Rick) Nelson, one of the two sons on *The Adventures of Ozzie and Harriet*, began to perform rock-and-roll numbers regularly on the series, with the nicely symbiotic result that TV exposure boosted his record sales even as his music making became central to the show's continuing popularity.

From very early on, TV also provided showcases devoted entirely to the new music, the most prominent early examples being Dick Clark's *American Bandstand* in the United States, which began as a local Philadelphia program in 1952 before going national five years later, and *Juke Box Jury* in the United Kingdom, which premiered in 1959.

## ROCK AND FILM

From the opening strains of Bill Haley and His Comets' "Rock Around the Clock" in *Blackboard Jungle* (1955), the power of rock and roll on film was obvious. Hollywood, however, treated the new music as a fad, which director Frank Tashlin spoofed in *The Girl Can't Help It* (1956), the story of a talentless singer (played by Jayne Mansfield) who is transformed into a rock-and-roll star. Yet, despite its condescending attitude, the film includes gorgeously photographed performances by early rockers Little Richard, Gene Vincent, and Eddie Cochran. Also in 1956, Elvis Presley appeared in *Love Me Tender*, a Civil War-era melodrama that had little to do with rock and roll but sought to capitalize on Presley's stardom, a formula that would be used throughout his unremarkable movie career. Indeed, of Presley's films, only *Jailhouse Rock* (1957) captured rock's spirit.

### THE WILD ONE

Some of rock and roll's rebellious attitude and iconography were borrowed from films that had little or no music in them. Among the first was *The Wild One* (1953), in which Marlon Brando's portrayal of a brooding biker in a black leather jacket helped

# RICK NELSON

At age 17, in 1957, Rick Nelson (born Eric Hilliard Nelson, May 8, 1940, Teaneck, New Jersey, U.S.—died December 31, 1985, De Kalb, Texas) recorded a hit version of Fats Domino's "I'm Walkin'." Trading on the handsome, wholesome image he developed on his parents' television series, *The Adventures of Ozzie and Harriet,* which embodied middle-American values in the 1950s and early 1960s, Nelson launched a recording career that resulted in a bevy of Top Ten hits and contributed to rock and roll's mainstream acceptance. Yet, unlike Frankie Avalon and other teen idols who found fame on *American Bandstand*, Nelson created boisterous, rockabilly-flavoured rock and roll as well as gentler ballads. Moreover, first-rate songwriters such as Gene Pitney ("Hello, Mary Lou") and Johnny and Dorsey Burnette provided him with material, and his guitarist, James Burton—who later played with Elvis Presley—was one of early rock's most distinctive players. After topping the charts with "Poor Little Fool" (1958) and "Travelin' Man" (1961), Nelson's popularity waned in the mid-1960s. Having shed his boy-next-door image, he formed the Stone Canyon Band and explored country rock. His final hit, "Garden Party" (1972), described Nelson's frustration with the hostile reaction of the audience at an "oldies" concert. He was inducted into the Rock and Roll Hall of Fame in 1987, two years after his death in a plane crash.

launch an international interest in motorcycle gangs such as the Hell's Angels. The plot is loosely based on a 1947 incident in which the town of Hollister, California, was inundated by biker gangs. In the film, Brando and Lee Marvin played rival gang leaders Johnny and Chino, respectively. After Chino is arrested by a small-town sheriff (played by Robert

Keith), his gang goes on a rampage. When Johnny is seen attempting to escort the sheriff's daughter out of harm's way, his actions are misconstrued by the enraged townspeople. Though he is eventually exonerated of any wrongdoing, the film does not offer a true happy ending. The line of dialogue most cited from the film belongs to Brando. When his character is asked what he is rebelling against, he responds, "Whaddya got?"—thus expressing the angst of many young people eager to break free of the social conventions of the 1950s. This film marked the first time that movie audiences were exposed in any significant way to the existence of organized motorcycle gangs, and it spawned an entire genre based on the theme of the outlaw biker. By the time Roger Corman's biker film *The Wild Angels* was released in 1966, three years before the legendary *Easy Rider* appeared, the amount of violence and sex depicted onscreen made *The Wild One* look tame. Yet it was deemed so dangerous in its day that England banned its showing until 1968, and it was cited by sociologists as a factor in the era's spread of juvenile delinquency.

## REBEL WITHOUT A CAUSE

Released in 1955, *Rebel Without a Cause* is a classic tale of teenage rebellion and angst. The movie featured

*Movie still from* Rebel Without a Cause, *starring* (left to right) *Sal Mineo (1939–76), James Dean (1931–55) and Natalie Wood (1938–81).* John Kobal Foundation/Moviepix/Getty Images

iconic actor James Dean in one of his final roles; he died one month before the release. Dean played Jim, a troubled but sensitive teenager who, although rejecting his elders' values, desperately wants to belong and have purpose in his life. Soon after his family moves to a new town, he takes on violent gang members while finding comfort with fellow troubled teens Judy (played by Natalie Wood) and Plato (Sal Mineo).

Following in the steps of *The Wild One*, *Rebel Without a Cause* was one of the better movies that dealt with the increasingly popular topic of juvenile deliquency. The film was partially shot in black and white, but the studio then stopped production and reshot in colour. A strong supporting cast included Dennis Hopper, Edward Platt, and Jim Backus, who received praise for his memorable role as Dean's henpecked father. All three lead actors met untimely deaths. Dean died in a car crash at age 24; Mineo was stabbed to death at 37; and Wood drowned amid mysterious circumstances at 43. Their deaths only added to the cultish appeal that later surrounded the film.

## BLACKBOARD JUNGLE

By blaring "Rock Around the Clock" (1954) by Bill Haley and His Comets, *Blackboard Jungle* was the first major film to feature rock music on its soundtrack. Released in 1955, it highlighted violence in urban schools. Richard Dadier (played by Glenn Ford) is a well-meaning New York City teacher assigned to a high school where teenage delinquents led by Artie West (Vic Morrow) terrorize students and teachers alike. On Dadier's first day, fellow teacher Lois Hammond (Margaret Hayes) is nearly raped by a student. Dadier beats her assailant, but he and math teacher Joshua Edwards (Richard Kiley) are attacked by Artie and his gang in retaliation. Despite being badly beaten, Dadier is determined to reach his students. He eventually breaks Artie's hold over his classmates and persuades one of them, Gregory Miller (Sidney Poitier), to stay in school.

Blackboard Jungle was based on a popular 1954 novel by Evan Hunter. The film hit a nerve with its unusually brutal depiction of the social conditions of urban schools, and the music and the theme made the movie hugely popular with teenage audiences. Fights and riots broke out in many towns in England where the movie was shown. Morrow and Poitier received special praise for their roles as the chief delinquents. Poitier, ironically, later played a teacher in a similar British film, *To Sir, with Love* (1967).

*Film still of Elvis Presley in* Jailhouse Rock *(1957).* © 1957 Metro-Goldwyn-Mayer Inc.; photograph, Library of Congress, Washington, D.C..

## JAILHOUSE ROCK

Released in 1957, *Jailhouse Rock* starred Elvis Presley in his third screen role. Widely considered his best film, it is primarily distinguished by a memorable title song and creative production numbers. Vince Everett (played by Presley) is imprisoned for manslaughter following his participation in a bar brawl. While serving his sentence, and with the help of a fellow inmate, Everett discovers he has a knack for writing and performing music. Upon his release, he becomes a singing sensation but must navigate the pitfalls of both fame and new love. Peggy Van Alden (played by Judy Tyler) is the talent agent who helps him on his way up.

*Jailhouse Rock* presents "the King" at a time in his career when his talent was still raw and untamed. In most of his later cinematic endeavours, his business manager, Col. Tom Parker, forbade Presley to stray too far from a "safe" image, but the film's engrossing plot allows its star to play a character with a degree of emotional depth. The film's unquestionable highlight is the production number in which Presley performs the title song.

# Conclusion

There is no doubt that by the early 1960s popular music was all shook up. The journey that rhythm and blues and rock and roll had taken from the blues, country, gospel, and pop that had gone before had changed not just the landscape of popular music but was beginning to alter American, as well as British, society. Teenagers had discovered they were *teenagers*. At first they had to stay up late at night to hear their music on the radio, often from distant stations, served up for them by jive-talking hipster deejays. Then radio changed. Kids could hear the songs they loved all the time, over and over, as Top 40 radio took hold and "hooks" became the currency of polished three-minute pop. Both puppy love and hound dog sensuality had a voice. Rock and roll also made its way into television and the movies. It was everywhere, created by both black and white people. As they listened and watched, young people in particular began to create a new culture. And as they immersed themselves in this unfolding culture, more of them began to bridle at the fact that, in many places, black and white Americans went to separate schools, rode in different sections of buses, and did not share bathrooms. As the 1960s progressed, the politics of change (and reaction), along with the music of protest, were waiting in the wings.

# Glossary

**adventitious** Coming from another source.

**apotheosis** Quintessence; perfect example.

**arpeggio** Production of the tones of a chord in succession and not simultaneously.

**autoharp** Stringed instrument of the zither family popular for accompaniment in folk music and country and western music.

**ballad** Popular song, especially a slow romantic or sentimental one.

**banal** Trite, worn-out, commonplace.

**barbershop** Typically all-male or all-female popular choral form characterized by a cappella singing, with three voices harmonizing to the melody of a fourth voice.

**blue-eyed soul** Music created by white recording artists who faithfully imitated the soul music of the 1960s, a select few of whom were popular with black audiences as well as white listeners.

**blues** Form of American music originated by African Americans in the South. As a music form, the blues is typified by a melancholy state of mind and 8-, 12-, or 32-bar harmonic progressions that form the basis for blues improvisation.

**bohemia** Community of people living an unconventional life.

**boogie-woogie** heavily percussive style of blues piano in which the right hand plays riffs (syncopated, repeating phrases) against a driving pattern of repeating eighth notes (ostinato bass).

**bowdlerize** To modify (as a book or a song) by omitting or modifying parts considered vulgar or offensive.

**Brill Building** Located in New York City, the Brill Building was the hub of professionally written rock and roll. The 1960s equivalent of Tin Pan Alley, it reemphasized a specialized division of labour in which professional songwriters worked closely with producers and artists-and-repertoire personnel to match selected artists with appropriate songs.

**British blues** Early to mid-1960s musical movement based in London clubs that was an important influence on the subsequent rock explosion.

**British Invasion** Musical movement of the mid-1960s composed of

British rock-and-roll ("beat") groups whose popularity spread rapidly to the United States. The Beatles led the charge when they arrived in New York City on February 7, 1964.

**busk**  British term meaning to entertain, especially by singing or reciting on the street or in a pub for donations.

**contralto**  Singing voice having a range between tenor and mezzo-soprano.

**country music**  Style of 20th-century American popular music that originated among whites in rural areas of the South and West. The term "country and western music" (later shortened to "country music") was adopted by the recording industry in 1949 to replace the derogatory label "hillbilly music."

**cover**  To record a song previously recorded by someone else.

**disc jockey**  Person who conducts a program of recorded music on radio, on television, or at dance halls. Also spelled disk jockey.

**dominant**  Fifth tone of a major or minor scale.

**doo-wop**  Vocal style of rock and roll characterized by the a cappella singing of nonsense syllables in rhythmical support of the melody.

**dulcimer**  American folk instrument with three or four strings stretched over an elongate fretted sound box that is held on the lap and played by plucking or strumming.

**expurgate**  To cleanse of something morally harmful, offensive, or erroneous.

**falsetto**  An artificially high singing voice.

**folk rock**  Hybrid musical style that emerged in the United States and Britain in the mid-1960s combining the entertainment value of rock with the serious intent of folk, notably embodied in the work of singer-songwriter Bob Dylan.

**funk**  Rhythm-driven musical genre popular in the 1970s and early 1980s that combines traditional forms of black music (as blues, gospel, or soul) and features hard syncopated bass lines and drumbeats.

**gospel**  Religious songs of American origin associated with evangelism and popular devotion and marked by simple melody and harmony and elements of folk songs and blues.

**hillbilly**  Person from a backwoods area (as the mountains of the southern United States)—often used disparagingly.

**hip-hop**  Cultural movement that includes rap, deejaying (turntable manipulation), graffiti painting, and break dancing.

**jazz**  Musical form, often improvisational, developed by African Americans and influenced by both European harmonic structure and African rhythms.

**jew's harp** Musical instrument consisting of a thin wood or metal tongue fixed at one end to the base of a two-pronged frame. The player holds the frame to his or her mouth, which forms a resonance cavity, and plucks the instrument's tongue. The tongue produces only one pitch.

**jug band** Band using usually crude or improvised instruments (as jugs, washboards, and kazoos) to play blues, jazz, and folk music.

**jukebox** Coin-operated machine that plays songs selected from its list; developed in 1889 as cylinder phonograph with 4 ear-tubes for listening when a nickel was inserted; became common in public places in late 1930s as better technology amplified sound; name derived from southern inns called "jukes," which featured these machines.

**juke house** Small inexpensive establishment for eating, drinking, or dancing to the music of a jukebox or a live band. Also known as a juke joint.

**lexicographer** Author or editor of a dictionary.

**lugubrious** Mournful or gloomy, especially to an exaggerated degree.

**magnetic tape** Thin ribbon (as of plastic) coated with a magnetic material on which information (as sound or television images) may be stored.

**mawkish** Excessively and cloyingly sentimental.

**microtone** Musical interval smaller than a half tone.

**minstrel show** Indigenous American theatrical form popular from the early 19th to the early 20th century founded on what was conceived as a comic enactment of racial stereotypes. The tradition reached its zenith between 1850 and 1870. Also called minstrelsy.

**new wave** Taking its name from the French New Wave cinema of the 1950s, the new wave genre of popular music arose in the late 1970s. It fused an arty sensibility with the do-it-yourself principle of punk to produce catchy and often subversively humorous music.

**outlaw music** Movement of American country music in the 1970s spearheaded by Willie Nelson and Waylon Jennings. Sometimes called progressive country, outlaw music was an attempt to escape the formulaic constraints of the Nashville Sound (simple songs, the use of studio musicians, and lush production), country's dominant style in the 1960s.

**pathos** Element in experience or artistic representation evoking pity or compassion.

**pentatonic scale** Scale consisting of five tones; specifically, one in which the tones are arranged as a major scale with the fourth and seventh tones omitted.

**Pentecostal** Any of various Christian religious bodies that emphasize individual experiences of grace, spiritual gifts (such as speaking in tongues and faith healing), expressive worship, and evangelism.

**pickup** Magnetic bar affixed to a guitar providing the instrument with its distinctive, vibrating sound.

**plectrum** Small thin piece of ivory, wood, metal, horn, quill, or other material used in playing on plucked stringed musical instruments (as the banjo, lyre, mandolin).

**psychedelic rock** Music of the 1960s that featured song lyrics about psychedelic drugs and incorporated feedback and distortion, improvisation, and long instrumental solos.

**punk rock** Aggressive form of rock music in the mid and late '70s marked by extreme and often deliberately offensive expressions of alienation and social discontent.

**race music** Early- to mid-20th century name given to African American blues and jazz.

**ragtime** Music having rhythm characterized by strong syncopation in the melody with a regularly accented accompaniment in stride-piano style.

**rap** Musical style in which rhythmic and/or rhyming speech is chanted ("rapped") to musical accompaniment. This backing music can include digital sampling (music and sounds extracted from other recordings).

**Rastafarian** Member of a political and religious movement that originated in Jamaica Rastafarians believe in the divinity of Emperor Haile Selassie I of Ethiopia and in the eventual return of his exiled followers to Africa.

**rave-up** Hard-driving usually instrumental climactic section of a popular or country music song.

**reggae** Style of popular music that originated in Jamaica in the late 1960s and quickly emerged as the country's dominant music. By the 1970s it had become an international style that was particularly popular in Britain, the United States, and Africa. It was widely perceived as a voice of the oppressed.

**rhythm and blues** Popular music typically including elements of blues and African American folk music and marked by a strong beat and simple chord structure.

**rockabilly** Form of rock music originated by white performers in the American South, popular from the mid-1950s to 1960 with a revival in the late 1970s.

**rock and roll** Early form of rock music; also called rock & roll, though all three names often are seen as synonymous.

**rpm** Revolutions per minute, as in records that play (rotate) at 33 1/3, 45, or 78 revolutions per minute.

**scat** Way of using the voice like an instrument by singing meaningless syllables.

**shape-note hymnal** American hymnal incorporating many folk hymns and utilizing a special musical notation. The seven-note scale was sung not to the syllables do–re–mi–fa–sol–la–ti but to a four-syllable system brought over by early English colonists.

**skiffle** Form of music formerly popular in Great Britain featuring vocals with a simple instrumental accompaniment.

**sobriquet** Nickname.

**soul** Style of U.S. popular music sung and performed primarily by African American musicians, having its roots in gospel music and rhythm and blues.

**strychnine** Bitter poisonous alkaloid.

**subdominant** Fourth degree of a major or minor scale.

**surf music** Genre of popular music that arose in southern California in the early 1960s characterized by its distinctive guitar-based sound often featuring single-note riffs.

**swing** Style of jazz that came to prominence between 1935 and 1945, swing music has a compelling momentum that results from musicians' attacks and accenting in relation to fixed beats.

**syncopation** Temporary displacement of the regular metrical accent in music caused typically by stressing the weak beat.

**tonic** First degree of a major or minor scale constituting the tonal centre of a musical composition that has an established tonality. Also called keynote.

**top 40** Forty best-selling audio recordings for a given period and by extension accessible, popular music.

**tremolo** The rapid reiteration of a musical tone or of alternating tones to produce a vibrating effect.

**triad** Chord of three tones consisting of a root with its third and fifth and constituting the harmonic basis of tonal music.

**troubadour** One of a class of European lyric poets and poet-musicians who flourished from the 11th to the end of the 13th century and whose major theme was courtly love.

**tympani** Italian for drums, tympani (also spelled timpani) are orchestral kettledrums.

**vaudeville** American stage entertainment popular from the mid-1890s until the early 1930s consisting of various unrelated acts such as magicians, acrobats, comedians, trained animals, jugglers, singers, and dancers.

# Bibliography

## GENERAL

There is an extensive literature on rock that ranges from academic musicology and sociology through every kind of journalism to disposable gossip and poster books. Peter van der Merwe, *Origins of the Popular Style* (1989, reissued 1992), a scholarly study of pre-20th-century popular music, helps explain why a music first appearing at the margins of Western culture so quickly became the mainstream. Charlie Gillett, *The Sound of the City: The Rise of Rock and Roll,* 3rd. ed. revised and enlarged (2011), is still the best account of how rock and roll was first shaped in a variety of local American settings. Rock and roll's roots in black and white music are covered in *Country: The Music and the Musicians: From the Beginnings to the '90s,* 2nd ed. (1994), an informative overview of country music history published by the Country Music Foundation; and Charles Keil, *Urban Blues* (1966, reissued 1991), an illuminating anthropological study of African American musical culture in the late 1950s and early 1960s. Tim J. Anderson, *Making Easy Listening: Material Culture and Postwar American Recording* (2006), is a valuable overview of the changes in the American recording industry that made new ways of music making and listening possible.

The development of rock out of rock and roll was as much an ideological as a musical process, and the classic description of that ideology—of why and how rock drew from and came to articulate the contradictory impulses of American popular culture—is Greil Marcus, *Mystery Train,* 5th rev. ed. (2008), which, in its studies of particular musicians, was the first work to reveal the possibilities of rock criticism. Simon Frith and Howard Horne, *Art into Pop* (1987), studies how British rock sensibility was shaped by art school ideas and practices. Theodore Gracyk, *Listening to Popular Music; or, How I Learned to Stop Worrying and Love Led Zeppelin* (2007), is an illuminating philosophical investigation of rock fans' values.

Simon Frith and Andrew Goodwin (eds.), *On Record: Rock, Pop, and the Written Word* (1990), is a useful anthology of 30 years of scholarly writing on rock, from a variety of disciplinary perspectives. Paul Théberge, *Any Sound You Can Imagine: Making Music/Consuming Technology* (1997); and Mark Katz, *Capturing Sound: How Technology Has Changed Music*, rev. ed. (2010), are histories of the effects of technology on music making.

## BLUES

Works of history and criticism include Samuel B. Charters, *The Country Blues* (1959, reprinted 1975); Paul Oliver, *Screening the Blues* (also published as *Aspects of the Blues Tradition*, 1968), and *The Story of the Blues* (1969, reissued 1982); Giles Oakley, *The Devil's Music*, rev. ed. (1983); William Barlow, *"Looking Up at Down": The Emergence of Blues Culture* (1989); and Lawrence Cohn et al., *Nothing but the Blues: The Music and the Musicians* (1993). Paul Oliver, *Blues Fell This Morning: Meaning in the Blues*, 2nd ed. (1990), studies the historical context of blues lyrics.

## RHYTHM AND BLUES

Arnold Shaw, *Honkers and Shouters: The Golden Years of Rhythm and Blues* (1978, reissued 1986), presents an intermittently accurate portrait of the origins and development of rhythm and blues. Jerry Wexler and *David Ritz, Rhythm and the Blues: A Life in American Music* (1993), the autobiography of legendary producer Wexler, contains many insightful anecdotes about the early years of rhythm and blues. Charlie Gillett, *Making Tracks: Atlantic Records and the Growth of a Multi-Billion-Dollar Industry* (1974, reissued as *Making Tracks: The Story of Atlantic Records*, 1993), covers the history of Atlantic Records. Johnny Otis, *Listen to the Lambs* (1968), is the self-serving but fascinating autobiography of Los Angeles rhythm-and-blues kingpin Otis. Ray Charles and David Ritz, *Brother Ray: Ray Charles' Own Story* (1978, reissued 1992), is the autobiography of a major transitional artist.

## DOO-WOP

Arnold Shaw, *The Rockin' '50s: The Decade That Transformed the Pop Music Scene* (1974, reprinted 1987), is a behind-the-scenes autobiographical narrative of the music business of the 1950s with candid reminiscences of the racial aspects of the industry. Philip Groia, *They All Sang on the Corner: A Second Look at New York City's Rhythm and Blues Vocal Groups* (1983), presents a well-researched social history of the doo-wop scene in New York City. Robert Pruter, *Doowop: The Chicago Scene* (1996), offers authoritative analysis of the seminal doo-wop music world of Chicago, a city more traditionally identified with blues. Patti LaBelle, *Don't Block the Blessings: Revelations of a Lifetime* (1996), is an autobiographical narrative of the life and career of one of the greatest voices in rock music.

## ROCKABILLY

Colin Escott and Martin Hawkins, *Good Rockin' Tonight: Sun Records and the Birth of Rock 'n' Roll* (1991), presents a detailed survey of the label and its impact. Craig Morrison, *Go Cat Go!: Rockabilly Music and Its Makers* (1996), gives a comprehensive overview of the style.

## THE BEACH BOYS

David Leaf, *The Beach Boys* (1985), the first biography, is more reliable and musically astute than a later work by Steven Gaines, *Heroes and Villains: The True Story of the Beach Boys* (1986, reissued 1995). Timothy White, *The Nearest Faraway Place: Brian Wilson, the Beach Boys, and the Southern California Experience* (1994), is a comprehensive, more-than-175-year social history of the Beach Boys and their ancestors. Kingsley Abbott (ed.), *Back to the Beach: A Brian Wilson and the Beach Boys Reader*, rev. and updated ed. (2003), assembles assorted classic articles on the musicians.

## ELVIS PRESLEY

Peter Guralnick, *Last Train to Memphis: The Rise of Elvis Presley* (1994), takes the story only to 1958 but is well-written and compelling and establishes a groundwork for understanding what happened and often why. Peter Guralnick, *Careless Love: The Unmaking of Elvis Presley* (1999), is far less useful as a guide to understanding what happened, but the two volumes together nevertheless constitute the only accurate standard biography. The best critical essays are Greil Marcus, "Elvis: Presliad," in *Mystery Train: Images of America in Rock & Roll Music*, 4th rev. ed. (1997), pp. 120–175; Jon Landau, "In Praise of Elvis Presley," in *It's Too Late to Stop Now* (1972), pp. 77–82; and Dave Marsh, *Elvis* (1982, reissued 1992), which explore, in the voice of writers whose lives were changed by listening to him, why and how he overwhelmed a generation and transformed the culture of popular music. Stanley Booth, "Situation

Report: Elvis in Memphis, 1967," in *Rythm Oil: A Journey Through the Music of the American South* (1991), chapter 6, pp. 52–68, originally appearing as "A Hound Dog, to the Manor Born," *Esquire*, 69(2):106–108, 48–50 (February 1968), approaches the same questions from an explicitly Southern perspective. Greil Marcus, *Dead Elvis* (1991), contains a panoply of writings by Marcus and others that illuminate what happened to Presley as he ascended into the pantheon of true American legends in the wake of his death.

## PHIL SPECTOR

Mark Ribowsky, *He's a Rebel* (1989, reissued 2006), is a biography. Ronnie Spector and Vince Waldron, *Be My Baby: How I Survived Mascara, Miniskirts, and Madness, or My Life as a Fabulous Ronette* (1990), written by Spector's singer-wife, describes life in and out of the studio with Spector. Richard Williams, *Out of His Head: The Sound of Phil Spector* (1972); and John J. Fitzpatrick and James E. Fogerty, *Collecting Phil Spector: The Man, the Legend, and the Music* (1991), and Mick Brown, *Tearing Down the Wall of Sound: The Rise and Fall of Phil Spector* (2007), discuss Spector's life and work.

## GIRL GROUPS

Charlotte Greig, *Will You Still Love Me Tomorrow?: Girl Groups from the 50s On* (1989), is a definitive analysis of the girl group period. Lucy O'Brien, *She Bop II: The Definitive History of Women in Rock, Pop, and Soul*, rev. ed. (2002), examines the girl group sound in the wider context of women's rock history.

## MOTOWN

Nelson George, *Where Did Our Love Go?: The Rise & Fall of the Motown Sound* (1985, reissued 2007), is the best history of Motown Records, its triumphs, and its failures. Gerald Early, *One Nation Under a Groove: Motown and American Culture* (1995), provides a concise analysis of Motown within the context of historical trends in post-World War II American culture. David Morse, *Motown and the Arrival of Black Music* (1971), offers a very short but helpful early study of Motown and its significance. Ben Fong-Torres, *The Motown Album* (1990), is a first-rate pictorial history of Motown. The founder of Motown presents a useful autobiography in Berry Gordy, *To Be Loved: The Music, the Magic, the Memories of Motown: An Autobiography* (1994); Gordy's second wife, Raynoma, contributes an interesting though not always accurate account of Motown and her role in its early years in Raynoma Gordon Singleton, Bryan Brown, and Mim Eichelr, *Berry, Me, and Motown* (1990). Dr. Licks, *Standing in the Shadows of Motown: The Life and Music of Legendary Bassist James Jamerson* (1989), insightfully examines the life and music of one of Motown's key studio musicians. Otis Williams, a founding member of one of Motown's most enduring groups, wrote a good autobiography: Otis Williams and Patricia Romanowski, *Temptations* (1988). Another Motown stalwart, Mary Wilson, wrote a sometimes disputatious work: Mary Wilson, Patricia Romanowski, and Ahrgus Juilliard, *Dreamgirl: My Life as a Supreme* (1986).

## OTHER BIOGRAPHIES

Other useful biographies include Charles White, *The Life and Times of Little Richard: The Quasar of Rock,* updated ed. (1994), which features a discography and filmography; John Goldrosen and John Beecher, *Remembering Buddy: The Definitive Biography* (1987, reissued 1996); Ellis Amburn, *Buddy Holly: A Biography* (1995); and Philip Norman, *Rave On: The Biography of Buddy Holly* (1996). Chuck Berry, *Chuck Berry: The Autobiography* (1987); and Howard A. DeWitt, *Chuck Berry: Rock 'n' Roll Music*, 2nd ed. (1985), detail his life and career. Daniel Wolff et al., *You Send Me: The Life and Times of Sam Cooke* (1995), is an informative biography.

# Index